HOUSES

IMPRINT

PROJECT MANAGEMENT
Florian Kobler, Cologne

COLLABORATION
Sonja Altmeppen, Berlin
Mischa Gayring, Cologne

**EDITORIAL
COORDINATION**
Julia Krumhauer, Cologne

PRODUCTION
Ute Wachendorf, Cologne

DESIGN
Sense/Net Art Direction,
Andy Disl and Birgit Eichwede,
Cologne
www.sense-net.net

GERMAN TRANSLATION
Kristina Brigitta Köper, Berlin

FRENCH TRANSLATION
Jacques Bosser, Paris

PRINTED IN CHINA
ISBN 978-3-8365-4348-4

© 2013 TASCHEN GMBH
Hohenzollernring 53
D–50672 Cologne
www.taschen.com

ORIGINAL EDITION
© 2009 TASCHEN GMBH

ARCHITECTURE NOW!
HOUSES

HÄUSER / MAISONS
Philip Jodidio

1

TASCHEN

CONTENTS

INTRODUCTION

OF CASTLES AND CAVES

"The house," says the Swiss architect Mario Botta, "is intimately related to the idea of shelter. A cave carved out of the rock is like a mother's womb. This is the concept of the house that I defend. When I am tired of the world, I want to go home. There I can regain my energy to prepare for the next day's battle. As long as there is a man who needs a house, architecture will still exist… A house should be like a mother's womb."[1] Though there may be distinctions between a house and a home, the fact remains that the fundamental ideas of shelter, life and death are intertwined with the architecture of the commonplace in every place of dwelling, from cave to castle. The house can be a measure of civilization, wealth or, indeed, intelligence; it is a barometer of existence. Depending on the architect and the client, a house can be at the very cutting edge of architecture, casting aside notions of the past in search of a new paradigm; it can accept the rules of urbanism while standing them on their head. It can float in the air or emerge from the depths of the earth. Where factors of cost may limit civic architecture to tried and trusted methods, some houses break all the rules, and help architecture to move forward.

HOUSES NOW!

In the design of houses, much as in the art of architecture as a whole, there is no one style today, no dominant trend like the minimalism that seemed to sweep through residential architecture led by such figures as John Pawson. Minimalism is still fashionable in many circles, but so is the kind of glittering complexity seen in Jouin Manku's interiors for the house in Kuala Lumpur. Computers, used in an earlier phase to fashion extravagant blobs, have become part and parcel of architectural design, from the smallest house to the largest building, and this too has changed, and in many ways liberated, the design of houses. The new "maturity" displayed by architects in their use of computers might best be summed up by Michael Meredith of MOS, an Assistant Professor of Architecture at the Harvard Graduate School of Design (Floating House, Lake Huron, Ontario, Canada): "Computers are dumb, but they can do simple things real fast and architecture is now so complex that you can't keep all of it in your head."

The number of books and magazines published about houses has expanded substantially over the years. In some cases this is for practical reasons—people looking for ideas about how to build or decorate their own home—but there is also an element of curiosity. How do other people live, in particular those who have the means to do practically anything they want. Voyeurism is of course part of the architect's imagination in designs from the Glass House in Paris (Pierre Chareau, Maison de Verre, 1928–31) to the Glass House in New Canaan (Philip Johnson, 1949) and right up to the present. Well, if the architect can do it, so can the reader, so come along.

KING OF THE ROOST

In all fairness when people, even very rich ones, decide to build a house of 3000 square meters or more, they usually intend to receive large numbers of clients or friends. This is certainly the case of the house in Kuala Lumpur designed by the French furniture and interior designer Patrick Jouin and his partner Sanjit Manku (page 158). Built on a restricted site in the former embassy area of the Malaysian capital, the house is intended for the extended family of one of the country's most visible entrepreneurs. In a neighborhood whose architecture can only be described as heterogeneous, the architects have, at the request of their client, packed as many square meters into the site as possible. Their bold design also features numerous outdoor terraces and enclosed garden areas designed by Lugano-based Sophie Agata Ambroise. Taking into account the extended family structure of

1
*Bernardes + Jacobsen Arquitetura,
Guarujá House, Guarujá, São Paulo,
Brazil, 2004–06*

1

the client, with apartments for three generations, the architects have sought a new language for a country that has little visible indigenous architectural style aside from the rapidly disappearing colonial Orientalism still to be seen in the railway station and a few other older buildings in the city. The very size of the house may be apparent in its exterior bulk, with a large parking garage and ballroom facilities for guests occupying lower level spaces, leaving what appears to be a convivial and reasonably sized house above.

TWISTING THE COOKIE CUTTER

A number of the architects and houses featured in this volume engage the very substance of design to question rules, regulations and typologies, in a sense to reinterpret the house. David Adjaye's Sunken House (London, UK, 2007, page 9) certainly defies convention in excavating the entire site to basement level and then placing a cube entirely clad in stained garden decking within this space, leaving room for patios, also covered in decking. This orchestration of spaces and materials questions the concept of the ground on which a house is built, and the typology of the basement and of the patio. This might be termed the ultimate patio house if the austerity of its form and rather radical approach did not make it a challenging object, quite the opposite of the traditional patio house, a suburban fixture in the United Kingdom and in many other countries.

Another project with a radical design concept is the Wall House (Santiago, Chile, 2004–07) by FAR frohn&rojas. The architects chose to conceive this residence as a series of wall layers made of progressively lighter or more translucent materials. The inner core of the house, containing bathrooms, is made of concrete that is surrounded by bands of wood, where the kitchen, bedrooms and a dining area are enclosed, and finally the visible skin is made of high-insulation polycarbonate panels. In a sense, the ancient idea of the cave seems to be at play here, at least in the positioning and the choice of materials. The innermost concrete heart of the house is its most solid and ultimately protective element. Living spaces given to change and movement are built of wood and the final layer of outside covering, a skin in an almost physiological sense, is translucent plastic. The anthropomorphic aspects of this layering would seem apparent, with bones, organs and skin being the parallels for the architectural choices made. Perhaps, most fundamentally, the architects have made a conscious decision to allow the walls to dictate the plan, which is quite the opposite of the usual procedure, where plan dominates. It is encouraging to see that despite centuries, if not millennia of residential design, some young architects still feel that they can change the way a house is designed. Undoubtedly, contemporary life styles and aesthetics are also factors in the liberty that Frohn and Rojas have claimed with their Wall House.

BETWEEN SEA AND SKY

The French speak of "*une vue imprenable*"—literally a view that cannot be taken, or taken away from its "owner." So often houses are built in locations that offer a view. For those who are sensitive to nature, a mountain view or an ocean vista offer the spectacle of constant change with the hours of the day and seasons of the year. To escape from the view into a house with its intimate spaces and inevitably closed vistas (the cave), the owner need only look forth from a balcony to see a version of the infinite. Making use of views and integrating them into the very conception of a house is a rewarding part of an architect's task in these instances. Rather than the full protection of the cave, the house with a view exposes its fragility to sometimes hostile elements. The kind of bareness to the elements offered by a spectacular view is particularly well suited to modern architecture, with its resistant materials and capacity to glaze large surfaces, even opposing the winds.

2
FAR frohn&rojas, Wall House,
Santiago, Chile, 2004–07

3 + 4 + 5
David Adjaye, Sunken House,
London, UK, 2007

2

The house in Guarujá (São Paulo, Brazil, 2004–06) by the Rio architects Bernardes + Jacobsen combines the kind of luxuriant natural setting only available in a climate like that of Brazil, with a view of the Atlantic from the heights of a steeply sloped site. This house underlines to what extent house architecture is influenced by climate. The outdoor terraces that render exterior and interior almost indistinguishable in this house would be impossible in many climates, no matter how attractive the view. The ambiguity between interior and exterior, long practiced in Japan, is a popular theme in contemporary architecture in general, but it would be difficult to practice it in a more logical and complete way than on the wooden terraces of this house.

TREE HOUSES AND PLASTIC HOUSES

As opposed to daring to hang over the edge, or to seeking in a sense to dominate the force of nature, other houses accept their setting, blending into it in many ways. Theirs is a proximity to nature that is not related to infinite views, but to the green of the forest for example. One of the more surprising and humorous interpretations of this theme is seen in the Silicon House (La Florida, Madrid, Spain, 2006) by SELGASCANO. The residence of the architects, this house was built with an almost fanatic respect for living trees on the site, which dictated the forms and placement of the residence. Offering generous views toward this greenery, the interior of the house surprisingly adapts a fully synthetic vocabulary, focusing on plastics or rubber. Even the strip window looking out on the trees is made of Plexiglas. The orange and blue colors chosen for the house are also not likely to be confused with their natural setting.

Another North American project that approaches its natural setting with a decided emphasis on blending in is Antoine Predock's Logjam House (Rio Blanco, Colorado, USA, 2007). This building makes physical use of large, natural tree trunks, felled and partially inserted into the architecture. Built amidst Ponderosa pines, the project is the result of Predock's vision of the very trees he has built around being cut down at some point in the future. The house, seen by the architect as a form of life, thus emerges from the natural setting of the pines. Rather than simply looking out onto the forest, which it does as well of course, the house in some sense becomes a part of its environment. Though modern and amply glazed, the house also contains the reminiscence of a childhood tree house, a kind of life within nature that many children experience, especially in such forest settings.

HOUSE FOR ART, HOUSE FOR BOOKS

Architects, of course, frequently design houses with the specific interests of the client in mind. Sometimes, these abiding passions become the *raison d'être* of a lodging. In the two cases cited here, the owners may well sleep elsewhere, reserving their architectural wonders for their real area of interest. The Casa Kike (Cahuita, Costa Rica, 2006–07, page 50) by Gianni Botsford is described as a "writer's retreat," though its two-pavilion design does allow for a smaller pavilion with a bedroom and bathroom. The main structure, lifted 1.2 meters off the ground on wooden stilts, is literally lined with books and is composed of an intricate pattern of beams and columns. On the exterior, this shed-like design is clad in corrugated steel sheeting, blending in with local architecture. The architect has combined a respect for the environment with a knowledge of Costa Rican dwellings to create a sophisticated synthesis of cultures, surrounding his client, Keith Botsford, with the books he loves.

Michael Meredith and Hilary Sample, the husband and wife team who form MOS, have designed a studio for the artist, Terry Winters, in Upstate New York (2007, page 228). Here, too, the idea of a shed is present in the zinc-clad monolithic form. Column-free space and an open, glazed end with

3   4   5

an exterior porch offer contact with the natural setting while giving the interior a sense of complete freedom. The only architectural element within the building is its central gray box containing a kitchen, archives and a washroom. Although clearly intended as an art studio, the very openness of the building is indicative of a general trend in residential architecture to break the usual hierarchies of interior space and allow users to determine their own activities as they will.

HUNKERING DOWN IN THE WILD

It is true that areas like the Western United States or parts of Latin America offer the possibility of construction in wilderness locations—a luxury not possible in densely crowded Japan for example. The very nature of such sites clearly changes the architecture and the problems it seeks to solve. No carefully pierced steel screen to hide the neighbors—rather a logic of openness, or perhaps one of creating limits where there are none. Two American examples show differing approaches related to their geographic situations. Will Bruder's Feigin Residence (Reno, Nevada, 2005–06, page 58) is a 560-square-meter house located on an enormous 2612-hectare site, and sits low in the land, curving like Richard Serra's Cor-ten steel *Snake*, according to the architect. Indeed, Bruder uses weathered steel plate for a retaining wall, and continues the serpentine curving theme developed here and in the roof of the house in its interiors.

Sean Godsell's Glenburn House (Glenburn, Victoria, Australia, 2004–07, page 120) is set in 20 hectares of farmland an hour and a half from Melbourne. Intending to offer panoramic views of the countryside while protecting its occupants from heat and wind, the architect quite simply embedded the house partially in the hilltop where it is situated. Responding to requests from the clients, the architect made use of sustainable strategies such as double glazing, solar collectors for power and hot water, and rainwater harvesting. It should be noted that although ecological concerns are not a specific theme in this book, they are naturally more and more present in contemporary houses. Fortunately, most architects have gone beyond feeling that a building must look "green" to be responsible. The Glenburn House is a case in point, with its distinctive modern appearance in a largely natural setting—it is ecological without being overbearing in its "message," and that seems to be the sign of a trend.

RIDERS ON THE STORM

This book is directly inspired by the *Architecture Now!* series (TASCHEN), now in its eigth volume. It has long been apparent that houses have been a frequent source of architectural innovation, and yet their rules and dimensions are clearly different from those of civic architecture for example. What can be done on a small scale may, however, herald the future of larger buildings as well. Architect's houses may indeed be more an affair of the rich than of the more financially modest, but an intelligent client and a good architect can permit experimentation and discoveries that would not be possible otherwise. The houses published here range from a floor area of 3250 square meters to the 36 square meters of the Quinta Monroy. What these two extremes share is that most basic of human needs, shelter from the storm.

Philip Jodidio, Grimentz, April 25, 2008

1Interview with Mario Botta, Lugano, Switzerland, August 16, 1998.

EINLEITUNG

VON BURGEN UND HÖHLEN

„Das Haus", so der Schweizer Architekt Mario Botta, „ist eng mit Vorstellungen von einem Zufluchtsort verbunden. Eine in den Felsen geschlagene Höhle ist wie ein Mutterleib. Dieses Konzept vom Haus verfechte ich. Wann immer ich von der Welt genug habe, will ich nach Hause gehen. Dort kann ich neue Kraft tanken für die Auseinandersetzungen des nächsten Tages. Solange es Menschen gibt, die Häuser brauchen, wird es Architektur geben … Ein Haus sollte wie der Schoß der Mutter sein."[1] Selbst wenn es Unterschiede zwischen Haus und Heim geben mag, so bleibt doch die Tatsache bestehen, dass die fundamentalen Vorstellungen von der Zuflucht, vom Leben und vom Tod eng mit der traditionellen Architektur der Wohnstatt verbunden sind, von der Höhle bis zur Burg. Ein Haus kann etwas über den Zivilisationsstand aussagen, über den Grad des Wohlstands oder sogar der Intelligenz; es ist ein Barometer der Existenz. Je nach Architekt und Auftraggeber kann ein Haus baulich avantgardistisch sein, historische Vorstellungen außer Acht lassen und nach neuen Paradigmen suchen; es kann sich den Regeln des Städtebaus fügen und sie zugleich auf den Kopf stellen. Es kann in luftiger Höhe schweben oder sich aus der Tiefe der Erde erheben. Während Kostenfaktoren das Bauen im öffentlichen Sektor meist auf die bewährten Methoden beschränken, gelingt es manchen privaten Wohnbauten, sämtlichen Regeln zu trotzen und den Fortschritt der Architektur voranzutreiben.

HOUSES NOW!

In der Gestaltung von Häusern ebenso wie in der Kunst der Architektur im Allgemeinen gibt es heutzutage keinen eindeutigen Stil, wie etwa den Minimalismus, der die Architektur des Wohnbaus unter Federführung z. B. von John Pawson lange zu dominieren schien. Der Minimalismus ist in vielen Kreisen nach wie vor populär, aber ebenso glamouröse Interieurs, wie etwa in dem Haus von Jouin Manku in Kuala Lumpur. Computer, die früher zum Einsatz kamen, um extravagante „Blobs" zu realisieren, sind inzwischen zum integralen Bestandteil des architektonischen Entwurfs geworden. Auch dies hat die Gestaltung der Häuser verändert und in vielerlei Hinsicht befreit. Die neue „Reife", die Architekten beim Einsatz von Computern an den Tag legen, lässt sich vielleicht am besten mit einem Kommentar von Michael Meredith von MOS zusammenfassen: „Computer sind dumm, aber sie können bestimmte Dinge unglaublich schnell erledigen, und die Architektur ist heute so komplex, dass man nicht alles im Kopf behalten kann."

Die Anzahl der Bücher und Zeitschriften über Häuser hat in den letzten Jahren merklich zugenommen. Menschen suchen nach Anregungen, um ihr eigenes Haus zu bauen oder einzurichten, ebenso spielt hier auch die Neugier eine Rolle. Wie leben andere Leute, insbesondere jene, die die Mittel haben, so gut wie alles zu realisieren, wonach ihnen der Sinn steht? Und natürlich spielt auch der Voyeurismus eine Rolle in den Visionen so mancher Architekten, etwa in Entwürfen wie dem Glashaus in Paris (Pierre Chareau, Maison de Verre, 1928–31) oder dem Glass House in New Canaan (Philip Johnson, 1949), und das bis in die Gegenwart. Was der Architekt kann, kann der Leser schon längst – fühlen Sie sich eingeladen.

EINE NUMMER GRÖSSER

Der Fairness halber sei zugestanden, dass jemand, der sich entschließt, ein Haus von 3000 m^2 Größe oder mehr zu bauen, normalerweise davon ausgeht, große Gruppen, Kunden oder Freunde, zu Gast zu haben. Dies trifft sicherlich auf das Haus in Kuala Lumpur zu, das der französische Möbel- und Innenraumdesigner Patrick Jouin und sein Partner Sanjit Manku (Seite 158) geplant haben. Das Haus wurde auf einem begrenzten Grundstück im ehemaligen Botschaftsviertel der malaysischen Hauptstadt erbaut und dient der ausgedehnten Großfamilie eines der bekanntesten Unternehmer des Landes als Domizil. Wunsch des Auftraggebers war es, auf dem Grundstück, das inmitten eines höchst heterogen bebauten Stadtteils liegt, so viel

6
Antoine Predock, Logjam House,
Rio Blanco, Colorado, USA, 2007

6

Grundfläche wie nur möglich zu realisieren. Der gewagte Entwurf umfasst zahlreiche Außenterrassen und abgegrenzte Gärten, die von der Schweizerin Sophie Agata Ambroise gestaltet wurden. Da die Architekten die ausgedehnte Großfamilie des Bauherrn zu berücksichtigen hatten, planten sie Wohneinheiten für drei Generationen. Dabei waren sie auf der Suche nach einer neuen Formensprache für ein Land, das einen kaum sichtbaren einheimischen Baustil hat. Die unglaubliche Größe des Hauses manifestiert sich in seinem massigen Baukörper. In den unteren Geschossebenen liegen eine große Garage und ein Tanzsaal für Gäste, darüber erhebt sich das eigentliche, gastliche und durchaus überschaubare Haus.

AUS DER REIHE TANZEN

Eine ganze Reihe von Architekten, die in diesem Band vorgestellt werden, nutzen den Entwurfsprozess, um bestehende Regeln, Vorschriften und Typologien zu hinterfragen und das Haus neu zu interpretieren. David Adjayes Sunken House (London, 2007, Seite 9) sprengt jede Konvention. Das Grundstück wurde zunächst bis auf Kellerniveau ausgehoben, um dort einen vollständig mit gebeiztem Holz verschalten Kubus und Terrassen zu errichten, die mit dem gleichen Bohlenbelag versehen sind. Dieser Umgang mit Raum und Materialien stellt sowohl die Vorstellung vom Grund, auf dem ein Bau zu errichten ist, infrage, als auch die Typologien von Keller und Terrasse bzw. Innenhof. Fast könnte das Haus als Hofhaus gelten, wären da nicht die Strenge der Form und der vergleichsweise radikale Ansatz, die den Bau zur Herausforderung werden lassen – im Gegensatz zum traditionellen Hofhaus bzw. Haus mit Terrasse.

Ein Projekt mit radikalem Designkonzept ist das Wall House (Santiago, Chile, 2004–07) von FAR frohn&rojas. Die Architekten entschieden sich, das Haus als Folge verschiedener Wandschichten aus zunehmend leichteren bzw. lichtdurchlässigeren Materialien anzulegen. Der innerste Kern des Hauses mit den Badezimmern besteht aus Beton. Um ihn herum sind Bänder aus Holz angeordnet, die die Küche, das Schlafzimmer und einen Essbereich umfassen. Die sichtbare Außenhaut des Baus besteht aus hochisolierenden Polykarbonatpaneelen. In gewisser Weise scheint hier das uralte Bild von der Höhle hineinzuspielen, zumindest in Anordnung und Wahl der Materialien. Der Kern des Hauses aus Beton ist sein massivstes und letztlich auch schützendstes Element. All jene Wohnbereiche hingegen, die eher Wandel und Bewegung erleben, wurden aus Holz gebaut, und die abschließende Außenschicht, fast eine Haut im physiologischen Sinn, besteht aus lichtdurchlässigem Kunststoff. Die anthropomorphen Aspekte dieser Schichtstruktur liegen auf der Hand, Parallelen zwischen der architektonischen Vorgehensweise und dem menschlichen Knochenbau, inneren Organen und Haut bieten sich an. Wesentlich war möglicherweise die Entscheidung der Architekten, den Grundriss ganz bewusst von den Wänden diktieren zu lassen, was im Grunde eine Umkehrung des üblichen Planungsvorgangs ist, bei dem der Grundriss dominiert. Es ist ermutigend zu sehen, dass trotz der jahrhundertealten Geschichte des Wohnbaus manche jungen Architekten nach wie vor überzeugt sind, die Art und Weise, wie Häuser gebaut werden, wandeln zu können.

ZWISCHEN HIMMEL UND MEER

Im Französischen gibt es den Ausdruck „une vue imprenable" – was so viel heißt wie eine Aussicht, die ihrem „Besitzer" nicht genommen werden kann. So werden Häuser oft an Orten mit Aussicht gebaut. Will sich der Besitzer vom Blick in sein Haus hinein, mit seinen intimen Räumen und begrenzten Ausblicken lösen, muss er nur von seinem Balkon blicken, um eine Variante des Unendlichen zu entdecken. In solchen Fällen ist es eine bereichernde Aufgabe für den Architekten, Aussichten in die Konzeption des Hauses einzubeziehen. Anders als der umfassende Schutz, den die Höhle bietet, setzt sich ein Haus mit Aussicht in all seiner Angreifbarkeit den mitunter feindlichen Elementen aus. Dieser Art von Entblößung kommt besonders die moderne Architektur entgegen mit ihren widerstandsfähigen Materialien und der Möglichkeit, große Flächen selbst bei starken Windlasten umfassend zu verglasen.

7

8

Das Haus in Guarujá (São Paulo, Brasilien, 2004–06), ein Entwurf des Architekturbüros Bernardes + Jacobsen aus Rio de Janeiro, liegt auf einem steil abfallenden Gelände. Es bietet nicht nur ein üppiges landschaftliches Umfeld, sondern auch Ausblick auf den Atlantik. Das Haus führt vor Augen, wie sehr die architektonische Gestaltung von den klimatischen Gegebenheiten abhängig ist. Die Terrassen, durch die Außen- und Innenraum nahezu ununterscheidbar werden, wären in vielen Klimazonen schlicht undenkbar, ganz gleich, wie beeindruckend der Ausblick auch wäre. Das mehrdeutige Spiel mit Innen- und Außenraum, seit Langem in Japan praktiziert, ist ein beliebtes Thema in der zeitgenössischen Architektur im Allgemeinen, doch lässt sich nur schwer vorstellen, wie man es logischer oder umfassender umsetzen könnte, als es die Holzterrassen dieses Hauses zeigen.

BAUMHÄUSER UND KUNSTSTOFFHÄUSER

Statt gewagt über einem Abgrund zu schweben oder danach zu streben, die Kräfte der Natur zu bezwingen, nehmen andere Häuser ihr Umfeld an und verschmelzen mit ihm. Ihre Nähe zur Natur hängt nicht von weiten Panoramablicken ab, sondern eher vom Grün der Wälder. Eine überraschende und humorvolle Interpretation des Themas zeigt die Casa de Silicona (La Florida, Madrid, Spanien, 2006) von SELGASCANO. Das Domizil der Architekten wurde mit Respekt vor den Bäumen auf dem Gelände gebaut, woraus sich auch Form und Platzierung des Hauses ergaben. Das Innere des Hauses bietet einen großzügigen Blick ins Grüne. Es bedient sich überraschenderweise eines rein synthetischen Vokabulars und nutzt besonders Kunststoffe und Gummi. Auch die Orange- und Blautöne, die für das Haus gewählt wurden, lassen kaum eine Verwechslung mit dem natürlichen Umfeld zu.

Ein weiteres nordamerikanisches Projekt, das sich seiner landschaftlichen Umgebung mit dem ausdrücklichen Ziel stellt, mit ihr zu verschmelzen, ist Antoine Predocks Logjam House (Rio Blanco, Colorado, USA, 2007). Das Haus arbeitet mit den massiven, naturbelassenen Baumstämmen, die gefällt und teilweise in die Architektur eingebunden wurden. Das zwischen Gelbkiefern gebaute Haus entstand aus Predocks Vision, dass die Bäume, um die herum er baute, irgendwann in der Zukunft gefällt werden könnten. So entwickelte sich das Haus, in dem der Architekt eine Lebensform sieht, aus dem natürlichen kiefernbewachsenen Umfeld. Doch statt nur Ausblick in den Wald zu bieten, wird das Haus in gewisser Weise Teil seiner Umgebung. Trotz der modernen großzügigen Verglasung weckt es auch Erinnerungen an Baumhäuser aus Kindertagen, an ein Leben in der Natur.

EIN HAUS FÜR DIE KUNST, EIN HAUS FÜR BÜCHER

Natürlich entwerfen Architekten Häuser mit Blick auf die spezifischen Interessen ihrer Auftraggeber. Und manchmal werden diese Passionen zur Raison d'Être eines Hauses. In den zwei hier besprochenen Beispielen könnten die Eigentümer sogar ihre architektonischen Schmuckstücke ganz ihrer Passion überlassen und selbst woanders schlafen. Die Casa Kike (Cahuita, Costa Rica, 2006–07, Seite 50) von Gianni Botsford ist ein „Rückzugsort für einen Schriftsteller". Der Entwurf sieht den kleineren der beiden Pavillons für Schlaf- und Badezimmer vor. Der Hauptbau, der auf Holzstützen 1,2 m hoch über dem Boden schwebt, wird von Büchern umsäumt und besteht aus einem Muster aus Trägern und Stützen. Außen wurde das schuppenähnliche Gebäude mit Wellblech ummantelt und knüpft so an die regionaltypische Architektur an. Es gelingt dem Architekten, einen respektvollen Umgang mit der Umwelt mit seiner Kenntnis costa-ricanischer Wohnformen zu verbinden und so eine gelungene Synthese der Kulturen zu schaffen.

Michael Meredith und Hilary Sample, das Ehepaar des Büros MOS, entwarfen ein Atelier für den Künstler Terry Winters in Upstate New York (2007, Seite 228). Auch hier taucht – in Gestalt eines zinkverkleideten Monolithen – das Motiv des Schuppens wieder auf. Mit seiner verglasten Stirnseite und einer Außenveranda öffnet sich der gänzlich stützenfreie Raum zur Umgebung; zugleich bietet der Innenraum unein-

7 + 8
Sean Godsell, Glenburn House,
Glenburn, Victoria, Australia,
2004–07

9
Gianni Botsford Architects, Casa Kike,
Cahuita, Costa Rica, 2006–07

geschränkte Freiheit. Das einzige architektonische Element innerhalb des Gebäudes ist der zentral positionierte graue Kubus, in dem sich Küche, Archiv und ein kleines Bad befinden. Obwohl der Bau eindeutig als Künstleratelier angelegt ist, ist seine ausgeprägte Offenheit dennoch Hinweis auf einen grundlegenden Trend in der Wohnbauarchitektur, der die üblichen Hierarchien der Innenraumgestaltung aufbricht.

AUSGESETZT IN DER WILDNIS

Gegenden wie der Westen der Vereinigten Staaten oder Teile Lateinamerikas erlauben es, in der Wildnis zu bauen – ein Luxus, der etwa im dicht besiedelten Japan nicht möglich ist. Schon allein die Beschaffenheit solcher Baugrundstücke hat Einfluss auf die Architektur und die Problemstellungen, die sie zu lösen versucht. Hier geht es nicht um einen aufwendig gestanzten Stahlschirm, der die Nachbarschaft verbirgt, sondern vielmehr um eine Logik der Offenheit oder möglicherweise sogar darum, Grenzen zu schaffen, wo keine sind. Zwei Beispiele aus den USA illustrieren verschiedene Herangehensweisen an die jeweilige geografische Lage. Will Bruders Feigin Residence (Reno, Nevada, 2005–06, Seite 58) ist ein 560 m² großes Haus auf einem gewaltigen 2612 ha großen Grundstück. Es scheint auf dem Boden zu kauern und windet sich wie eine Schlange, dem Architekten zufolge eine Anspielung auf Richard Serras „Snake", eine Skulptur aus Cor-Ten-Stahl. Und tatsächlich setzt Bruder patinierte Stahlplatten als Böschungsmauer ein, in der sich der schlängelnde Schwung fortsetzt, der sich als Thema durch das Projekt zieht, etwa auch im Dach und Interieur des Hauses.

Sean Godsells Glenburn House (Glenburn, Victoria, Australien, 2004–07, Seite 120) liegt auf 20 ha Farmland, etwa anderthalb Stunden von Melbourne entfernt. Um weite Blicke in die Landschaft zu ermöglichen und die Bewohner dennoch vor Hitze und Wind zu schützen, versenkte der Architekt das Haus teilweise in dem Hügel, an dem es liegt. Auf Wunsch der Auftraggeber bemühte sich der Architekt um Nachhaltigkeit und nutzte Doppelverglasung, Sonnenkollektoren für Strom und Warmwasser sowie Regenwassergewinnung. Ökologische Belange, auch wenn sie in diesem Band nicht speziell thematisiert werden, sind im zeitgenössischen Hausbau immer stärker präsent. Glücklicherweise haben sich die meisten Architekten von der Vorstellung verabschiedet, ein Haus müsse „grün" aussehen, um umweltverträglich zu sein. Das Glenburn House mit seinem modernen Erscheinungsbild in einem natürlichen Umfeld ist ein gutes Beispiel hierfür – es ist ökologisch, ohne seine „Botschaft" aufdrängen zu wollen.

RIDERS ON THE STORM

Dieses Buch wurde unmittelbar von der Reihe *Architecture Now!* (TASCHEN) inspiriert, die inzwischen aus acht Bänden besteht. Schon lange ist offensichtlich, dass private Wohnbauten oft Inspirationsquellen für architektonische Innovation waren. Was sich im kleinen Maßstab realisieren lässt, mag durchaus Vorbote größer dimensionierter Bauten sein. Von Architekten geplante Wohnbauten mögen zwar noch immer eher ein Privileg der Wohlhabenden sein – doch ein kluger Auftraggeber und ein guter Architekt lassen Experimente und Entdeckungen zu, die andernfalls nicht realisierbar wären. Die hier vorgestellten Häuser reichen von einer Grundfläche von 3250 m² bis zu einer Fläche von 36 m² in der Quinta Monroy. Diesen beiden Extremen ist gemein, dass sie einem der grundlegendsten Bedürfnisse des Menschen gerecht werden: Zuflucht vor den Stürmen des Lebens zu bieten.

Philip Jodidio, Grimentz, 25. April 2008

---

1 Interview mit Mario Botta, Lugano, Schweiz, 16. August 1998.

INTRODUCTION

DE CAVERNES ET DE CHÂTEAUX

« L'idée de maison, explique l'architecte suisse Mario Botta, est intimement liée à celle d'abri. Une caverne creusée dans la roche est comme un ventre maternel. C'est le concept de maison que je défends. Lorsque je suis fatigué du monde, je veux retourner dans ma maison. Là, je peux me recharger en énergie et me préparer aux batailles du lendemain. Tant qu'un homme aura besoin d'une maison, l'architecture existera… Une maison devrait être comme le ventre d'une mère. »[1] L'architecture de l'habitat, quel qu'il soit, caverne ou château, est profondément intriquée aux idées fondamentales de refuge, de vie et de mort. La maison peut être une façon de mesurer le degré de civilisation, de richesse, voire d'intelligence. Elle est un baromètre de la vie. Selon l'auteur et le client, une maison peut être d'avant-garde et balayer les idées anciennes à la recherche d'un nouveau paradigme. Elle peut accepter les règles de l'urbanisme, quitte à les inverser. Elle peut flotter dans l'air ou surgir des profondeurs de la terre. Alors que les facteurs économiques risquent de cantonner l'architecture publique à des méthodes éprouvées, certaines maisons bousculent toutes les règles et aident globalement l'architecture à progresser.

HOUSES NOW !

Aujourd'hui, la création architecturale en général et l'architecture résidentielle en particulier n'obéissent pas à un style unique ou à une tendance dominante, comme l'a longtemps été le minimalisme sous l'impulsion de personnalités comme John Pawson. Il reste à la mode dans de nombreux cercles, mais la complexité scintillante des intérieurs aménagés par Jouin Manku dans sa maison malaisienne l'est aussi. L'ordinateur, naguère utilisé pour dessiner des blobs extravagants, est devenu un outil trivial. Appliqué à la conception de toutes petites résidences ou de vastes bâtiments, la simulation informatique a modifié et, à bien des égards, libéré le travail sur la maison. Cette nouvelle « maturité » semble assez bien résumée par Michael Meredith, de MOS, assistant en architecture à la Harvard Graduate School of Design (Floating House, lac Huron, Ontario, Canada) : « Les ordinateurs sont stupides, mais ils peuvent accomplir des tâches simples très vite et l'architecture est une discipline tellement complexe qu'il est impossible de tout avoir en tête. »

Les livres et magazines consacrés aux maisons sont de plus en plus nombreux. Certains lecteurs y pêchent des astuces et des idées pour construire et décorer leur maison, mais beaucoup les feuillettent par pure curiosité. Pour savoir comment vivent les autres, surtout ceux qui ont les moyens de réaliser tous leurs désirs… Le voyeurisme participe bien sûr à l'imagination de l'architecte, de la Maison de verre de Pierre Chareau à Paris (1928–31) à la Glass House de Philip Johnson (New Canaan, 1949), jusqu'à aujourd'hui. Si l'architecte peut le faire, le lecteur peut en rêver…

LA REINE DU PERCHOIR

En tout logique, lorsque des gens, souvent très riches, décident de construire une maison de 3000 m2 ou plus, c'est parce qu'ils ont l'intention d'y recevoir beaucoup de monde. C'est le cas de la maison édifiée à Kuala Lumpur par l'architecte d'intérieur et designer de mobilier Patrick Jouin et son associé Sanjit Manku (page 158). Édifiée sur un terrain assez modeste dans l'ancien quartier des ambassades de la capitale malaisienne, cette résidence est destinée à la famille élargie d'un des hommes d'affaires les plus en vue du pays. Dans un environnement dont l'architecture est au mieux qualifiable d'hétérogène, les architectes, à la demande de leur client, ont empilé autant de

10
SELGASCANO, Silicon House,
La Florida, Madrid, Spain, 2006

10

mètres carrés utiles que possible. Cet audacieux projet bénéficie également de nombreuses terrasses et jardins clos dessinés par Sophie Agata Ambroise de Lugano. Prenant en compte la taille imposante de la famille du client, qui nécessitait assez d'appartements pour trois générations, les architectes ont cherché à définir un nouveau langage pour ce pays qui n'a guère de style architectural notable en dehors d'un orientalisme colonial désuet dont témoignent encore la gare et quelques bâtiments plus anciens. L'impressionnante masse extérieure de la maison s'explique par la présence d'un vaste garage et d'une salle de bal aux niveaux inférieurs, qui servent de socle à ce qui paraît être une résidence agréable de taille raisonnable en partie supérieure.

TORDRE LA RÈGLE

Un certain nombre de résidences présentées dans ce volume s'attaquent à la substance même du projet pour remettre en question les codes, les règles et les typologies et réinterpréter la maison. La Sunken House de David Adjaye (Londres, 2007) défie clairement les conventions : la totalité du terrain a été creusée jusqu'au sous-sol ; le nouveau volume ainsi libéré accueille un cube bardé de bois teinté s'ouvrant sur une série de patios. Cette orchestration des espaces et des matériaux remet en cause aussi bien le concept du sol sur lequel une maison s'appuie que la typologie du sous-sol et du patio. On pourrait parler d'un archétype de maison à patio si l'austérité de ses formes et la radicalité de son concept ne la rendait si provocante, à l'opposé de la maison à patio classique, omniprésente dans les banlieues du Royaume-Uni et ailleurs.

Autre projet radical : la Wall House de FAR frohn&rojas (Santiago du Chili, 2004–07). Cette maison se présente comme une succession concentrique de parois réalisées dans des matériaux de plus en plus légers et transparents. Le noyau central en béton qui contient les salles de bain est entouré de bandeaux de bois derrière lesquels s'organisent la cuisine, les chambres et une salle à manger, cloisonnées par des panneaux de polycarbonate isolant. On retrouve ici l'idée de la caverne archaïque, du moins dans le positionnement et le choix des matériaux. Le noyau de béton est l'élément le plus solide et le plus protecteur de la maison. Les espaces de séjour prévus pour le mouvement sont en bois et la couche extérieure en plastique translucide. Cette stratification est aussi à l'image du corps humain : os, organes et peau. Les architectes ont laissé les murs dicter le plan, contrairement à la procédure habituelle où le plan prime. Il est encourageant de constater que, malgré des siècles voire des millénaires de travail sur la maison, certains jeunes architectes pensent encore qu'ils peuvent modifier la manière dont on la conçoit. Les modes de vie et les styles esthétiques contemporains jouent à l'évidence un rôle crucial dans la liberté que Frohn et Rojas revendiquent dans cette Wall House.

ENTRE CIEL ET MER

Nous rêvons tous d'une « vue imprenable », et les maisons individuelles sont souvent édifiées dans des sites ouvrant sur un horizon dégagé. Une perspective sur les montagnes ou sur l'océan offre le spectacle du changement perpétuel de la nature au fil des saisons. Pour s'échapper du foyer, de ses espaces clos et de ses perspectives contraintes (la caverne), il suffit de regarder dehors pour percevoir l'infini. Intégrer paysages et perspectives à la conception de la maison fait partie des aspects les plus passionnants du travail d'architecte. Plutôt que la protection de la caverne, la maison dotée d'une vue spectaculaire s'expose à l'hostilité des éléments. Cet apparent état de vulnérabilité convient à l'architecture moderne, qui dispose de matériaux résistants et peut se permettre de grandes surfaces vitrées, même face au vent.

De toute la hauteur de son site escarpé, la maison construite à Guarujá par les architectes de Rio de Janeiro Bernardes + Jacobsen (São

11   12

Paulo, Brésil, 2004–06) combine un cadre naturel tropical luxuriant et une vue magnifique sur l'Atlantique. Elle montre dans quelle mesure l'architecture des maisons est influencée par le climat. Ces terrasses qui empêchent presque toute distinction entre dedans et dehors seraient impensables sous d'autres cieux, quel que soit l'attrait du paysage. L'ambiguïté entre l'intérieur et l'extérieur, cultivée de tout temps au Japon et prisée des architectes contemporains, s'exprime avec une fluidité et une logique sans pareilles dans les terrasses en bois de cette résidence.

MAISONS DANS LES ARBRES ET MAISONS EN PLASTIQUE

À l'opposé de l'audace que suppose une situation en porte-à-faux en bord de falaise ou une ouverture téméraire aux forces naturelles, d'autres demeures se fondent dans leur cadre de façon plus douce. Elles recherchent une proximité avec la nature qui n'est pas liée à l'infini des perspectives, mais à la verdure de la forêt par exemple. Une des interprétations les plus surprenantes et humoristiques de ce thème est la maison Silicone de SELGASCANO (La Florida, Madrid, Espagne, 2006). Les architectes ont construit leur résidence personnelle dans un respect quasi fanatique des arbres préexistants, qui ont dicté son implantation et ses formes. En privilégiant des vues généreuses sur la nature, ils ont adopté pour l'intérieur un vocabulaire synthétique à base de plastiques et de caoutchouc. Même le bandeau des fenêtres donnant sur les arbres est en Plexiglas. Ce bleu et cet orange ne risquent pas de se confondre avec les couleurs du cadre naturel.

Autre projet d'Amérique du Nord qui cherche résolument la fusion avec son environnement naturel, la Logjam House d'Antoine Predock (Rio Blanco, Colorado, États-Unis, 2007), dont la structure, percée de gros troncs d'arbres tombés, est implantée dans une pinède de Ponderosa. Elle intègre aussi la vision de ces arbres qui seront un jour abattus. Cette résidence dans laquelle l'architecte transpose une forme de vie émerge harmonieusement de son environnement naturel. Elle ne se contente pas de donner sur la forêt, elle en fait partie. Bien que moderne et amplement vitrée, elle n'est pas sans rappeler l'esprit d'une maison dans les arbres, ce mode de vie primitif et ludique qu'adorent les enfants et les adultes.

MAISON POUR L'ART, MAISON POUR LES LIVRES

Bien entendu, les architectes conçoivent leurs maisons en fonction des intérêts et des goûts de leur client, des passions parfois si envahissantes qu'elles deviennent la raison d'être de la résidence. Dans les deux cas suivants, il se pourrait même que les propriétaires aillent dormir dehors, tant ces merveilles architecturales sont faites pour d'autres hôtes qu'eux. La Casa Kike de Gianni Botsford (Cahuita, Costa Rica, 2006–07, page 50) est décrite comme « la retraite d'un écrivain », dont le plus petit des deux pavillons abrite une chambre et une salle de bains. La structure principale, composée d'une imbrication de poutres et de colonnes est surélevée de 1,2 m sur des pilotis de bois et littéralement doublée de livres. À l'extérieur, la couverture en tôle d'acier ondulée se fond dans le bâti local. L'architecte a combiné respect pour l'environnement et connaissance de l'habitat du Costa Rica pour créer une synthèse culturelle sophistiquée et entourer son client, Keith Botsford, des quelques 16 000 livres qu'il aime.

Michael Meredith et Hilary Sample, les époux qui ont créé l'agence MOS, ont conçu l'atelier de l'artiste Terry Winters dans l'État de New York (2007, page 228). On retrouve ici l'idée de shed dans cette forme monolithique habillée de zinc. Un grand volume sans colonne dont une extrémité est entièrement vitrée et un porche établissent le contact avec le cadre naturel, tout en générant à l'intérieur un sentiment de liberté totale. Le seul élément architectural interne est la boîte centrale grise contenant la cuisine, les archives et une salle d'eau. Bien que dessiné

11 + 12
Will Bruder + Partners, Feigin Resi-
dence, Reno, Nevada, Usa, 2005–06

13
Jouin Manku, House in Kuala Lumpur,
Malaysia, 2004–08

13

pour répondre aux besoins d'un atelier d'artiste, ce plan ouvert illustre la tendance générale de l'architecture résidentielle à rompre avec les hiérarchies habituelles de l'espace intérieur et à laisser les utilisateurs déterminer leurs activités selon leurs désirs.

TAPIE DANS LA NATURE

Il est vrai que l'Ouest des États-Unis ou certaines régions d'Amérique latine permettent de construire dans des zones quasiment sauvages, luxe impossible dans un pays aussi densément peuplé que le Japon, par exemple. La nature même de ces sites influe à l'évidence sur l'architecture et les problèmes à résoudre. Inutile de prévoir des écrans d'acier perforés pour se cacher des voisins, mieux vaut rechercher une logique d'ouverture ou, peut-être, créer des limites là où elles n'existent pas. Ces exemples américains montrent deux façons d'aborder la situation géographique. La Feigin Residence de Will Bruder (Reno, Nevada, 2005–06, page 58) est une maison de 560 m2 implantée sur une immense propriété de 2612 hectares. L'architecte la décrit tapie dans le paysage, comme une sculpture en acier Corten de la série Snakes signée Richard Serra. Bruder utilise d'ailleurs des tôles d'acier patiné pour un mur de soutènement et reprend le thème de la courbe sinusoïdale dans la toiture et à l'intérieur.

La Glenburn House de Sean Godsell (Glenburn, Victoria, Australie, 2004–07, page 120) est située sur 20 hectares de terres agricoles à une heure et demie de voiture de Melbourne. Pour offrir des vues panoramiques sur la campagne tout en protégeant les habitants de la chaleur et du vent, l'architecte l'a en partie enterrée au sommet d'une colline. À la demande de son client, Godsell a adopté des stratégies de développement durable comme le double vitrage, les panneaux photovoltaïques fournissant l'électricité et l'eau chaude et la récupération des eaux de pluie. Si les préoccupations écologiques ne font pas l'objet d'un chapitre particulier dans ce livre, elles sont de plus en plus présentes dans les maisons contemporaines. Heureusement, la plupart des architectes ont dépassé l'idée qu'une construction devait « avoir l'air écolo » pour devenir pleinement éco-responsables. La maison Glenburn en est un exemple. Assumant son aspect moderne dans un cadre naturel, elle est écologique sans surjouer son « message ». Ce pourrait être le signal d'une tendance.

LES CAVALIERS DE LA TEMPÊTE

Ce livre est directement inspiré de la série Architecture Now ! de TASCHEN, qui en est aujourd'hui à son huitième volume. La maison est depuis longtemps considérée comme une source d'innovation architecturale, bien qu'elle subisse des contraintes plus importantes et nombreuses que l'architecture publique, par exemple. Les petits projets peuvent aussi servir de terrain d'expérimentation pour des constructions ultérieures de dimensions plus ambitieuses. Si les maisons d'architectes s'adressent le plus souvent à une clientèle riche, la collaboration entre un bon architecte et un client intelligent, même modeste, peut ouvrir la voie à des découvertes qui n'auraient pas été possibles dans d'autres conditions. La surface des maisons présentées ici va de 3250 m2 au sol aux 36 m2 de la Quinta Monroy. Au-delà de cette amplitude, ces deux extrêmes ont en partage le besoin le plus viscéral de l'être humain : se protéger de la tempête.

Philip Jodidio, Grimentz, 25 avril 2008

1   Entretien avec Mario Botta, Lugano, Suisse, 16 août 1998.

Deck House ▶

FELIPE ASSADI +
FRANCISCA PULIDO ARCHITECTS

Felipe Assadi + Francisca Pulido Architects
Carmencita 262, oficina 202
Las Condes, Santiago
Chile

Tel: +56 234 5558
E-mail: info@assadi.cl
Web: www.felipeassadi.com

FELIPE ASSADI was born in 1971. He received his degree in Architecture from the Finis Terrae University (Santiago, 1996) and his M.Arch degree from the Pontificia Universidad Católica de Chile in Santiago in 2006. He teaches at the Andrés Bello University in Santiago. **FRANCISCA PULIDO** also received her architecture degree from the Finis Terrae University in 1996 and teaches at the Andrés Bello University. They created Assadi & Pulido in 1999 on an informal basis, incorporating the firm in 2006. Their work, concentrated on private residences for the moment, includes the Schmitz House (Calera de Tango, Santiago, 2001); the Bar El Tubo (Lima, Peru, 2003); the Park Theater (Santiago, 2004); the 20x20 House (Santiago, 2005); the Gatica House (Rancagua, 2006); the Russo Club (Talca, 2006); the Serrano House (Santiago, 2006); the Deck House (Alto Rungue, Santiago, 2006, published here); and the Guthrie House (Santiago, 2007), all in Chile unless stated otherwise.

FELIPE ASSADI wurde 1971 geboren. Er machte seinen Abschluss in Architektur an der Universidad Finis Terrae (Santiago, 1996) und erwarb 2006 einen M.Arch. an der Pontificia Universidad Católica de Chile in Santiago. Assadi lehrt an der Universidad Andrés Bello in Santiago. Auch **FRANCISCA PULIDO** schloss ihr Architekturstudium 1996 an der Universidad Finis Terrae ab und lehrt an der Universidad Andrés Bello. Gemeinsam gründeten sie Assadi & Pulido 1999 zunächst informell, 2006 folgte die offizielle Firmengründung. Ihr Werk, das sich bislang auf private Wohnbauten konzentriert, umfasst u. a. die Casa Schmitz (Calera de Tango, Santiago, 2001), die Bar El Tubo (Lima, Peru, 2003), das Teatro del Parque (Santiago, 2004), die Casa 20x20 (Santiago, 2005), die Casa Gatica (Rancagua, 2006), den Russo Club (Talca, 2006), die Casa Serrano (Santiago, 2006), das Deck House (Alto Rungue, Santiago, 2006, hier vorgestellt) sowie die Casa Guthrie (Santiago, 2007), alle in Chile, sofern nicht anders vermerkt.

FELIPE ASSADI, né en 1971, est diplômé en architecture de l'Universidad Finis Terrae (Santiago du Chili, 1996) et M.Arch de la Pontificia Universidad Católica de Chile de Santiago en 2006. Il enseigne à l'Universidad Andrés Bello à Santiago. **FRANCISCA PULIDO** est également diplômée de l'Universidad Finis Terrae en 1996 et enseigne à l'Universidad Andrés Bello. Ils ont créé Assadi & Pulido en 1999 sur une base informelle, ne fondant la société qu'en 2006. Pour le moment, ils travaillent essentiellement au Chili et sur des projets de résidences privées dont la Casa Schmitz (Calera de Tango, Santiago, 2001) ; le Bar El Tubo (Lima, Pérou, 2003) ; le Teatro del Parque (Santiago, 2004) ; la Casa 20x20 (Santiago, 2005) ; la Casa Gatica (Rancagua, 2006) ; le Russo Club (Talca, 2006) ; la Casa Serrano (Santiago, 2006) ; la Casa Deck (Alto Rungue, Santiago, 2006, publiée ici) et la Casa Guthrie (Santiago, 2007).

DECK HOUSE

Alto Rungue, Santiago, Chile, 2006

House area: 150 m². Deck area: 370 m².
Client: not disclosed. Cost: not disclosed

The site of this house suggested the idea of a large terrace from which to view the Coast mountain range. Working from the basic idea of a large deck made of native oak over which the structure of the house would be placed, essentially housing living areas that in a sense serve the deck itself. The living area in this instance is defined as including not only a kitchen and dining room, but also the master bedroom. In fact, the sleeping area is intentionally conceived with a dormitory-like configuration, eliminating the hierarchy implicit in the concept of a master bedroom. The husband and wife architecture team describes the interior as a "capsule of glass incorporated in the folding deck." The deck clearly wraps around the floor-to-ceiling glass block that forms the actual interior spaces. This deck runs from the lowest level where a swimming pool is located, up to the roof. Assadi compares the folding of the deck to that of a chaise longue, integrating the pool at one extremity and the roof-solarium at the other. Round windows in the rooftop patio bring light into the house. Asked originally to design a 140-square-meter house that could easily be reproduced, the architects rejected the very principle of the commission to create "a unique living space, unrepeatable and lacking the very essence of a catalog product—an identifiable façade."

Das Grundstück des Hauses legte nahe, eine großzügige Terrasse mit Blick auf die Küstenkordillere anzulegen. Grundidee des Entwurfs war eine große Terrasse aus einheimischem Eichenholz, auf die auch die Hauskonstruktion selbst gesetzt wurde, wobei der Wohnbereich des Hauses im Grunde der Terrasse untergeordnet ist. Der Wohnbereich umfasst Küche und Essbereich sowie auch das Hauptschlafzimmer. Es wurde bewusst als Schlafsaal konzipiert, wodurch die übliche Raumhierarchie, die das Konzept des Hauptschlafzimmers impliziert, aufgelöst wurde. Die Architekten, die auch privat ein Paar sind, beschreiben das Interieur als „in die stufenförmige Terrasse integrierte Glaskapsel". Der vom Boden bis zur Decke verglaste Kasten, der das Innere bildet, wird von der Terrasse quasi umfangen. Die Terrasse reicht von dem tiefsten Punkt mit dem Swimmingpool bis zum Dach des Hauses. Assadi vergleicht die Faltung der Terrasse, in die an einem Ende ein Pool, am anderen Ende eine Sonnenterrasse integriert sind, mit einer Strandliege. Kleine, in die Dachterrasse integrierte Fenster lassen Licht in das Haus. Ursprünglich lautete der Auftrag, ein leicht zu reproduzierendes 140 m² großes Haus zu entwerfen. Diesen Ansatz lehnten die Architekten jedoch ab; sie wollten einen „unverwechselbaren Wohnraum schaffen, der unwiederholbar ist und auf das Schlüsselmerkmal eines Katalogprodukts verzichtet – eine erkennbare Fassade".

L'environnement de cette maison suggérait à lui seul l'idée de créer une vaste terrasse d'où regarder la chaîne des montagnes côtières. Les architectes ont donc travaillé sur le principe d'une plate-forme en chêne local, sur laquelle serait implantée la maison regroupant les espaces de vie qui desservent en un sens la terrasse. La zone de vie comprend la cuisine, la salle à manger, mais aussi la chambre principale. En fait, la partie réservée au sommeil prend volontairement une configuration de dortoir, éliminant la hiérarchie implicite au concept classique de chambre principale. Le couple d'architectes décrit l'intérieur telle « une capsule de verre intégrée à une terrasse en forme de pli ». Celle-ci enveloppe le bloc de verre toute hauteur qui constitue le volume intérieur. Elle part du niveau inférieur où elle intègre la piscine pour remonter, se redresser, se replier et former la toiture qui inclut un solarium. Assadi compare ces plis à la forme d'une chaise longue. De petites verrières dans le toit éclairent l'intérieur. Alors qu'il leur avait été demandé au départ de concevoir une maison de 140 m² facilement reproductible, les architectes ont rejeté cette idée pour créer « un espace de vie unique, qui ne peut être répété, et qui exclut ce qui fait l'essence même d'un produit de catalogue : une façade identifiable. »

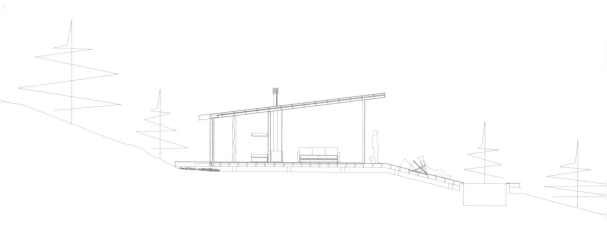

As seen in the section above or in the photos to the right, the house is clearly the result of the idea of a continuous, folded deck, extending from the front of the broadly glazed residence to its roof.

Wie der Aufriss oben und die Fotos rechts zeigen, wurde das Haus offensichtlich aus der Grundidee eines durchgängigen, „gefalteten" Holzdecks entwickelt, das sich von der Front des großzügig verglasten Baus bis über sein Dach zieht.

Comme le montre la coupe ci-dessus ou les photographies de droite, la maison tire son concept d'une idée de plate-forme continue, qui se plie de la partie avant largement vitrée jusqu'au toit.

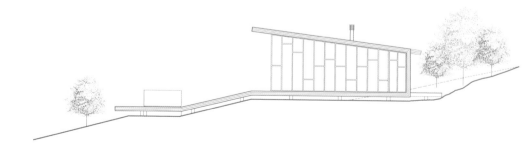

With its full-height glazing opening onto a pool and a magnificent view, the house seems to participate actively in the leisure activities of its owners, perched on a hillside between the mountains and the sky.

Mit seiner raumhohen Glasfront, die sich dem Pool und der überwältigenden Aussicht zuwendet, wirkt das Haus, als nähme es aktiv am Freizeitvergnügen seiner Bewohner teil. Der Bau schmiegt sich an den Abhang zwischen Bergen und Himmel.

Par sa façade vitrée toute en hauteur qui donne sur une piscine et un panorama magnifique, la maison perchée à flanc de colline entre les montagnes et le ciel semble participer activement aux activités de loisirs de ses propriétaires.

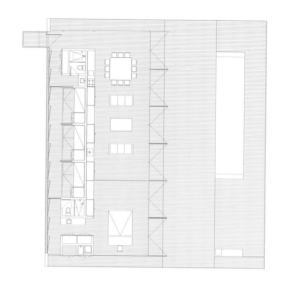

The high windows of the house can be opened almost entirely. The furnishing and interior design correspond to the rigorous geometry of the plan. Above, wooden slats filter the sunlight coming into the house.

Die hohen Fenster des Hauses lassen sich fast vollständig öffnen. Möbel und Innengestaltung knüpfen an die konsequente Geometrie des Grundrisses an. Holzlamellen (oben) filtern das einfallende Sonnenlicht.

Les hautes fenêtres peuvent s'ouvrir presque entièrement. Les aménagements et le mobilier intérieurs répondent à la géométrie rigoureuse du plan. Ci-dessus, des lattes de bois filtrent la lumière solaire.

Guarujá House ►

BERNARDES + JACOBSEN ARQUITETURA

Bernardes + Jacobsen Arquitetura
Rua Corcovado 250 / Jardim Botânico
22460-050 Rio de Janeiro, RJ / Brazil

Tel/Fax: +55 21 2512 7743
E-mail: bjrj@bja.com.br / Web: www.bja.com.br

Thiago Bernardes was born in Rio de Janeiro in 1974. The office of **BERNARDES + JACOBSEN** was created in 1980 by his father, Cláudio Bernardes, and Paulo Jacobsen, pioneers of a new type of residential architecture based on an effort to combine contemporary design and Brazilian culture. Thiago Bernardes worked in his father's office from 1991 to 1996, when he left to create his own firm, working on more than 30 residential projects between that date and 2001. With the death of his father, Thiago Bernardes reintegrated the firm and began to work with Paulo Jacobsen, who was born in 1954 in Rio de Janeiro. Jacobsen had studied photography in London, before graduating from the Bennett Methodist Institute in 1979. The office of Bernardes + Jacobsen currently employs approximately 50 people in Rio de Janeiro and São Paulo, and they work on roughly 40 projects per year. Some of their significant projects include the Gerdau Headquarters (Porto Alegre, 2005); the Villa Isabela (Henriksberg, Finland, 2005); the Hotel Leblon (Rio de Janeiro, 2005); the CF House, Angra dos Reis, Rio de Janeiro, 2001–06, published here); the Guarujá House (São Paulo, 2004–06, also published here); the MPM Agency Main Office (São Paulo, 2006); and the TIM Festival 2007 (Rio de Janeiro, 2007), all in Brazil unless stated otherwise. Recent work includes the Boa Vista Houses (São Paulo, 2007); the Eco Resort Houses (Bahia, 2007), both in Brazil; the St. James Villa (St. James Island, Virgin Islands, 2007); a summer house (Doha, Qatar, 2006–10); and a number of residential projects.

Thiago Bernardes wurde 1974 in Rio de Janeiro geboren. 1980 gründete sein Vater Cláudio Bernardes gemeinsam mit Paulo Jacobsen das Büro **BERNARDES + JACOBSEN**. Die beiden Architekten waren Pioniere einer neuen Form von Wohnbauarchitektur, die zeitgenössisches Design und brasilianische Kultur miteinander verbinden wollte. Zwischen 1991 und 1996 arbeitete Thiago Bernardes im Büro seines Vaters und gründete schließlich sein eigenes Büro, mit dem er zwischen 1996 und 2001 über 30 Hausprojekte realisierte. Nach dem Tod seines Vaters fusionierte Thiago Bernardes die beiden Firmen und arbeitete nun mit Paulo Jacobsen. Der 1954 in Rio de Janeiro geborene Jacobsen hatte in London Fotografie studiert, bevor er 1979 seinen Abschluss am Instituto Metodista Bennett machte. Das Büro Bernardes + Jacobsen hat zurzeit rund 50 Mitarbeiter in Rio de Janeiro und São Paulo, die pro Jahr an etwa 40 Projekten arbeiten. Eine Auswahl ihrer wichtigsten Arbeiten umfasst u. a. den Hauptsitz der Gerdau-Gruppe (Porto Alegre, 2005), die Villa Isabela (Henriksberg, Finnland, 2005), das Hotel Leblon (Rio de Janeiro, 2005), das CF House in Angra dos Reis (Rio de Janeiro, 2001–06, hier vorgestellt), das Haus in Guarujá (São Paulo, 2004–06, ebenfalls hier vorgestellt), den Hauptsitz der Agentur MPM (São Paulo, 2006) sowie Bauten für das TIM-Festival 2007 (Rio de Janeiro, 2007), alle in Brasilien, wenn nicht anders vermerkt. Neuere Projekte sind u. a. die Wohnanlage Boa Vista (São Paulo, 2007), der Eco Resort (Bahia, 2007), beide in Brasilien, die St. James Villa (St. James Island, Jungferninseln, 2007) sowie ein Sommerhaus (Doha, Katar, 2006–10) und mehrere private Wohnbauten.

Thiago Bernardes est né à Rio de Janeiro en 1974. L'agence **BERNARDES + JACOBSEN** a été créée en 1980 par son père, Cláudio Bernardes, et Paulo Jacobsen, pionniers d'un nouveau type d'architecture résidentielle reposant sur une volonté d'associer la conception d'esprit contemporain à la culture brésilienne. Thiago Bernardes a travaillé dans l'agence paternelle de 1991 à 1996, puis a fondé sa propre structure, intervenant sur plus de 30 projets résidentiels de 1996 à 2001. Après le décès de son père, il a réintégré son agence et commencé à collaborer avec Paulo Jacobsen, né en 1954 à Rio de Janeiro. Jacobsen avait étudié la photographie à Londres, avant d'être diplômé de l'Instituto Metodista Bennett en 1979. L'agence Bernardes + Jacobsen emploie actuellement environ 50 personnes à Rio et São Paulo, pour une quarantaine de projets réalisés chaque année. Parmi leurs réalisations les plus significatives : le siège de Gerdau (Porto Alegre, 2005) ; la Villa Isabela (Henriksberg, Finlande, 2005) ; l'Hotel Leblon (Rio de Janeiro, 2005) ; la maison CF (Angra dos Reis, Rio de Janeiro, 2001–06, publiée ici) ; la maison Guarujá (São Paulo, 2004–06, également publiée ici) ; le siège de l'agence MPM (São Paulo, 2006) et le TIM Festival 2007 (Rio de Janeiro, 2007), toutes au Brésil. Parmi leurs travaux récents : les maisons Boa Vista (São Paulo, 2007) ; les maisons Eco Resort (Bahia, 2007), au Brésil ; la villa St. James (St. James Island, Îles Vierges, 2007) ; une maison d'été (Doha, Qatar, 2006–10) et plusieurs autres projets résidentiels.

GUARUJÁ HOUSE

Guarujá, São Paulo, Brazil, 2004–06

Site area: 1550 m². Floor area: 1300 m². Client: not disclosed. Cost: not disclosed.
Team: Fabiana Porto, Gabriel Bocchile, Marco Aurélio Viterbo (Interior design), Andrés Galvez

In this vacation house for a couple with two children, intended also to accomodate friends, the architects have set the living spaces, balcony, and swimming pool with a spectacular view toward the ocean. The street side reveals only a "discreet, flat and horizontal façade." The landscape and vegetation on the site were preserved to the greatest extent possible. A steel-frame building enclosed with glass and wood, the house is set on such a steep slope that it was possible to use a structural platform 18 meters above the ground as a kind of basement play area for the children, "giving the sensation of a ground-floor house, set at the level of the tops of the trees." The architects and the client profit from a remarkable natural setting for this house, where an easy transition between interior and exterior, and the generous views redefine the meaning of the "vacation house" in a specifically Brazilian context.

Für dieses Haus, das einem Paar mit zwei Kindern als Feriendomizil dient und in dem auch Freunde beherbergt werden können, haben die Architekten Wohnräume, Balkon und Pool mit spektakulärem Ausblick auf das Meer angelegt. Die Straßenseite zeigt lediglich eine „diskrete, flache und horizontale Fassade". Landschaft und Vegetation auf dem Grundstück wurden, soweit irgend möglich, unberührt gelassen. Das Haus, eine glas- und holzummantelte Stahlrahmenkonstruktion, liegt an einem steil abfallenden Hang, sodass mit der 18 m über dem Boden stehenden Plattformkonstruktion ein Bereich zum Spielen für die Kinder entstand. Auf diese Weise „hat man das Gefühl, in einem ebenerdigen Haus zu sein, das in den Baumwipfeln schwebt". Architekten und Auftraggeber profitieren von der außergewöhnlichen landschaftlichen Lage des Hauses. Ein nahtloser Übergang zwischen Innen- und Außenraum und die großzügigen Ausblicke definieren das „Ferienhaus" in einem spezifisch brasilianischen Kontext neu.

Pour cette maison de vacances destinée à un couple, ses deux enfants et les amis qu'ils reçoivent, les architectes ont orienté les espaces de vie, le balcon et la piscine vers une vue spectaculaire sur l'océan. De la rue on n'aperçoit qu'une « façade discrète, plate et horizontale ». L'aménagement paysager et la végétation du terrain ont été conservés dans la mesure du possible. La maison à ossature d'acier, panneaux de verre et de bois est implantée sur une pente si escarpée qu'il a été possible de créer une plate-forme structurelle à 18 mètres au-dessus du sol pour créer une sorte d'aire de jeux en « sous-sol » pour les enfants « donnant la sensation d'une maison en rez-de-chaussée, posée au niveau du sommet des arbres ». Ce cadre remarquable a permis aux architectes et à leurs clients de ménager des transitions aisées entre l'intérieur et l'extérieur et de bénéficier de perspectives généreuses sur l'océan, qui donnent un nouveau sens au concept de « maison de vacances » dans ce contexte spécifiquement brésilien.

Perched above the water, the Guarujá House has a continuous wooden deck that opens toward a pool whose water appears to flow over the edge, integrating the architecture into the site.

Das über dem Meer schwebende Guarujá House hat eine durchgängige Holzterrasse, die sich zum Pool hin öffnet. Das Wasser scheint über die Beckenkante zu fließen und integriert die Architektur in das Gelände.

Perchée au-dessus de l'océan, la maison Guarujá présente une terrasse continue en bois qui donne sur une piscine à débordement, ce qui renforce l'intégration de l'architecture au site.

Surrounded by lush vegetation on a steeply sloped site, the house integrates itself into the environment using tree-like columns and its own green planters.

Inmitten üppiger Vegetation liegt das Haus auf einem steil abfallenden Grundstück. Baumähnliche Stützpfeiler und Pflanzen in Kübeln binden den Bau in sein Umfeld ein.

Implantée au cœur d'une végétation luxuriante sur un terrain en forte pente, la maison s'intègre à l'environnement grâce à ses colonnes en forme d'arbre et de grandes jardinières.

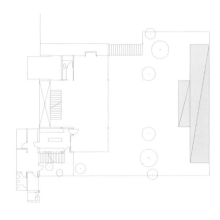

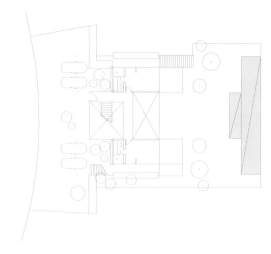

The luxuriant vegetation and quasi-tropical climate allow for the house to be almost entirely open, making the difference between inside and outside almost imperceptible.

Dank der üppigen Vegetation und des geradezu tropischen Klimas war es möglich, das Haus fast völlig offen zu gestalten, wodurch der Unterschied von Innen- und Außenraum kaum spürbar ist.

La végétation abondante et le climat quasi tropical ont permis de réaliser une maison presque entièrement ouverte. La différence entre l'intérieur et l'extérieur devient imperceptible.

Evening views show the dining room, with the vegetation of the site dominating the large window view, while an entrance picture shows the ways in which a view is framed looking directly through the architecture.

Abendliche Ansichten zeigen das Esszimmer mit Aussicht auf die Vegetation des Grundstücks; ein Foto vom Eingangsbereich zeigt, wie Ausblicke gerahmt werden, etwa durch eine Sichtachse direkt durch den Bau.

Une vue prise de la salle à manger à la tombée de la nuit, confrontée à la végétation environnante à travers sa vaste baie. Ci-dessous, vue de l'entrée montrant une perspective traversante cadrant une vue sur le paysage.

CF HOUSE

Angra dos Reis, Rio de Janeiro, Brazil, 2001–06

Site area: 1990 m². Floor area: 1024 m². Cost: not disclosed.
Team: Márcia Santoro, Inès Benevolo (Lighting design), Isabel Duprat (Landscape design)

The architect explains, "The first visit to the site convinced us that anything we built would create an obstacle to the sight of the sea and the wind flows." The large house is set close to the sea at the lowest available level on the site. Visitors thus arrive from above, and the architects have placed a pond on the roof, "camouflaging the building against the background of the sea and reflecting the sky, making the lightest effect possible." The steel-frame structural design makes use of 30-centimeter beams and allows for 9 meters between columns. The private areas and bedrooms are located at the top of the house near the entrance, while public spaces are situated below. A large, open balcony is intended to allow the house to "breathe" and thus "the circulation between the street and the sea is an enormous garden." The open volumes of the house and the extensive use of wood with fine green steel columns, stone and a light color scheme make the transparency sought by the architects apparent. "The materials chosen," they conclude, "are intended to make the house disappear."

Der Architekt erklärt: „Der erste Besuch des Bauplatzes überzeugte uns davon, dass alles, was wir bauen würden, dem freien Blick auf das Meer und den Winden im Weg stehen würde." Das große Haus ist dicht am Meer gebaut, auf dem tiefstmöglichen Punkt des Grundstücks. Und so nähern sich die Besucher von oben. Außerdem haben die Architekten auf dem Dach des Hauses einen Teich angelegt, der „das Gebäude vor dem Meer kaschiert und den Himmel spiegelt, um den größtmöglichen Effekt von Leichtigkeit zu erzielen". Der Entwurf der Stahlrahmenkonstruktion sieht 30-cm-Träger vor, was einen Stützenabstand von 9 m erlaubt. Die Privatbereiche und Schlafzimmer befinden sich im oberen Teil des Hauses in der Nähe des Eingangs, während die Gemeinschaftsbereiche im unteren Geschoss liegen. Ein großer, offener Balkon lässt das Haus „atmen", die „Verkehrsflächen zwischen Straße und Meer sind ein riesiger Garten". Die offen gestalteten Baukörper des Hauses und die ausgeprägte Verwendung von Holz in Kombination mit schmalen grünen Stahlstützen, Stein und einer hellen Farbpalette vermitteln die von den Architekten angestrebte Transparenz. „Die gewählten Materialien", merken sie zusammenfassend an, „sollen das Haus verschwinden lassen."

« La première visite du site nous avait convaincus que tout ce que nous pourrions édifier ferait obstacle à la vue sur la mer et au souffle du vent », expliquent les architectes. Cette grande demeure se dresse à proximité de l'océan, dans la partie basse de son terrain. Les visiteurs y accèdent donc par le haut, et un bassin a été aménagé sur le toit « camouflant la construction par rapport à l'océan et reflétant le ciel, pour obtenir l'effet de plus grande légèreté possible ». L'ossature en acier fait appel à des poutres de 30 centimètres de section qui autorisent des portées de 9 mètres entre colonnes. Les parties privatives et les chambres se trouvent au niveau supérieur près de l'entrée, au-dessus des espaces de réception. Un vaste balcon ouvert permet à la maison de « respirer », et « la circulation entre la rue et l'océan est un énorme jardin ». Le volume ouvert de la maison et l'utilisation extensive du bois et de fines colonnes d'acier peintes en vert, de la pierre et d'une gamme de couleurs claires rendent encore plus perceptible la transparence voulue par les architectes : « Les matériaux choisis tentent de faire disparaître la maison », concluent-ils.

The CF House rises up from its site with a lightness generated by thin pilotis. The ground level shelters covered spaces that are neither really indoors nor outdoors.

Das CF House erhebt sich mit großer Leichtigkeit auf schmalen pilotis über den Baugrund. Im Erdgeschoss liegen geschützte Räume, die weder ganz Innen- noch ganz Außenraum sind.

La maison CF posée sur l'eau s'élève avec légèreté sur de fins pilotis. Le rez-de-chaussée abrite des espaces couverts qui ne sont ni réellement intérieurs, ni extérieurs.

The light canopied structure sits largely above the ground allowing for such picturesque settings as the picnic table above, looking over the pool and the water beyond.

Der leichte Bau mit seinem Baldachindach wurde größtenteils über dem Boden aufgeständert, wodurch malerische Räume entstehen, etwa der Picknicktisch oben mit Blick auf den Pool und das Meer im Hintergrund.

La structure légère avec ses auvents est détachée du sol, permettant des aménagements originaux, telle cette table de pique-nique qui fait face à la piscine et la mer au-delà.

BLANK STUDIO

Blank Studio
1441 East Sunnyside Drive
Phoenix, AZ 85020
USA

Tel: +1 602 331 3310
Fax: +1 602 331 3525
E-mail: studio@blankspaces.net
Web: www.blankspaces.net

Matthew Trzebiatowski was born in Wisconsin in 1972 and received an M.Arch degree in Architecture from the University of Wisconsin at Milwaukee School of Architecture and Urban Planning (SARUP) in 1997. He is a registered architect in Arizona and Wisconsin and is currently a faculty member at Collins College of Design and Technology. Trzebiatowski established **BLANK STUDIO** in 2001 with his wife, Lisa, while working with an internationally recognized architectural studio in Phoenix. Lisa Trzebiatowski was born in Michigan in 1976 and received a B. A. in Psychology and a Master's degree in Clinical Social Work from the University of Wisconsin at Milwaukee in 1999, in addition to completing fine arts studies and publishing research in the field of experimental psychology. Their work includes the Xeros Residence (Phoenix, Arizona, 2004–06, published here); a Social Condenser for Superior (Superior, Arizona, 2006); Yoga Deva (Gilbert, Arizona, 2007); a Visitor Information Center and Community Park (Superior, Arizona, 2007), all in the USA, and their Landsnet Towers in Iceland (2008).

Matthew Trzebiatowski wurde 1972 in Wisconsin geboren und schloss sein Studium 1997 mit einem M.Arch. an der Milwaukee School of Architecture and Urban Planning (SARUP) an der University of Wisconsin ab. Er ist eingetragener Architekt in Arizona und Wisconsin und Fakultätsmitglied am Collins College of Design and Technology. Trzebiatowski gründete **BLANK STUDIO** 2001 gemeinsam mit seiner Frau Lisa, während er für ein international renommiertes Architekturbüro in Phoenix tätig war. Lisa Trzebiatowski wurde 1976 in Michigan geboren und schloss ihr Psychologiestudium mit einem B. A. ab. 1999 erwarb sie einen Master in klinischer Sozialarbeit an der University of Wisconsin in Milwaukee. Darüber hinaus schloss sie ein Kunststudium ab und veröffentlichte Studien in experimenteller Psychologie. Zu ihren Projekten zählen die Xeros Residence (Phoenix, Arizona, 2004–06, hier vorgestellt), der Social Condenser (Superior, Arizona, 2006), die Yogaschule Yoga Deva (Gilbert, Arizona, 2007), ein Informationszentrum für Touristen mit öffentlichem Park (Superior, Arizona, 2007–), alle in den USA, und ihre Landsnet Towers in Island (2008).

Matthew Trzebiatowski, né dans le Wisconsin en 1972, est M.Arch (Milwaukee School of Architecture and Urban Planning (SARUP), University of Wisconsin, 1997). Il est architecte licencié en Arizona et au Wisconsin et enseigne actuellement au Collins College of Design and Technology. Il a fondé **BLANK STUDIO** en 2001 avec son épouse, Lisa, tout en travaillant pour une agence de réputation internationale à Phoenix. Lisa Trzebiatowski, née dans le Michigan en 1976, est B. A. en psychologie et a passé un mastère en travail social clinique (University of Wisconsin, Milwaukee, 1999), avant de poursuivre des études d'art et des recherches en psychologie expérimentale. Parmi leurs réalisations : la Xeros Residence (Phoenix, Arizona, 2004–06, publiée ici) ; un équipement social (Superior, Arizona, 2006) ; Yoga Deva (Gilbert, Arizona, 2007); un Centre d'information des visiteurs et parc public (Superior, Arizona, 2007), tous aux États-Unis, et leurs Landsnet Towers en Islande (2008).

XEROS RESIDENCE

Phoenix, Arizona, USA, 2004–06

Floor area: 153 m² (or 209 m² including covered exterior spaces, terraces and balconies).
Clients: Matthew and Lisa Trzebiatowski. Cost: not disclosed

This house, with a two-story lower level design studio, was built in an area developed in the 1950s near the North Phoenix Mountain Preserve at the juncture of two dead-end streets. Access to the residence is gained via an exterior steel staircase leading to an upper level balcony that leads to the public area (living, dining, kitchen). The "master suite/media room" is a cantilevered volume with a glazed wall on the north offering views of the mountains. Naturally weathered exposed steel is the main building material, with corrugated steel cladding and unfinished woven steel wire mesh shade screens. Interior surfaces are finished in exposed concrete, plaster, dark plum colored plywood, and the exposed structural steel frame. The architects state that the choice of the name of the house (*xeros* from the Greek for "dry") is a "reminder that all design solutions should be in direct response to the environment in which the project exists." The use of an opaque façade to the west and a small footprint allowing the presence of low-water use vegetation are cited by Blank Studio as "environmentally responsible decisions."

Das Haus mit einem im Erdgeschoss liegenden zweistöckigen Designstudio wurde an der Mündung zweier Sackgassen gebaut. Die Gegend selbst war in den 1950er-Jahren unweit des Naturschutzgebiets North Phoenix Mountain Preserve baulich erschlossen worden. Zugang zum Haus erhält man über eine nach außen verlegte Stahltreppe, die auf einen Balkon im Obergeschoss führt, der die Gemeinschaftsbereiche (Wohnzimmer, Esszimmer, Küche) erschließt. Das Hauptschlafzimmer mit Bad ist zugleich „Medienraum" und als auskragender Baukörper mit einer Glaswand gestaltet, die den Blick nach Norden auf die Berge freigibt. Hauptbaumaterialien sind korrodierter, frei liegender Stahl sowie eine Verkleidung aus Wellblechplatten und Lichtschutzblenden aus unbehandeltem Drahtgeflecht. Das Innere wird von Sichtbeton, Putz, dunklen, pflaumenfarben gebeizten Furnierplatten und dem offen liegenden Stahlrahmenskelett dominiert. Die Architekten erklären, dass der Name des Hauses (xeros, griechisch für trocken) eine „Erinnerung daran sein will, dass jede Art von Entwurf eine unmittelbare Reaktion auf das Umfeld sein sollte, in dem sich das Projekt befindet". Die Wahl einer opaken Westfassade und die kleine Grundfläche, die Raum für Pflanzen mit geringem Wasserbedarf lässt, sind laut Blank Studio „umweltbewusste Entscheidungen".

Cette maison, équipée d'un atelier de dessin sur deux niveaux en partie inférieure, a été construite dans un quartier loti au cours des années 1950 près de la North Phoenix Moutain Reserve, au croisement de deux impasses. L'accès à la résidence se fait par un escalier extérieur métallique qui conduit au niveau supérieur à un balcon ouvert sur la zone de vie : séjour, repas, cuisine. La « chambre principale/salle média » est un volume en porte-à-faux comprenant un mur de verre orienté vers le nord, offrant une vue sur les montagnes. L'acier naturellement patiné laissé apparent est le principal matériau de construction utilisé, ainsi qu'un habillage en tôle ondulée et des écrans solaires en textile d'acier brut. À l'intérieur, les matériaux sont le béton apparent, le plâtre, un contreplaqué teinté rouge-violet foncé et l'ossature en acier laissée apparente. Les architectes font remarquer que le nom de la maison xeros (« sec » en grec) « rappelle que toute solution de conception doit répondre directement à l'environnement dans lequel le projet doit exister ». L'utilisation d'une façade opaque à l'ouest et une faible empreinte au sol suggérant la présence d'une végétation faible consommatrice d'arrosage sont citées par Blank Studio comme des « décisions volontairement écologiques ».

Though it is constituted of rectilinear, geometric elements, the Xeros Residence alternates opacity and transparency, as well as materials, in a surprising way.

Trotz ihrer geradlinigen, geometrischen Formen behauptet sich die Xeros Residence als überraschendes Wechselspiel aus Geschlossenheit, Transparenz und Materialien.

Constituée d'éléments géométriques orthogonaux, la Xeros Residence alterne pourtant d'une façon surprenante opacité, transparence et matériaux.

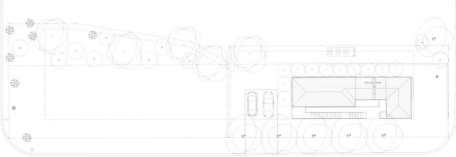

The basically rectangular design of the house is seen in the site plan above and in the photo taken at nightfall. Elements of the architecture are cantilevered or made to protrude in an unexpected way, belying the initial impression of austerity.

Die im Grunde rechteckige Anlage des Hauses zeigt sich am Grundriss oben und auf dem Foto, das bei Einbruch der Nacht entstand. Einzelne Elemente kragen auf unerwartete Weise hervor und strafen den ersten Eindruck von Strenge Lügen.

La conception orthogonale de la maison se confirme sur le plan du terrain ci-dessus et cette photo prise à la tombée de la nuit. Certains éléments en porte-à-faux se projettent de manière inattendue, remettant en cause une austérité apparente.

Below, drawings show the simplicity of the basic design, while a spiraling staircase and a double-height volume (right) demonstrate the ability of the architects to extract spatial excitement from rigorous geometry.

Zeichnungen (unten) belegen die Schlichtheit des Grundentwurfs. Zugleich beweisen eine Wendeltreppe und ein Raum von doppelter Geschosshöhe (rechts), wie gekonnt die Architekten verstehen, aus strenger Geometrie räumliche Spannung zu entwickeln.

Ci-dessous, les croquis montrent la simplicité du plan de départ. À droite, un escalier en colimaçon et un volume double hauteur illustrent la capacité des architectes à élaborer des surprises spatiales à partir d'une géométrie très rigoureuse.

Steel, concrete and glass express
themselves openly in this minimally
articulated but eloquent space.

Stahl, Beton und Glas finden unein-
geschränkten Ausdruck in diesem
minimalistischen und dennoch
eindrucksvollen Bau.

L'acier, le béton et le verre s'expriment librement dans cet espace
éloquent, bien que d'articulation
minimale.

The plan of the house shows its simplicity with the area including the spiral staircase on the lower plan (right) and the living room space above, seen in the photo.

Der Grundriss des Hauses zeigt seine Schlichtheit, etwa den Raum mit Wendeltreppe, im Erdgeschoss (rechts). Das Foto unten zeigt den darüber gelegenen Wohnraum.

Le plan de la maison montre toute sa simplicité dans la zone comprenant l'escalier en spirale du niveau inférieur (à droite) et le volume du séjour situé juste au-dessus (image ci-dessous).

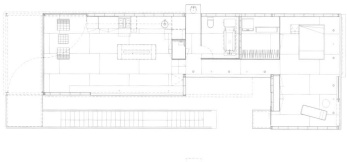

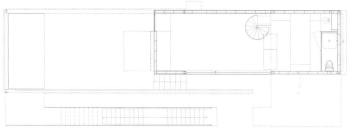

Casa Kike ►

GIANNI BOTSFORD ARCHITECTS

Gianni Botsford Architects
83–84 Berwick Street
London W1F 8TS
UK

Tel: +44 20 74 34 22 77
Fax: +44 20 74 34 99 77
E-mail: info@giannibotsford.com
Web: www.giannibotsford.com

GIANNI BOTSFORD was born in Venice, Italy, in 1960. He attended Kingston Polytechnic in London and received an AA Diploma from the Architectural Association School of Architecture (1996). He taught at the AA from 2000 to 2002. His built work includes retail premises for Giovanni Valentino (Milan, Italy, 1998); the Stuart House, office refurbishment (Peterborough, 2001); the Tolworth Tower, master plan and commercial refurbishment (Tolworth, Surrey, 2003); the South Bar House, office refurbishment (Banbury, 2004); the Light House (London, 2005); the Travelodge Hotel (Peterborough, 2006); the Casa Kike (Cahuita, Costa Rica, 2006–07, published here); and the Garden Apartment, apartment refurbishment (London, 2007), all in the UK unless stated otherwise. Recent work includes the Betil Residence (Ortakent, Turkey, 2007–08); the Garden House (London, 2007–); a building for the Halow Trust (Guildford, Surrey, 2007–); and a Residential Tower located on West 21st Street (New York, New York, 2008–).

GIANNI BOTSFORD wurde 1960 in Venedig, Italien, geboren. Er studierte an der Kingston Polytechnic in London und erwarb ein Diplom an der Architectural Association School of Architecture (1996). Dort war er zwischen 2000 und 2002 als Dozent tätig. Zu seinen gebauten Projekten zählen u. a. Ladenräume für Giovanni Valentino (Mailand, Italien, 1998), die Renovierung der Büroräume im Stuart House (Peterborough, 2001), der Masterplan und Umbau der Gewerbefläche des Tolworth Tower (Tolworth, Surrey, 2003), die Renovierung der Büroräume im South Bar House (Banbury, 2004), das Light House (London, 2005), das Travelodge Hotel (Peterborough, 2006), die Casa Kike (Cahuita, Costa Rica, 2006–07, hier vorgestellt) sowie die Sanierung des Garden Apartment (London, 2007), alle in Großbritannien, sofern nicht anders vermerkt. Neuere Projekte sind u. a. das Haus Betil (Ortakent, Türkei, 2007–08), das Garden House (London, 2007–), ein Gebäude für den Halow Trust (Guildford, Surrey, 2007–) sowie ein Apartmenthochhaus auf der West 21st Street (New York, 2008–).

GIANNI BOTSFORD né à Venise, Italie, en 1960, a étudié à Kingston Polytechnic à Londres avant d'être diplômé de l'Architectural Association School of Architecture (1996). Il a enseigné à l'AA de 2000 à 2002. Parmi ses réalisations : des magasins pour Giovanni Valentino (Milan, Italie, 1998) ; la Stuart House, rénovation de bureaux (Peterborough, 2001) ; la Tolworth Tower, plan directeur et opération de rénovation commerciale (Tolworth, Surrey, 2003) ; la South Bar House, rénovation de bureaux (Banbury, 2004) ; la Light House (Londres, 2005) ; le Travelodge Hotel (Peterborough, 2006) ; la Casa Kike (Cahuita, Costa Rica, 2006–07, publiée ici) et le Garden Apartment, rénovation d'appartement (Londres, 2007). Parmi les projets récents : la Betil Residence (Ortakent, Turquie, 2007–08) ; la Garden House (Londres, 2007–) ; d'un immeuble pour le Halow Trust (Guildford, Surrey, 2007–) et une tour résidentielle sur la West 21st Street (New York, 2008–).

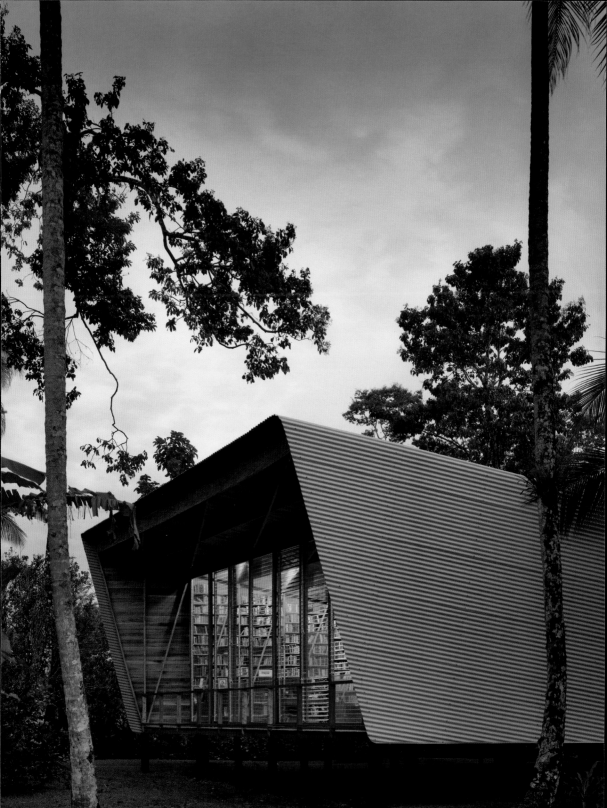

CASA KIKE

Cahuita, Costa Rica, 2006–07

Floor area: 112 m². Client: Keith Botsford.
Cost: $110 000

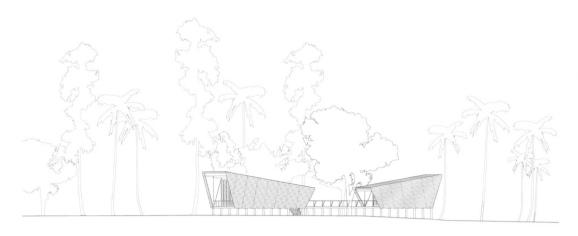

The "writer's retreat" is a lightweight timber structure raised 1.2 meters above the ground on wooden stilts, using a local technique intended to create the minimum impact on the environment. The two pavilions in the shape of parallelograms are designed with load-bearing 10-meter-long beams made of local Laurel, Cachá and Surá woods. The intricate pattern of diagonal beams and columns is intended to contrast with the corrugated steel sheeting used as external cladding. Such sheeting is typical of inexpensive Costa Rican dwellings. An existing one-story house in the style of local beach-front buildings remains on the site. To be refurbished, the older house will contain guest quarters and the main kitchen, while the writer lives in the new structure. At the insistence of the client, no trees were cut during construction, and environmental software was used to plot sun movements, prevailing winds and desired views in order to obtain the best positioning of the structure. The larger new pavilion was designed for daytime work and contemplation, with a roof rising from 3 meters at one end to 4.75 meters on the seaside glazed and louvered façade. The second pavilion, two-thirds the size of the first one, includes a bedroom and bathroom, with its higher façade oriented toward the jungle. A walkway, including a small pool, links the buildings and is intended as an outdoor living space.

Der „Rückzugsort für einen Schriftsteller" ist eine Leichtbaukonstruktion aus Holz, die auf Holzstelzen 1,2 m über dem Boden schwebt – ein Rückgriff auf eine regionale Bautechnik, um so wenig wie möglich in die Umwelt einzugreifen. Der Entwurf der beiden wie Parallelogramme geformten Pavillons basiert auf 10 m langen Trägern aus regionalen Hölzern wie Laurel, Cachá und Surá. Das aufwendige Muster aus diagonalen Trägern und Stützen kontrastiert mit den Wellblechplatten der Außenverkleidung (solche Platten sind typisch für einfache costa-ricanische Bauten). Ein auf dem Grundstück bereits bestehendes einstöckiges Gebäude im Stil regionaler Strandhäuser wurde erhalten. Nach der Sanierung wird das alte Gebäude Gästezimmer und die Hauptküche umfassen, während der Schriftsteller selbst den Neubau bewohnt. Auf ausdrücklichen Wunsch des Bauherrn wurden beim Bau keine Bäume gefällt. Mithilfe besonderer Software wurden der Sonnenlauf, vorherrschende Winde und die gewünschte Aussicht berechnet, um den unter Umweltaspekten idealen Standort für die Konstruktion zu ermitteln. Der größere der neuen Pavillons dient der Arbeit und Kontemplation. Sein Dach steigt von 3 m auf der einen Seite bis zu 4,75 m auf der verglasten, mit Lüftungsschlitzen versehenen Fassade zum Meer hin an. Der zweite Pavillon misst etwa zwei Drittel des größeren Baus, hier befinden sich Schlaf- und Badezimmer. Seine höhere Fassadenseite ist zum Dschungel hin orientiert. Ein Pfad, an dem ein kleiner Pool liegt, verbindet die Gebäude und dient als Wohnraum unter freiem Himmel.

Cette « retraite d'écrivain » est une construction légère en bois reposant sur des pilotis de 1,2 mètre de haut, une pratique locale pour exercer un impact minimum sur l'environnement. Les deux pavillons en forme de parallélogrammes reposent sur des poutres porteuses de 10 mètres de long en bois locaux : laurier, cachá et surá. La disposition des poutres et colonnes imbriquées en diagonale contraste avec l'habillage extérieur en tôle d'acier ondulé. Ce type d'habillage est typique des constructions bon marché du Costa-Rica. Une maison d'un seul niveau qui existait sur le terrain dans le style des constructions de front de mer locales a été conservée. Une fois rénovée, elle contiendra des pièces pour invités et la cuisine principale, tandis que l'écrivain vivra dans la construction principale. Le client a insisté pour qu'aucun arbre ne soit coupé, et un logiciel a servi à calculer les mouvements du soleil, les vents dominants et les vues souhaitées afin de positionner au mieux la maison. Le plus grand pavillon est conçu pour le travail et la contemplation. Son toit s'élève à 3 mètres d'un côté et 4.75 mètres du côté de la mer où s'élève une façade vitrée protégée par des persiennes. Le second pavillon, des deux tiers de la taille du premier, comprend une chambre et une salle de bains. Sa façade la plus haute est orientée vers la jungle. Un passage doté d'un petit bassin relie les bâtiments et permet de vivre à l'extérieur.

The simplicity of the architecture is rendered expressive by the dramatic shape of this "shed" and by the fact that the buildings are lifted off the ground on low pilotis.

Die schlichte Architektur gewinnt durch die dramatische Form dieser „Hütte" und das Aufständern der Bauten auf niedrigen pilotis an Expressivität.

La simplicité de cette architecture est néanmoins rendue expressive par la forme spectaculaire de cet « appentis » et sa surélévation du sol au moyen de pilotis.

Above, a view across the wooden deck connecting the structures shows the lightness and transparenciy of the architcture. Below, the house sits in a nearly pristine wooded environment, and its design is simple and largely based on wood.

Ein Blick über das Holzdeck (oben) das die Gebäude miteinander verbindet, macht die Leichtigkeit und Transparenz der Architektur deutlich. Das Haus liegt inmitten eines nahezu unberührten Waldgrundstücks (unten). Der Entwurf ist schlicht und basiert überwiegend auf Holz.

Ci-dessus, la prise de vue sur la terrasse en bois qui réunit les deux constructions montre la transparence et la légèreté de l'architecture. Ci-dessous, la maison dans son cadre boisé très naturel possède un style simple et largement basé sur l'utilisation du en bois.

Right, a site plan showing the two connected new structures vis-à-vis other, older houses on the property. Below, the shell-like structure and deck seen from a different angle.

Ein Lageplan (rechts) zeigt die beiden miteinander verbundenen Neubauten vis-à-vis der älteren Gebäude auf dem Grundstück. Unten die muschel-artige Konstruktion und das Holzdeck aus einer anderen Perspektive.

À droite, un plan du terrain montrant les deux structures, leur connexion et leur relation avec les maisons plus anciennes existantes. Ci-dessous, la structure en coque et la terrasse, vues sous un angle différent.

Books line the library but do not cut it off from the forest environment seen through the floor-to-ceiling windows, protected by wooden slats (left above).

Bücher säumen die Wände der Bibliothek, lösen sie jedoch nicht aus dem Kontext ihrer waldigen Umgebung, die durch die deckenhohen, mit Holzjalousien geschützten Fenster sichtbar ist.

La bibliothèque n'est pas isolée de l'environnement boisé, que l'on aperçoit à travers les grandes baies toute en hauteur protégées par des lames de bois (ci-dessus, à gauche).

The architecture is simple but
eloquent, fitting into its forest
environment with a minimal amount
of damage to the trees and site.

*Die Architektur ist schlicht und den-
noch ausdrucksstark und wurde unter
geringstmöglicher Beeinträchtigung
von Baumbestand und Grundstück in
die waldige Umgebung integriert.*

*Simple mais éloquente, cette
architecture se glisse dans son
environnement forestier en exerçant
le minimum d'impact sur les arbres
et le site.*

WILL BRUDER + PARTNERS

Will Bruder + Partners Ltd
2524 North 24th Street
Phoenix, AZ 85008
USA

Tel: +1 602 324 6000
Fax: +1 602 324 6001
E-mail: studio@willbruder.com
Web: www.willbruder.com

Born in Milwaukee, Wisconsin, in 1946, **WILL BRUDER** has a B. F.A. in Sculpture from the University of Wisconsin-Milwaukee (1969), and is self-trained as an architect. He apprenticed under Paolo Soleri (1967–68) and Gunnar Birkerts (1969–70). He obtained his architecture license in 1974 and created his own studio the same year. He has taught and lectured at Massachusetts Institute of Technology (MIT), Arizona State University and the "cable works," School of Architecture, Institute of Technology, Otaniemi Espoo, Finland (1993). His most important built work is the Phoenix Central Library in Phoenix (Arizona, 1989–95). Further projects include the Deer Valley Rock Art Center (Phoenix, Arizona, 1994); the Teton County Library and Riddell Advertising (Jackson, Wyoming, 1997); and the Temple Kol Ami (Scottsdale, Arizona, 1992–94, 2002–03). The Nevada Museum of Art (Reno, 2003) was given a Design Honor Award by the American Institute of Architects (AIA). Construction on the Hercules Public Library in California was completed in 2006. Other recent work includes the Feigin Residence (Reno, Nevada, 2005–06, published here); the Mezzo, multi-family housing (Phoenix, Arizona, 2006–08); and the Dial/Henkel Headquarters and R&D Facility (Scottsdale, Arizona, 2006–08), all in the USA. Ongoing projects include the CBD101/Creative Business District/Mixed-Use (Glendale, Arizona, 2006–16); and the 2012/2020 Capital District Vision (Phoenix, Arizona, 2007–20).

WILL BRUDER, 1946 in Milwaukee, Wisconsin, geboren, schloss sein Studium der Bildhauerei an der University of Wisconsin in Milwaukee mit einem B. F.A. (1969) ab, als Architekt ist er Autodidakt. Seine Lehrjahre absolvierte er bei Paolo Soleri (1967–68) und Gunnar Birkerts (1969–70). Seine Zulassung als Architekt erhielt er 1974, noch im selben Jahr gründete er sein eigenes Büro. Er lehrte und hielt Vorträge am Massachusetts Institute of Technology (MIT), an der Arizona State University sowie am Institut für Architektur der Technischen Hochschule Helsinki in Otaniemi Espoo, Finnland (1993). Sein bedeutendstes bisher realisiertes Projekt ist die Phoenix Central Library in Phoenix (Arizona, 1989–95). Zu seinen Projekten zählen außerdem das Deer Valley Rock Art Center (Phoenix, Arizona, 1994), die Teton County Library sowie ein Gebäude für Riddell Advertising (Jackson, Wyoming, 1997) und der Tempel Kol Ami (Scottsdale, Arizona, 1992–94, 2002–03). Das Nevada Museum of Art (Reno, 2003) wurde mit einem Ehrenpreis für Design vom American Institute of Architects (AIA) ausgezeichnet. Der Bau der Hercules Public Library in Kalifornien konnte 2006 beendet werden. Weitere aktuelle Projekte sind u. a. die Feigin Residence (Reno, Nevada, 2005–06, hier vorgestellt), das Mehrfamilienhaus Mezzo (Phoenix, Arizona, 2006–08) und die Zentrale sowie Forschungs- und Entwicklungsabteilung von Dial/Henkel (Scottsdale, Arizona, 2006–08), alle in den USA. In Arbeit sind u. a. das CBD101/Creative Business District/Mischgebiet (Glendale, Arizona, 2006–16) und die 2012/2020 Capital District Vision (Phoenix, Arizona, 2007–20).

Né à Milwaukee, Wisconsin, en 1946, **WILL BRUDER** a obtenu son B. F.A. en sculpture (University of Wisconsin-Milwaukee,1969) et est architecte autodidacte. Il a fait son apprentissage auprès de Paolo Soleri (1967–68) et Gunnar Birkerts (1969–70). Il a obtenu sa licence professionnelle en 1974 et ouvert son agence la même année. Il a enseigné et été assistant au Massachusetts Institute of Technology (MIT), à l'Arizona State University et par réseau « cable works » à l'École d'architecture de l'institut de technologie à Otaniemi Espoo en Finlande (1993). Son œuvre réalisée la plus importante est la Bibliothèque centrale de Phoenix (Arizona, 1989–95). Parmi ses autres réalisations : le Deer Valley Rock Art Center (Phoenix, Arizona, 1994) ; la bibliothèque du comté de Teton, l'agence Riddell Advertising (Jackson, Wyoming, 1997) ; le temple Kol Ami (Scottsdale, Arizona, 1992–94, 2002–03) et la bibliothèque publique d'Hercules (Californie, 2006). Son Nevada Museum of Art (Reno, 2003) a reçu un prix d'honneur de conception décerné par l'American Institute of Architects (AIA). Parmi ses autres œuvres récentes : la Feigin Residence (Reno, Nevada, 2005–06, publiée ici) ; Mezzo, logements pour familles (Phoenix, Arizona, 2006–08) ; et le siège et centre de R&D de Dial/Henkel (Scottsdale, Arizona, 2006–08), toutes aux États-Unis. Il travaille actuellement sur les projets de CBD101 / Creative Business District / à usage mixte (Glendale, Arizona, 2006–16) et la 2012 / 2020 Capital District Vision (Phoenix, Arizona, 2007–20).

FEIGIN RESIDENCE

Reno, Nevada, USA, 2005–06

Floor area: 560 m². Client: Stuart Feigin. Cost: not disclosed.
Team: Will Bruder (Design Architect), Richard Jensen (Managing Partner), John Puhr (Project Architect)

Set on a site commensurate with the open vistas of the American West (2612 hectares), the Feigin Residence is approached from below along an S-shaped drive. A weathered steel plate retaining wall evokes Richard Serra's *Snake* sculpture. The house is entered between canyon walls and opens to a 220° glazed view of the mountain horizon in the distance. Living, dining, and library areas are "unified under the gentle curve of the warped shed roof." A sunken water court lined in weathered steel plate offers a view toward the Carson Range near Lake Tahoe. A curving passage leads from the dining area to a media room and twin home offices, and guest areas beyond. As the architect says, "Exterior spaces are conceived as an extension of the interior. Courtyard gardens, like pearls on a string, meter the serpentine passage with light and air. The dramatic, down-slope, floating lawn tray projects from the living pavilion as it reaches for the horizon. The secret garden, accessed by a hidden stair, provides a 360° view of the surrounding landscape." Aside from weathered steel plate, aluminum plate cladding is also used outside, while within, polished concrete floors, white Venetian plaster or black plate steel walls contrast with abundant glazing. Bruder concludes, "As a quiet canvas for the carefully choreographed dance of movement and light, the sculptural form gives rhythm to the owner's life—a statement of quality and quiet away from the chaos of the world below."

Man nähert sich der Feigin Residence von unten über eine S-förmige Auffahrt. Das Grundstück ist den Weiten des amerikanischen Westens entsprechend bemessen (2612 ha). Eine Böschungsmauer aus korrodiertem Stahl erinnert an Richard Serras Skulptur „Snake". Das Haus betritt man durch eine Mauerschlucht. Es öffnet sich mit einer 220-Grad-Panoramaglasfront zu den Bergen am Horizont. Wohn-, Ess- und Bibliotheksbereich werden „unter dem sanft geschwungenen Pultdach" zusammengeführt. Ein von korrodierten Stahlplatten gesäumter, abgesenkter Hof mit einem Teich bietet Ausblick auf die Carson-Gebirgskette in der Nähe des Lake Tahoe. Ein geschwungener Korridor führt vom Essbereich zu einem Medienraum und einem doppelten Arbeitszimmer sowie zu dahinter gelegenen Gästezimmern. Der Architekt erklärt: „Die Außenräume wurden als Weiterführung des Innenraums entworfen. Hofgärten ziehen sich rhythmisch wie Perlen auf einer Schnur die sich schlängelnde Passage entlang und lassen Licht und Luft hinein. Der dramatische, nach unten abfallende, scheinbar schwebende Rasen erstreckt sich vom Wohnpavillon in Richtung Horizont. Der über eine versteckte Treppe erschlossene geheime Garten erlaubt einen 360-Grad-Rundumblick auf die Umgebung." Abgesehen von korrodierten Stahlplatten kommen am Außenbau auch Aluminiumplatten zum Einsatz. Innen kontrastieren polierte Betonfußböden, weißer venezianischer Putz oder Wandplatten aus geschwärztem Stahl mit den großzügigen Glasfronten. Bruder fasst zusammen: „Die skulpturale Form des Hauses fungiert als stille Leinwand für den sorgsam choreografierten Tanz von Licht und Bewegung – ein Statement der Qualität und Stille, weitab vom Chaos der Welt, die sich zu seinen Füßen ausbreitet."

L'accès à cette résidence implantée sur un terrain de 2612 ha, à l'échelle des perspectives infinies de l'Ouest américain, se fait en contrebas par une allée d'accès en forme de « S ». Un mur de soutènement en tôle d'acier patiné évoque la sculpture *Snake* de Richard Serra. L'accès à la maison se fait par un passage entre deux murs en canyon. Elle s'ouvre à 220° sur le panorama des montagnes dans le lointain. Les zones de vie, de repas et la bibliothèque sont « unifiées sous la courbe délicate du toit légèrement incliné ». D'une cour entourée de murs d'acier patiné et occupée par un bassin en creux, on aperçoit la chaîne de Carson, près de Lake Tahoe. Un passage incurvé conduit de la salle à manger à la pièce consacrée aux médias, aux deux bureaux jumeaux puis à la partie réservée aux invités. Pour Bruder : « Les espaces extérieurs sont conçus comme une extension de l'intérieur. Comme des perles sur un fil, des cours jardins ponctuent ce passage en apportant l'air et la lumière. Un plan de pelouse spectaculairement suspendu se projette du pavillon jusqu'à l'horizon. Un jardin secret accessible par un escalier dérobé offre une vue à 360° sur le paysage environnant. » En dehors de la tôle d'acier patiné, on trouve à l'extérieur des habillages en tôle d'aluminium et à l'intérieur des sols en béton, du plâtre blanc à finition de style vénitien ou des murs en tôle d'acier noirci qui contrastent avec d'abondants vitrages. « Comme une toile de fond pour un ballet soigneusement chorégraphié de mouvements et de lumière, la forme sculpturale [de la maison] apporte une affirmation de qualité et de sérénité loin du chaos du monde en contrebas. »

The low-lying house is inscribed in its
site almost like a natural formation,
emerging like a curved slope in the
images to the left.

Der sich duckende Bau wurde fast
wie eine geologische Formation in
das Gelände eingeschrieben. Auf den
Bildern links tritt er wie ein gewölbter
Hang hervor.

De proportions surbaissées, la
maison s'inscrit dans son paysage
comme une formation quasi naturelle.
Sur les images ci-contre, elle semble
émerger de la pente.

Below, an open fireplace and decoration that plays on the curving plan of the house, allowing for views of the spectacular if rather arid scenery. To the right, a site plan shows how the architecture corresponds to the topography.

Unten ein offener Kamin. Die Innenausstattung greift den geschwungenen Grundriss des Hauses spielerisch auf, der Ausblicke in die dramatische, wenn auch sehr trockene Landschaft erlaubt. Ein Lageplan (rechts) illustriert, wie die Architektur mit der Topografie korrespondiert.

Ci-dessous, la cheminée à foyer ouvert et la décoration jouent avec les courbes de la maison, face au panorama spectaculaire bien qu'assez aride. À droite, un plan du terrain montre comment l'architecture s'est adaptée à la topographie.

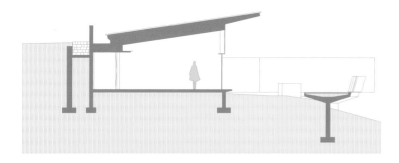

With its glazed elevations inserted into the site and rusted steel walls marking the exterior, the house exudes the image of a desert encampment. Interior volumes and the furniture are often curved like the house, and colors are muted.

Das verglaste Profil wurde in das Grundstück hineingebaut, rostiger Stahl prägt den Außenbau, das Haus wirkt wie ein Wüstenlager. Innenräume und Möbel sind in vielen Fällen geschwungen wie das Haus selbst. Die Farbpalette ist gedämpft.

À travers ses façades vitrées prises dans le sol et ses murs en acier patiné, la maison évoque l'image d'un camp du désert. Comme l'architecture extérieure, l'intérieur et le mobilier sont souvent de forme incurvée. Les couleurs sont assourdies.

NANCY COPLEY

Nancy Copley Architect, PLLC
180 Dug Road
Accord, NY 12404
USA

Tel: +1 914 626 0689
ncopley@ulster.net
www.architectcopley.com

NANCY COPLEY was born in Virginia and studied in New York at the Pratt Institute (B.Arch, 1956). She opened her own office in Upstate New York in 1972. Her own explanation is quite clear: "A degree in Architecture did not give me the skills to create buildings. I bought a wooded property in Ulster County, New York, in 1959 to give myself the opportunity to build with my hands and learn from nature… It became clear to me that nature teaches textures and color, light and shades, and that moving water creates music in the environment and reflects light that is filtered through the trees. As a building reflects these attributes, it comes alive." Her projects include the Jewish Institute for Geriatric Care (New Hyde Park, New York); the Woodland Apartments (Stone Ridge, New York); the Turtle Rock Apartments (New Paltz, New York); the Davis Residence on the Hudson (Highland, New York); the restoration of the oldest wood framed houses in Kingston (New York); and the residence published here: Copley Residence (Accord, New York, 1980–2008)—as the architect puts it, "25 years of hands-on stone work, a tower 13 meters high in my residence, landscaping the natural setting with boulders, large slabs of blue stone and woodland plants."

NANCY COPLEY wurde in Virginia geboren und studierte in New York am Pratt Institute (B.Arch., 1956). Ihr eigenes Büro eröffnete sie 1972 in Upstate New York. Sie selbst schildert recht anschaulich: „Ein Abschluss in Architektur versetzte mich noch nicht in die Lage zu bauen. Und so kaufte ich 1959 ein Waldgrundstück in Ulster County, New York, um mit meinen eigenen Händen bauen und von der Natur lernen zu können … Mir wurde bewusst, dass uns die Natur Texturen und Farben lehrt, Licht und Schatten, und dass bewegtes Wasser Musik in der Landschaft schafft und Licht reflektiert, das durch den Filter der Bäume fällt. Wenn ein Gebäude diese Eigenschaften hat, erwacht es zum Leben." Zu ihren Projekten zählen u. a. das Jewish Institute for Geriatric Care (New Hyde Park, New York), die Woodland Apartments (Stone Ridge, New York), die Turtle Rock Apartments (New Paltz, New York), die Davis Residence am Hudson (Highland, New York), die Restaurierung der ältesten Fachwerkhäuser in Kingston (New York) sowie das hier vorgestellte Haus, die Copley Residence (Accord, New York, 1980–2008), die die Architektin wie folgt beschreibt: „ein 25-jähriger praktischer Arbeitsprozess mit Stein, ein 13 m hoher Turm, die Gestaltung der natürlichen Umgebung mit Feldsteinen, großen Platten aus blauem Stein und Waldpflanzen".

NANCY COPLEY est née en Virginie et a étudié à New York au Pratt Institute (B.Arch, 1956). Elle a ouvert sa propre agence dans le nord de l'État de New York en 1972. Sa présentation est éclairante : « Le diplôme en architecture ne me donnait pas la capacité de créer des bâtiments. J'ai acheté une propriété boisée dans le comté d'Ulster, dans l'État de New York, en 1959 pour me donner la possibilité de construire de mes mains et d'apprendre de la nature… Il m'est paru de plus en plus clairement que la nature enseigne les textures et la couleur, l'ombre et la lumière, et que l'eau vive crée une musique et reflète la lumière qui filtre à travers les arbres. » Parmi ses réalisations : le Jewish Institute for Geriatric Care (New Hyde Park, New York) ; l'immeuble Woodland Apartments (Stone Ridge, New York) ; l'immeuble Turtle Rock Apartments (New Paltz, New York) ; la résidence Davis sur l'Hudson (Highland, New York) ; la restauration des plus anciennes maisons à ossature en bois de Kingston (New York) et la résidence Copley (Accord, New York, 1980–2008, publiée ici), décrite par l'architecte comme « 25 années de travail manuel de la pierre, une tour de 13 mètres de haut, l'aménagement du cadre naturel au moyen de rochers, de grandes dalles de pierre bleue et de plantes des bois ».

COPLEY RESIDENCE

Accord, New York, USA, 1980–2008

Floor area: 279 m². Client: Nancy Copley.
Cost: $2.5 million

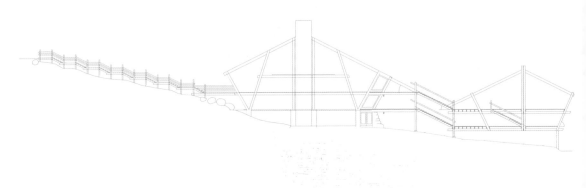

The house sits in its site like an almost natural extrusion, perhaps bringing to mind some of the designs of Frank Lloyd Wright.

Das Haus ragt beinahe wie ein natürliches Gebilde aus dem Gelände und erinnert an einige Entwürfe von Frank Lloyd Wright.

La maison est posée dans son cadre à la manière d'une extrusion naturelle, ce qui peut rappeler certains projets de Frank Lloyd Wright.

Given the unusual nature of this house, developed over more than 25 years, the words of the architect seem best to explain the project: "The inspiration for my house grew from this beautiful sloping land enriched with strong oaks, hickories, beech and the sculptural forms of boulders. I developed a form that complemented the land and vertical lines from the trees. Four triangular planes developed as a protective roof over a diamond shaped plan. Each quadrant oriented directly to the sun as it rotates from the East in the morning bathing the living area, then moving around to the South in the living room and dining area. A large glass roof between the South and West quadrant allows the west sun to warm the living room, indoor garden and kitchen. Exterior walls slope at a 64° angle to complement the triangular surfaces of the copper roof. In the winter months the glass façades permit warmth through the day when the sun is low. In the summer, leaves on the trees screen the spaces from the heat. Skylights between each of the four quadrants articulate the structure at the roof." A significant element of the house is the blue stone tower, 13 meters high, located between the East and North quadrants: the tower contains bathrooms and fireplaces, but also a pipe organ that uses five meters of vertical space.

Angesichts der Tatsache, dass dieses außergewöhnliche Haus im Lauf von über 25 Jahren organisch gewachsen ist, scheint die persönliche Beschreibung der Architektin dem Projekt am ehesten gerecht zu werden: „Die Inspiration für mein Haus erwuchs aus dem wunderschönen hügeligen Grundstück mit seinen großen Eichen, Hickorynussbäumen, Buchen und den skulpturalen Findlingen. Und so entwarf ich eine Form als Pendant zur landschaftlichen Umgebung und den vertikalen Linien der Bäume. Über einem rautenförmigen Grundriss fügen sich vier dreieckige Ebenen zu einem Dach. Jeder Bereich ist exakt nach der Sonne ausgerichtet, ihrem Lauf vom Osten her, der den Wohnbereich am Morgen in Licht taucht und mittags dann vom Süden her den Wohn- und Essbereich. Ein großes Dachfenster zwischen südlichem und westlichem Bereich lässt die wärmende Sonne von Westen her in Wohnbereich, Innengarten und Küche hinein. Passend zu den dreieckigen Flächen des Kupferdachs sind die Außenwände in einem Winkel von 64 Grad geneigt. In den Wintermonaten, wenn die Sonne tief steht, lassen die Glasfassaden den ganzen Tag über Wärme in das Haus. Im Sommer schützt das Laub der Bäume vor der Hitze. Oberlichtfenster zwischen den vier Bereichen gliedern das Dach des Baus." Auffälliges Element ist der 13 m hohe Turm aus blauem Stein, der zwischen Nord- und Ostbereich liegt: Dort befinden sich Badezimmer und Kamine, doch auch eine Orgel, die 5 m der Raumhöhe einnimmt.

La nature très inhabituelle de cette maison, réalisée en plus de 25 ans, est particulièrement bien exprimée par l'architecte elle-même : « L'inspiration de ma maison vient de ce superbe terrain en pente que magnifient de grands chênes, des noyers, des hêtres et la forme sculpturale des rochers. J'ai imaginé une forme en complément de la terre et de la verticalité des arbres et qui s'y intègre. Quatre secteurs triangulaires forment une toiture protectrice posée sur un plan en diamant. Chacun des quatre secteurs est orienté vers le soleil, et son déplacement de l'est le matin, où il baigne le séjour, vers le sud ensuite pour éclairer le séjour et la zone des repas. Entre les secteurs sud et ouest, un grand toit de verre permet au soleil couchant de réchauffer le séjour, le jardin intérieur et la cuisine. Les murs extérieurs s'inclinent à 64° pour venir s'adapter aux pans triangulaires de la toiture en cuivre. Pendant les mois d'hiver, les façades vitrées laissent pénétrer la chaleur du soleil qui est alors en position basse. En été, les feuilles des arbres protègent les volumes intérieurs du gain solaire. Des verrières disposées entre chacun des quatre quadrants articulent la structure par rapport au toit. » Particulièrement importante est la présence de la tour en pierre bleue, de 13 mètres de haut, entre les secteurs est et nord. Elle contient les salles de bains et les cheminées, mais également un orgue à tuyaux qui occupe cinq mètres de haut de cet espace vertical.

The architect herself has worked over the years on the rock environment of the house, contributing to the overall impression of communion with nature. The simple plan to the right shows the geometric design.

Jahrelang legte die Architektin selbst Hand an bei der Gestaltung des felsigen Geländes und trug so zum Eindruck einer harmonischen Einheit von Haus und Natur bei. Der schlichte Grundriss rechts veranschaulicht den geometrischen Entwurf.

L'architecte elle-même a travaillé pendant des années sur le cadre rocheux de sa maison pour renforcer le sentiment de communion avec la nature. À droite, un plan simplifié montre le caractère très géométrique du projet.

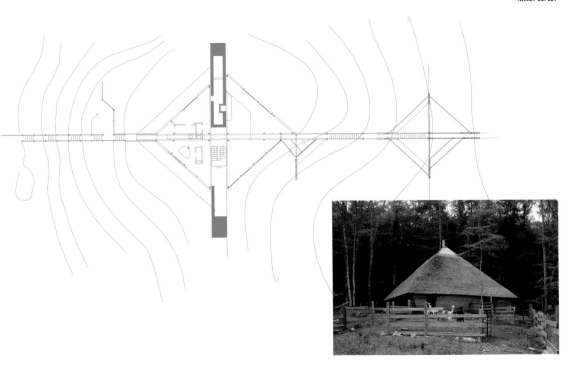

The low sloping roof seen from the interior allows ample natural light into the largely wooden volumes.

Der Blick von innen auf das niedrige, schräg abfallende Dach veranschaulicht den großzügigen Lichteinfall in die überwiegend mit Holz gestalteten Räume.

Vu de l'intérieur, le toit à forte pente laisse pénétrer un abondant éclairage naturel dans les volumes en grande partie habillés de bois.

Furniture, the stairway and the interior presence of rough stones continue the communion with the forest environment announced by the outside of the house, yet its soaring volumes are nonetheless surprising.

Im Interieur setzt sich die Harmonie mit der waldigen Umgebung fort, die sich bereits am Außenbau ankündigt, wie Mobiliar, Treppe und der unbehauene Stein zeigen. Dennoch überraschen die hohen Räume.

Le mobilier, l'escalier et la présence de pierres brutes à l'intérieur prolongent la communion avec la forêt qui s'aperçoit à l'extérieur. Le jaillissement des volumes n'en reste pas moins surprenant.

Casa no Gerês ▶

CORREIA/RAGAZZI ARQUITECTOS

Graça Correia/Roberto Ragazzi
Rua Azevedo Coutinho 39 4° Sala 44
4100–100 Porto
Portugal

Tel/Fax: +351 226 067 047
E-mail: correiaragazzi@gmail.com
Web: www.correiaragazzi.com

Graça Correia was born in Porto in 1965. She graduated from Porto University's Architecture Faculty in 1989, working from then until 1995 with Eduardo Souto de Moura. She created her own firm in 1995, and began in 2000 to develop projects in partnership with Souto de Moura. Roberto Ragazzi was born in Poggio Rusco, Italy, in 1969. He graduated from the IUAV (Istituto Universitario di Architettura di Venezia) in Italy in 1997. Between 1998 and 1999 he worked on architectural modeling for exhibitions and competitions in Alvaro Negrello's studio in Porto. Between 2000 and 2005 he worked as a project collaborator/coordinator in the office of Virginio Moutinho. In 2005, both architects established **CORREIA/RAGAZZI ARQUITECTOS**, through which they develop individual and shared projects, one of which is the house in Gerês published here (Caniçada, Vieira do Minho, 2003–06). Their recent work includes the remodeling of an apartment in Porto (2007–); a collaboration with Eduardo Souto de Mouro on a project to convert the historic buildings of the Fábrica Robinson, including a project for the Escola de Hotelaria de Portalegre and its Auditorium (2007); and a Multi-Family Dwelling and Office building in Portalegre (2008), all in Portugal.

Graça Correia wurde 1965 in Porto geboren. 1989 machte sie ihren Abschluss an der Architekturfakultät der Universität Porto und arbeitete anschließend bis 1995 bei Eduardo Souto de Moura. 1995 gründete sie ihr eigenes Büro und begann 2000, gemeinsam mit Souto de Moura Projekte zu entwickeln. Roberto Ragazzi wurde 1969 in Poggio Rusco, Italien, geboren. Seinen Abschluss machte er 1997 am IUAV (Istituto Universitario di Architettura di Venezia) in Italien. Zwischen 1998 und 1999 arbeitete er im Büro von Alvaro Negrello in Porto in der Modellerstellung für Ausstellungen und Wettbewerbe. Von 2000 bis 2005 war er als Projektmitarbeiter/-koordinator im Büro von Virginio Moutinho tätig. 2005 gründeten die beiden ihr gemeinsames Büro **CORREIA/RAGAZZI ARQUITECTOS** und entwickeln seitdem eigene ebenso wie gemeinsame Projekte, wie etwa das hier vorgestellte Haus in Gerês (Caniçada, Vieira do Minho, 2003–06). Zu ihren jüngeren Arbeiten zählen u. a. der Umbau eines Apartments in Porto (2007–), der Umbau der historischen Gebäude der Fábrica Robinson einschließlich eines Projekts für die Escola de Hotelaria de Portalegre und deren Hörsaal (2007) in Zusammenarbeit mit Eduardo Souto de Moura sowie ein Mehrfamilienhaus und Bürogebäude in Portalegre (2008), alle in Portugal.

Graça Correia, née à Porto en 1965, diplômée de la faculté d'architecture de l'université de Porto (1989), a travaillé jusqu'en 1995 pour Eduardo Souto de Moura. Elle a créé sa propre agence en 1995, et a commencé en 2000 à intervenir sur des projets en partenariat avec Souto de Moura. Roberto Ragazzi, né à Poggio Rusco, Italie, en 1969, est diplômé de l'IUAV (Istituto Universitario di Architettura di Venezia) en 1997. De 1998 à 1999, il réalise des maquettes architecturales pour des expositions et des concours au sein du studio d'Alvaro Negrello à Porto. De 2000 à 2005, il est collaborateur et coordinateur de projets dans l'agence de Virginio Moutinho. En 2005, tous deux fondent **CORREIA/RAGAZZI ARQUITECTOS**, agence dans laquelle ils réalisent des projets personnels ou communs, comme cette maison à Gerês publiée ici (Caniçada, Vieira do Minho, 2003–06). Parmi leurs interventions récentes, toutes au Portugal : la rénovation d'un appartement à Porto (2007–) ; un projet de conversion des bâtiments historiques de la Fábrica Robinson en collaboration avec Eduardo Souto de Mouro, incluant un projet pour l'école hôtelière de Portalegre et son auditorium (2007), et un immeuble de bureaux et de logements à Portalegre (2008).

CASA NO GERÊS

Caniçada, Vieira do Minho, Portugal, 2003–06

Site area: 4060 m². Floor area: 120 m².
Client: Joáo Telmo Ferreira. Cost: not disclosed

The site for this house is located in a protected natural area near the Cavado River. The clients required the use of concrete because of the humid site, and the preservation of all trees on the grounds. The clients were a couple with a child who wished to have a guest area, preferably disconnected from the main house. Storage areas for water skis, an extra shower and bath were also part of the program. A ruin on the site dictated the reduced size of the final scheme. The architects imagined the house as a metaphorical stranded boat in reference to Adalberto Libera's Malaparte House on Capri. The construction system used refers to naval design but also, apparently, to the Less table by Jean Nouvel. The partially buried design is described by the architect as a "weightless intervention enhanced by an overhanging section that shoots off the riverbank cliff, maximizing the transparent appearance as seen from the river, reducing land occupancy." Birch panels are used for the interior cladding. The existing ruin, built of granite, was recuperated and transformed into the required storage area and a small guest area, including a bathroom and bedroom lined with birch panels.

Der Bauplatz für dieses Haus liegt in einem Naturschutzgebiet in der Nähe des Flusses Cavado. Wegen des feuchten Baugrunds und um sämtliche Bäume auf dem Grundstück erhalten zu können, entschieden sich die Bauherren für Beton als Baumaterial. Die Auftraggeber, ein Paar mit Kind, wünschten sich außerdem einen Gästebereich, der idealerweise vom Haupthaus getrennt sein sollte. Lagerraum für Wasserskier, eine Dusche und ein Bad zusätzlich gehörten ebenfalls zum Programm. Eine Ruine auf dem Grundstück machte es letztlich notwendig, den ursprünglichen Entwurf zu verkleinern. Die Architekten stellten sich das Haus metaphorisch als gestrandetes Boot vor, eine Anspielung auf Adalberto Liberas Haus Malaparte auf Capri. Das Konstruktionssystem nimmt Anleihen beim nautischen Design und anscheinend auch bei Jean Nouvels Tischentwurf „Less". Den zum Teil versenkten Bau beschreibt der Architekt als „schwerelose Intervention, die zusätzlich von einem auskragenden Baukörper betont wird, der über das Kliff am Flussufer ragt. So wird die Transparenz von der Flussseite her maximiert und die Landnutzung reduziert". Der Innenraum wurde mit Birkenholzpaneelen vertäfelt. Die vorhandene Ruine, ein Granitbau, wurde wieder hergerichtet und zum gewünschten Lagerraum sowie zu einem kleinen Gästebereich einschließlich eines mit Birkenholz vertäfelten Bade- und Schlafzimmers umgebaut.

Le terrain de cette maison est situé dans une zone naturelle protégée à proximité d'un fleuve, le Canado. Les clients voulaient une construction en béton, car le site est humide, et conserver tous les arbres préexistants. Ce couple et son enfant souhaitaient qu'une partie de la maison soit réservée aux amis, mais déconnectée de la maison principale. Des rangements pour des skis nautiques et des salles d'eau supplémentaires faisaient également partie du programme. Une ruine existant sur le terrain a dicté la taille réduite du projet final. Les architectes ont imaginé la maison comme une métaphore de bateau échoué, en référence à la villa de Malaparte à Capri par Adalberto Libera. Le système constructif se réfère à des principes de construction navale mais aussi, apparemment, à la table « Less » de Jean Nouvel. Le plan, en partie enterré, est décrit par les architectes comme « une intervention impondérable mise en exergue par la partie en porte-à-faux projetée de la falaise qui domine la rive, et optimisée par l'aspect de transparence que l'on perçoit du fleuve, ainsi que par l'emprise au sol réduite ». L'intérieur est doublé de panneaux de bouleau. La ruine en granit a été récupérée et transformée en stockage et, petite chambre d'amis une équipée d'une salle de bains également lambrissée de bouleau.

The rectangular house is dramatically
cantilevered over its sloped riverside
site, with large openings facing out
onto the natural environment.

Der geradlinige Bau kragt dramatisch
über das abschüssige Grundstück am
Fluss aus. Große Fenster öffnen sich
zur landschaftlichen Umgebung.

De forme rectangulaire, la maison
est en porte-à-faux spectaculaire
au-dessus du fleuve. De grandes
baies donnent sur l'environnement
naturel.

The concrete slab of the structure
looks as though it might have been
placed accidentally near the edge of
the hill. The simplicity of the design
is confirmed by the drawings below.

Die Betonplatte wirkt, als habe man
sie versehentlich am Abhang abge-
legt. Die Schlichtheit des Entwurfs
wird durch die Zeichnungen unten
bestätigt.

La dalle de béton qui forme la
base de la maison semble avoir été
déposée accidentellement au bord de
la pente. La simplicité du projet se lit
sur les croquis.

The architects play deftly on the contrast between the heavy opacity of the concrete walls and the large glazed openings that reflect and open on the natural setting.

Die Architekten spielen offensichtlich mit dem Kontrast zwischen der Geschlossenheit der massiven Betonwände und den großen Fensterflächen, die sich zur natürlichen Umgebung hin öffnen und diese spiegeln.

Les architectes ont joué habilement du contraste entre la lourde opacité des murs de béton et les grandes ouvertures vitrées qui donnent sur le cadre naturel, ou qui le reflètent.

A relatively austere décor leaves the drama and variety of the house to the site, and to the changing seasons near the riverbank.

Das eher strenge Interieur des Hauses tritt bewusst hinter die dramatische Wirkung und den Facettenreichtum des Grundstücks sowie den Wechsel der Jahreszeiten am Fluss zurück.

Le décor intérieur, relativement austère, respecte le caractère spectaculaire de l'implantation de la maison et la variété des points de vue. Il met en valeur le changement des saisons sur les rives du fleuve.

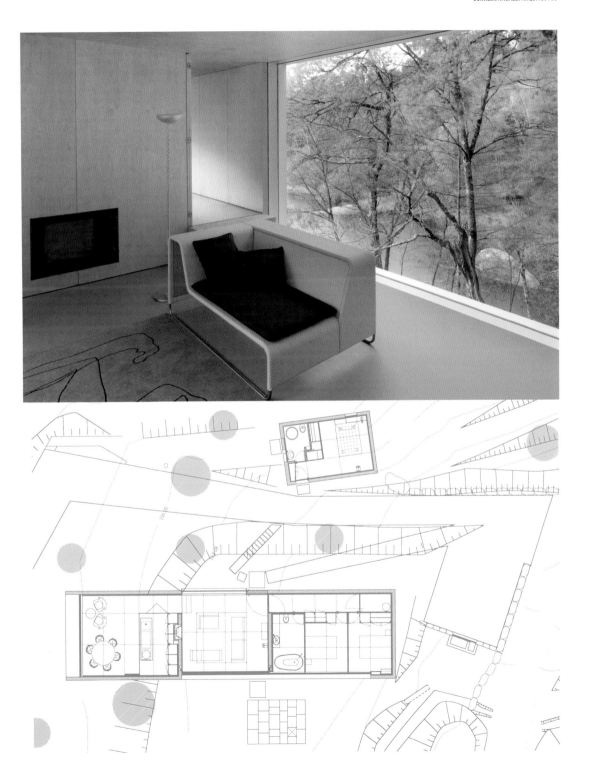

DURBACH BLOCK ARCHITECTS

Durbach Block Architects
Level 2, 9 Roslyn Street
Potts Point
Sydney, NSW 2011
Australia

Tel: +61 2 8297 3500
Fax: +61 2 8297 3510
E-mail: mail@durbachblock.com
Web: www.durbachblock.com

NEIL DURBACH received his B.Arch degree from the University of Cape Town, South Africa, in 1972. He attended the School of Environmental Design at the University of California (1979) before working in the office of Stanley Saitowitz in San Francisco (1981), then creating his own firm in Sydney in 1989. He was Co-Creative Director for the Australian Pavilion at the 2008 Venice Architecture Biennale. **CAMILLA BLOCK** received her B.Arch degree from the University of Sydney in 1991, creating Durbach Block with Neil Durbach in 1993. Their work includes Twin Peaks, two courtyard houses (Queens Park, Sydney, NSW, 2003); the Spry House (Point Piper, Sydney, NSW, 2004); the Holman House (Dover Heights, Sydney, NSW, 2003–05, published here); the Brick Pit Ring, an Environmental Interpretive Center and outdoor exhibition (Sydney Olympic Park Authority, Sydney, NSW, 2005); the Sixel Miller Cottage (Watsons Bay, Sydney, NSW, 2006); the Sussan Sportsgirl Headquarters (Richmond, Melbourne, Victoria, 2007); and the Park Street Commercial Building (Sydney, NSW, 2008), all in Australia.

NEIL DURBACH schloss 1972 sein Studium an der Universität von Kapstadt, Südafrika, mit einem B.Arch. ab. Er besuchte die School of Environmental Design an der University of California (1979) und war anschließend im Büro von Stanley Saitowitz in San Francisco (1981) tätig. 1989 gründete er in Sydney sein eigenes Büro. Er war Co-Kreativdirektor für den australischen Pavillon auf der Architekturbiennale 2008 in Venedig. **CAMILLA BLOCK** machte ihren B.Arch. 1991 an der Universität von Sydney und gründete 1993 gemeinsam mit Neil Durbach das Büro Durbach Block. Zu ihren Projekten zählen u. a. Twin Peaks, zwei Hofhäuser (Queens Park, Sydney, NSW, 2003), das Spry House (Point Piper, Sydney, NSW, 2004), das Holman House (Dover Heights, Sydney, NSW, 2003–05, hier vorgestellt), der Brick Pit Ring, ein Umweltzentrum mit Freiluftausstellung (Sydney Olympic Park Authority, Sydney, NSW, 2005), das Sixel Miller Cottage (Watsons Bay, Sydney, NSW, 2006), die Zentrale für Sussan Sportsgirl (Richmond, Melbourne, Victoria, 2007) sowie das Park Street Commercial Building (Sydney, NSW, 2008), alle in Australien.

NEIL DURBACH est B.Arch de l'université du Cap, Afrique du Sud, en 1972. Il a étudié à la School of Environmental Design, University of California (1979), avant de travailler dans l'agence de Stanley Saitowitz à San Francisco (1981), puis de créer sa propre agence à Sydney en 1989. Il a été co-directeur de création du Pavillon australien à la Biennale d'architecture de Venise 2008. **CAMILLA BLOCK**, B.Arch de l'université de Sydney en 1991, a fondé Durbach Block avec Neil Durbach en 1993. Parmi leurs réalisations, toutes en Australie : Twin Peaks, deux maisons à cour (Queens Park, Sydney, NSW, 2003) ; la Spry House (Point Piper, Sydney, NSW, 2004) ; la Holman House (Dover Heights, Sydney, NSW, 2003–05, publiée ici) ; le Brick Pit Ring, un centre environnemental d'interprétation et d'exposition en plein air (Sydney Olympic Park Authority, Sydney, NSW, 2005) ; le Sixel Miller Cottage (Watsons Bay, Sydney, NSW, 2006); le siège de Sussan Sportsgirl (Richmond, Melbourne, Victoria, 2007) et le projet du Park Street Commercial Building (Sydney, NSW, 2008).

HOLMAN HOUSE

Dover Heights, Sydney, NSW, Australia, 2003–05

Floor area: 400 m². Clients: Antony and Jennifer Holman.
Cost: not disclosed. Collaborator: David Jaggers

Located at the edge of a 70-meter-high cliff, the plan of this house is a reference to a painting by Pablo Picasso entitled *The Bather*. According to the architects, "It contains a complex series of fluid living spaces set within a meandering perimeter that arcs, folds and stretches in response to sun, landscape and views. Living and dining areas cantilever out over the ocean, allowing dramatic views up and down the coast. The lower floor forms a base that is built from rough stonewalls like an extension of the cliff below. These walls continue along the cliff edge to form a series of eccentric terraced gardens and a vase-shaped rock pool." Partially cantilevered over the ocean, the house offers spectacular views in a particularly precarious mode with large glazed faces practically hanging over the void. Unlike other nearby houses that seem to shy away from the cliff edge, the Holman House embraces the emptiness, affirming its truly modern character.

Der Grundriss des am Rand eines 70 m hohen Kliffs gelegenen Hauses spielt auf Pablo Picassos Gemälde *Die Badende* an. Den Architekten zufolge „besteht es aus einer komplexen Folge fließend ineinander übergehender Wohnräume, die von einer sich schlängelnden Umgrenzung eingefasst werden, die auf Sonne, Landschaft und Ausblicke reagiert, indem sie Kurven beschreibt, Falten schlägt und sich wieder ausdehnt. Wohn- und Essbereiche kragen über das Meer aus und erlauben dramatische Ausblicke auf die Küste. Die unteren Etagen bilden eine Basis aus grob behauenen Steinmauern, die wie eine Fortsetzung des darunter liegenden Kliffs wirken. Die Mauern ziehen sich weiter am Kliff entlang und umfassen exzentrische Gärten und einen wie eine Vase geformten Pool." Das teilweise über das Meer auskragende Haus bietet auf gewagte Weise spektakuläre Aussichten, da die großen Glasfronten quasi über dem Abgrund zu schweben scheinen. Anders als Häuser in der Nachbarschaft, die vor dem Kliff zurückzuschrecken scheinen, öffnet sich das Holman House dem Nichts und betont seinen wahrhaft modernen Charakter.

Implantée sur l'arête d'une falaise de 70 mètres de haut, cette maison se réfère dans son plan à une peinture de Picasso intitulée *Le Baigneur*. Selon la présentation des architectes : « Le plan regroupe une série complexe d'espaces de vie fluides disposés en un méandre qui se tend, se plie et se dilate en réponse au soleil, au paysage et aux perspectives. Les zones de séjour et de repas se projettent en porte-à-faux au-dessus de l'océan et bénéficient ainsi de vues spectaculaires sur toute la côte. Le niveau inférieur, qui constitue la base, est en murs de pierre brute comme une sorte d'extension de la falaise. Ils se poursuivent le long de l'arête pour former une série de jardins en terrasses excentrés et une piscine en forme de vase creusée dans le rocher. » En partie suspendue au-dessus de l'océan, la maison offre des vues à couper le souffle grâce à sa position quasi précaire : ses grandes baies vitrées s'étendent pratiquement au-dessus du vide. À la différence des demeures voisines qui semblent s'écarter du rebord de la falaise, la maison Holman embrasse le vide et affirme du coup son caractère résolument moderne.

Seen from below (left), the house
appears to mimic the cliff edge on
which it sits in a stepped pattern,
albeit in a color pattern and choice
of materials that make its "artificial"
nature apparent.

Von unten gesehen (links) wirkt das
Haus geradezu wie ein Echo der
Klippen, auf denen es treppenförmig
ruht. Farbpalette und Materialwahl
hingegen verraten seine „künstliche"
Natur.

Vue en contre-plongée (à gauche),
la maison semble reprendre la forme
de l'arête de la falaise sur laquelle
elle s'appuie, mais le choix des
matériaux et leur couleur rendent
sa nature « artificielle » évidente.

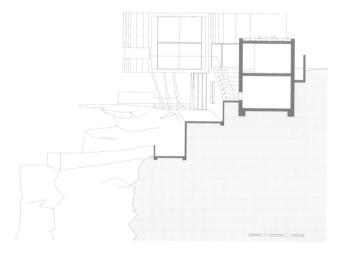

A chair and a small table seem to be an appropriate décor to take in the grandiose openness of this terrace.

Ein Sessel und ein Beistelltisch scheinen die angemessene Innenausstattung zu sein, um die grandiose Offenheit der Terrasse zu genießen.

Un fauteuil et une petite table forment un décor approprié face à l'ouverture grandiose de cette terrasse sur l'infini.

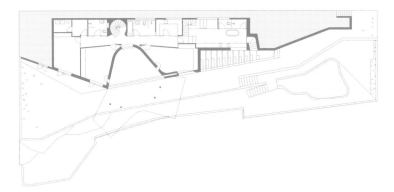

A sweeping curve in the open kitchen and large glazed surfaces recall the drama of the site. Sparse furnishing makes way for the play of light across the floors and wall surfaces.

Der kühne Schwung der offenen Küche und die großflächige Verglasung erinnern einmal mehr an die Dramatik des Grundstücks. Die sparsame Möblierung lässt Raum für Lichtspiele auf Böden und Wänden.

Les courbes de la cuisine ouverte et des parois vitrées rappellent le caractère spectaculaire du site. Le mobilier clairsemé laisse toute la place au jeu de la lumière sur les sols et les murs.

ELEMENTAL/ALEJANDRO ARAVENA

Alejandro Aravena Architects
Av. Los Conquistadores 1700, 25th Floor
Providencia, Santiago
Chile

Tel: +56 2 753 3000
Fax: +56 2 753 3016
E-mail: info@elementalchile.cl
Web: www.alejandroaravena.com, www.elementalchile.cl

ALEJANDRO ARAVENA graduated as an architect from the Universidad Católica (UC) of Chile in 1992. He studied architectural history and theory at the IUAV (Istituto Universitario di Architettura di Venezia, Italy, 1992–93). Aravena was a Visiting Professor at Harvard University (2000–05) and has been a Professor at the UC of Chile since 1994. He created Alejandro Aravena Arquitectos in 1994. Since 2006, he has been the Elemental Copec Professor at UC and Executive Director of Elemental, described as a "Do Tank affiliated to the Pontificia Universidad Católica de Chile and Copec, its focus is the design and implementation of urban projects of social interest and public impact." His professional work includes the project published here, Elemental Iquique (Iquique, 2004, 15th Santiago Biennale Grand Prix); the Mathematics (1998–99), Medical (2002–04), and Architecture (2004) Schools at UC (Santiago); the Pirihueico Lake House (2003–04); and the Siamese Towers at UC (Santiago, 2003–06), all in Chile. In 2006, he was chosen as the architect for the new facilities of St. Edward's University in Austin, Texas.

ALEJANDRO ARAVENA schloss sein Studium an der Universidad Católica de Chile (UC) 1992 als Architekt ab. An der IUAV (Istituto Universitario di Architettura di Venezia, Italien, 1992–93) studierte er Architekturgeschichte und -theorie. Aravena ist seit 1994 Professor an der UC in Chile und war Gastprofessor an der Harvard University (2000–05). 1994 gründete er sein Büro Alejandro Aravena Arquitectos. Seit 2006 hat er den Elemental-Copec-Lehrstuhl an der UC inne und ist leitender Direktor von Elemental, einem Büro, das sich als „praktischer Kreativpool der Pontificia Universidad Católica de Chile und der Copec versteht und dessen Schwerpunkt der Entwurf und die Umsetzung von gesellschaftlich relevanten und öffentlichkeitswirksamen Stadtplanungsprojekten ist". Zu Aravenas Projekten zählen das hier vorgestellte Elemental Iquique (Iquique, 2004, ausgezeichnet mit dem Großen Preis der 15. Biennale von Santiago), die Institute für Mathematik (1998–99), Medizin (2002–04) und Architektur (2004) an der UC (Santiago), die Casa del Lago Pirihueico (2003–04) sowie die „Siamesischen Zwillingstürme" der UC (Santiago, 2003–06), alle in Chile. 2006 erhielt er den Auftrag, die neuen Einrichtungen für die St. Edward's University in Austin, Texas, zu gestalten.

ALEJANDRO ARAVENA est diplômé en architecture de l'Universidad Católica (UC) du Chili (1992). Il a également étudié l'histoire et la théorie de l'architecture à l'Istituto Universitario di Architettura di Venezia (Italie, 1992–93). Professeur invité à Harvard University (2000–05), il enseigne à l'UC du Chili depuis 1994. Il a créé l'agence Alejandro Aravena Arquitectos en 1994. Depuis 2006, il est Elemental Copec Professor à l'UC et directeur exécutif d'Elemental, décrite comme un « Do Tank dépendant de la Pontificia Universidad Católica du Chili et de la Copec, qui a pour objet la conception et la mise en œuvre de projets urbains d'intérêt public à impact social ». Parmi ses réalisations figurent le projet publié ici, Elemental Iquique (Iquique, 2004, Grand Prix de la 15ᵉ Biennale de Santiago) ; les collèges de mathématiques (1998–99), de médecine (2002–04) et d'architecture (2004) de l'UC (Santiago) ; la maison du lac de Pirihueico (2003–04) et les tours siamoises de l'UC (Santiago, 2003–06), toutes au Chili. En 2006, il a été choisi pour concevoir les nouvelles installations de St. Edward's University à Austin, Texas.

ELEMENTAL IQUIQUE

Iquique, Chile, 2004

Floor area: 36 m² per unit (93 units total). Client: Chile-Barrio Program, Chilean Ministry of Housing. Cost: $7500 per unit.
Team: Alejandro Aravena, Alfonso Montero, Tomas Cortese, Andres Iacobelli

The Chile-Barrio Program, sponsored by the Chilean government, approached Elemental in 2003 about relodging 100 families that had illegally occupied a down-town 5000-square-meter site called the Quinta Monroy in the desert city of Iquique. The first priority was to maintain the families on the site, but to improve their living conditions with a limited budget. This decision was linked to the implantation of the residents in the district with the obvious advantages for their future employment and social well-being. Elemental's solution was to imagine a house on a given lot with a duplex apartment above it, allowing for two families to occupy the same plot of land. The architects explain, "Regarding the urban scale, what we identified to be a key issue in the economic take off of a poor family is the provision of physical space for the extensive family to develop. Families in the Quinta Monroy asked us to distribute them around four collective squares formed by around 20 families each, with controlled access." Using 9 x 9-meter lots, the architects first built a unit on the ground containing a bathroom, kitchen and loft space. Over that, they placed a concrete slab and a 6 x 6 x 5-meter duplex apartment also containing a kitchen, bathroom and double-height loft space. One side of each duplex is made of corrugated metal, "a soft wall that can not only be easily removed for growth purposes, but also works as the material for roofing the void between apartments."

Bei dem von der chilenischen Regierung geförderten Chile-Barrio-Programm befasste sich Elemental 2003 mit dem Anliegen, 100 Familien umzusiedeln, die ein 5000 m² großes Gebiet, die Quinta Monroy, im Zentrum der Wüstenstadt Iquique illegal besetzt hatten. Oberste Priorität war es, die Familien vor Ort wohnen zu lassen und ihre Lebensbedingungen im Rahmen eines begrenzten Budgets zu verbessern. Diese Entscheidung war mit dem Ziel verbunden, die Bewohner in den Bezirk zu integrieren, um ihre Aussichten auf Arbeit und ihr soziales Wohlergehen ganz offensichtlich zu steigern. Der Lösungsansatz von Elemental sah ein Haus pro Grundstück mit einer zwei-ten, darüber gelegenen Wohnung vor, sodass zwei Familien ein Grundstück bewohnen können. Die Architekten erläutern: „Was die städteplanerische Dimension anging, so schien es uns ein Schlüsselproblem für die wirtschaftliche Entwicklung armer Familien zu sein, Platz zu schaffen, damit die großen Familien wachsen können. Die Familien in der Quinta Monroy baten uns, sie um vier quadratische Plätze zu verteilen, die von je 20 Familien bewohnt würden und kontrollierten Zugang hätten." Auf Grundstücken von 9 x 9 m bauten die Architekten zunächst ein Erdgeschossmodul mit Bad, Küche und offenem Wohnraum. Darauf wurde eine Betonplatte gelegt, auf der sie eine zweite, 6 x 6 x 5 m große Wohnung mit ebenfalls Küche, Bad und doppelgeschossigem offenem Wohnraum setzten. Jeweils eine Seite der oberen Wohnungen besteht aus Wellblech, „eine weiche Wand, die nicht nur leicht zu entfernen ist, um die Wohnung zu vergrößern – mit dem Material wird zugleich der Freiraum zwischen den Wohnungen überdacht".

Les responsables du programme du Chile-Barrio, financé par le gouvernement chilien, ont contacté Elemental en 2003, afin de reloger 100 familles qui occu-paient illégalement un terrain de 5000 m², appelé la Quinta Monroy, situé au centre d'Iquique, une ville du désert. La première priorité était de maintenir ces familles sur place, mais aussi d'améliorer leurs conditions de vie dans le cadre d'un budget limité. La décision était liée à l'implantation de ces résidents dans le quartier pour leur permettre de trouver plus aisément du travail et de bénéficier de services sociaux. Le principe de la solution proposée par Elemental fut de construire sur chaque parcelle une maison surmontée d'un appartement en duplex, ce qui permettait à deux familles d'occuper le même terrain. Les architectes expliquent : « En terme d'échelle urbaine, nous avons identifié comme enjeu essentiel pour le démarrage économique d'une famille pauvre, l'offre d'un espace physique suffisant pour le développement d'une structure familiale élargie. Les occupants de la Quinta Monroy nous ont demandé de les répartir autour de quatre places regroupant environ 20 familles chacune, avec accès contrôlé. » Travaillant sur des parcelles de 9 x 9 m, les architectes ont d'abord construit une première unité de logement au sol contenant un espace de type loft, une cuisine et une salle de bains. Au-dessus, ils ont mis en place une dalle de béton, puis un appartement en duplex de 6 x 6 x 5 m contenant également un espace de type loft double hauteur, une cuisine et une salle de bains. L'une des façades de chaque duplex est en tôle ondulée, un « mur léger qui non seulement peut être supprimé si l'on veut agrandir, mais qui sert également de matériau de toiture pour l'espace vide entre les appartements ».

A series of images shows variations on the basic configuration and the possibility that owners have to extend their vital space, despite the city-center location of the project.

Diese Aufnahmen zeigen Variatio-nen der Basiskonfiguration und die Optionen der Hausbesitzer, ihren Wohnraum trotz der zentralen Stadt-lage des Projekts zu erweitern.

Cette suite d'images montre des variations sur une même base et la possibilité d'agrandir les espaces de vie, bien que le projet se trouve en centre-ville.

Though repetitive, the housing units appear cheerful and, above all, designed in order to allow for considerable variety and expansion.

Die einzelnen Wohneinheiten sind identisch, wirken aber dennoch fröhlich und wurden vor allem so konzipiert, dass erstaunliche Vielfalt und Erweiterungen möglich sind.

Malgré la répétitivité, les appartements restent chaleureux et se prêtent visiblement à une grande variété d'adaptations et d'extensions.

Simple lines allow for flexible living conditions that nonetheless show the presence of an architect; certainly a luxury, given the economic conditions under which this project was carried out.

Dank einfacher Linien lässt sich der Wohnraum flexibel nutzen und zeugt dennoch von der Handschrift eines Architekten – sicherlich ein Luxus angesichts der wirtschaftlichen Bedingungen des Projekts.

La simplicité des plans permet de s'adapter aux divers modes d'habitation non sans exprimer clairement l'intervention d'un architecte, un luxe face aux conditions économiques du projet.

Two images of inhabited interiors show the congenial aspect of residences that clearly would be much less agreeable had Alejandro Aravena and his team not been involved.

Zwei Bilder bewohnter Räume veranschaulichen, wie gelungen die Häuser sind, die sicherlich wesentlich weniger freundlich wären, hätten Alejandro Aravena und sein Team nicht ihre Hand im Spiel gehabt.

Deux photographies d'intérieurs aménagés montrent le caractère convivial d'appartements qui auraient certainement été moins agréables si Alejandro Aravena et son équipe n'étaient pas intervenus.

Wall House

FAR FROHN&ROJAS

FAR frohn&rojas
berlin::santiago de chile::los angeles
FAR Berlin Zentralbüro
Karl-Liebknecht-Str. 7 / 10178 Berlin

Tel: +49 30 240 48 205 / Fax: +49 30 288 83 312
E-mail: berlin@f-a-r.net / Web: www.f-a-r.net

Marc Frohn was born in Krefeld, Germany, in 1976. He attended the School of Architecture, RWTH Aachen (1995–98), the School of Architecture, Universitá degli Studi Federico II, Naples, Italy (Erasmus Scholarship, 1998–99), and the School of Architecture, University of Houston, Houston, Texas (Fulbright Scholarship, M.Arch, 1999–2001). He worked in the office of OMA/Rem Koolhaas in Rotterdam (2000), before attending the School of Architecture at Rice University, Houston, Texas (Rice Fellowship, M.Arch, 2001–04). He co-founded **FAR FROHN&ROJAS** with Mario Rojas Toledo in 2004 and has been in charge of concept development and is its design director. He has been a Professor at the Southern California Institute of Architecture SCI-Arc, Los Angeles, since 2007. Mario Rojas Toledo was born in Leverkusen, Germany, in 1973. He received his Diploma in Architecture and Engineering from the School of Architecture, RWTH Aachen (1995–2000), before working in the office of GMP in Aachen (1997–2004). A co-founder of FAR frohn&rojas with Marc Frohn, he is involved in project development and is technical director of the firm. As they describe it, "FAR frohn&rojas is a networked architectural design and research practice located in Cologne, Santiago and Mexico City." Their work includes the Hong Kong Design Center (Hong Kong, competition entry in cooperation with urban environments architects, 2006); the Centro Cultural Buenos Aires (competition entry with Rafailidis, 2006); the Wall House (Santiago, 2004–07, published here); the Yuejin Showroom (Santiago, 2006–); and the House in Heat (Rancagua, 2007–), all in Chile unless stated otherwise. FAR frohn&rojas received the prestigious AR award for emerging architecture in 2007.

Marc Frohn wurde 1976 in Krefeld geboren. Er studierte Architektur an der RWTH Aachen (1995–98), der Universitá degli Studi Federico II in Neapel (Erasmus-Stipendium, 1998–99) sowie an der University of Houston, Houston, Texas (Fulbright-Stipendium, M.Arch., 1999–2001). Er arbeitete für OMA/Rem Koolhaas in Rotterdam (2000), bevor er die Fakultät für Architektur an der Rice University, in Houston, Texas, besuchte (Rice-Stipendium, M.Arch., 2001–04). Gemeinsam mit Mario Rojas Toledo gründete er 2004 das Büro **FAR FROHN&ROJAS**, wo er für die Konzeptentwicklung verantwortlich und zugleich Designdirektor ist. Seit 2007 ist er Professor am Southern California Institute of Architecture SCI-Arc, Los Angeles. Mario Rojas Toledo wurde 1973 in Leverkusen geboren. Er schloss sein Studium der Architektur und des Ingenieurwesens an der RWTH Aachen mit dem Diplom ab (1995–2000) und arbeitete anschließend für GMP in Aachen (1997–2004). Bei FAR frohn&rojas ist er für die Projektentwicklung verantwortlich und Technischer Leiter des Büros. Den Architekten zufolge ist „FAR frohn&rojas ein Netzwerk für Architekturgestaltung und -forschung in Köln, Santiago und Mexico City". Zu ihren Projekten zählen das Hong Kong Design Center (Hongkong, Wettbewerbsbeitrag in Zusammenarbeit mit urban environments architekten, 2006), das Centro Cultural Buenos Aires (Wettbewerbsbeitrag mit Rafailidis, 2006), das Wall House (Santiago, 2004–07, hier vorgestellt), der Yuejin Showroom (Santiago, seit 2006) sowie das House in Heat (Rancagua, seit 2007), die letzten drei in Chile. 2007 erhielt das Büro den AR Award for Emerging Architecture.

Marc Frohn, né à Krefeld, Allemagne, en 1976, a étudié à l'école d'architecture RWTH Aachen (1995–98), à l'école d'architecture de l'Universitá degli Studi Federico II à Naples, Italie (bourse Erasmus, 1998–99), et à l'école d'architecture de l'université d'Houston, Texas (bourse Fulbright, M.Arch, 1999–2001). Il a travaillé dans l'agence d'OMA/Rem Koolhaas à Rotterdam (2000), avant d'étudier à Rice University, School of Architecture, Houston, Texas (bourse Rice, M.Arch, 2001–04). En 2004, il co-fonde **FAR FROHN&ROJAS** avec Mario Rojas Toledo, où il prend en charge le développement des concepts et la direction du design. Il enseigne au Southern California Institute of Architecture, SCI-Arc, à Los Angeles, depuis 2007. Mario Rojas Toledo, né à Leverkusen, Allemagne, en 1973, est diplômé en architecture et ingénierie de l'école d'architecture RWTH Aachen (1995–2000) et a travaillé pour l'agence GMP à Aachen (1997–2004). Co-fondateur de FAR frohn&rojas avec Marc Frohn, il est directeur technique de l'agence et intervient dans la mise au point des projets. Comme ils l'expliquent : « FAR frohn&rojas est une agence de recherche et de conception architecturale en réseau implantée à Cologne, Santiago du Chili et Mexico. » Parmi leurs interventions : le Design Center de Hong Kong (participation au concours en coopération avec urban environments architects, 2006) ; le Centre culturel de Buenos Aires (participation au concours avec Rafailidis, 2006) ; la Wall House (Santiago, 2004–07, publiée ici) ; le showroom Yuejin (Santiago, 2006–) et une maison à Heat (Rancagua, 2007–), la plupart au Chili. En 2007, FAR frohn&rojas a reçu le prestigieux AR Award for Emerging Architecture.

WALL HOUSE

Santiago, Chile, 2004–07

Floor area: 230 m². Client: Patricia Krause Senft. Cost: €135 000.
Project Team: Marc Frohn, Mario Rojas Toledo, Amy Thoner, Pablo Guzman, Isabel Zapata

Working for a retired couple living in a suburban area near the Pan-American Highway, the architects "developed the idea of a house based upon a series of separated wall layers which structure the house and progressively fade it out, starting from its solid, innermost core to its soft and delicate encasing." They sought a "gradual and hazy" transition between interior and exterior, using four layers each with a specific material and feeling. The innermost of these materials is a concrete core containing two bathrooms, surrounded by engineered wood shelving bands containing the kitchen, dining and guest rooms on the ground floor and a work studio above. Moving to the exterior, the third layer is a skin of high-insulation polycarbonate panels that make way for the living room and master bedroom. Finally, a soft fabric membrane, "typically used in greenhouse environments, acts as an energy screen, filtering out up to 70 % of the solar energy hitting the building, and at the same time creates a protective barrier against the mosquitoes and insects prevalent in the area," according to the architects.

Im Auftrag eines pensionierten Ehepaars entwickelten die Architekten in einer Vorortgegend unweit der Panamericana „die Idee, ein Haus mit einer Reihe unabhängiger Wandschichten zu bauen, die das Haus gliedern und es zunehmend transparenter werden lassen, von seinem massiven zentralen Kern bis hin zu seiner weichen, zarten Hülle". Die Architekten strebten nach einem „graduellen und diffusen" Übergang von innen nach außen, wobei sie vier Schichten einsetzten, die je ein spezifisches Material nutzen und ein eigenes Flair haben. Das innerste dieser Materialien ist ein Betonkern, in dem sich zwei Bäder befinden. Um ihn herum ziehen sich maßgefertigte „Bänder" aus Holzregalen, die Küche, Essbereich und Gästezimmer im Erdgeschoss einfassen. Darüber liegt ein Arbeitszimmer bzw. Atelier. Nach außen schließen sich als dritte Haut hochisolierende Paneele aus Polykarbonat an, die Wohn- und Hauptschlafzimmer umgeben. Wie die Architekten erläutern, folgt schließlich eine weiche Textilmembran, „wie sie für Gewächshäuser typisch ist. Sie dient als Energieschirm und filtert 70 % der auf das Gebäude treffenden Sonnenenergie und bildet zugleich eine Schutzhaut gegen die für die Gegend typischen Mücken und andere Insekten".

Pour ce projet destiné à un couple de retraités dans un quartier de banlieue près de l'autoroute panaméricaine, les architectes ont « mis au point l'idée d'une maison faite d'une succession de strates de murs indépendants qui structurent la maison tout en l'effaçant progressivement, partant d'un noyau central plein pour aller jusqu'à un gainage extérieur léger et délicat ». Ils ont recherché une transition « graduelle et vaporeuse » entre l'intérieur et l'extérieur, en quatre strates, chacune traitée dans une atmosphère et un matériau différents. Le cœur est un noyau en béton contenant deux salles de bains entourées de bandeaux de lattes de bois superposées contenant la cuisine, une zone de repas et des chambres d'amis au rez-de-chaussée, ainsi qu'un atelier au-dessus. En se déplaçant vers l'extérieur, la troisième strate est une peau en panneaux de polycarbonate à fort pouvoir isolant qui enclot le séjour et la chambre principale. « En final, une membrane textile, que l'on utilise habituellement dans les serres, fait fonction d'écran énergétique, filtrant jusqu'à 70 % de l'énergie solaire qui frappe la maison, tout en faisant office de barrière de protection contre les moustiques et les insectes qui pullulent dans la région », expliquent les architectes.

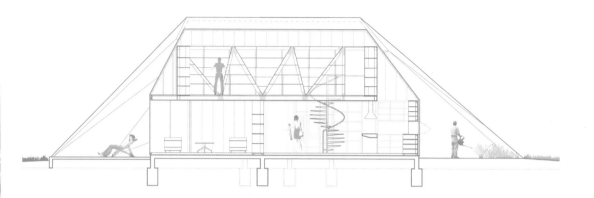

Both in an image and in a section drawing, the house clearly shows its relation to the design of a large tent, with the particularity of its successively less permeable layers arrayed from outside to inside.

Sowohl das Foto als auch die Schnittzeichnung verweisen eindeutig auf die Verwandtschaft des Entwurfs mit einem großen Zelt – allerdings mit der Besonderheit, dass die Wandschichten hier von außen nach innen immer massiver werden.

Sur la photographie et la coupe, la maison montre clairement son rapport avec un principe de tente et l'originalité de ses strates successives, de plus en plus perméables en allant vers l'extérieur.

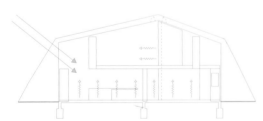

Drawings show how the light of the sun and convection currents are employed in the house. Above, the more protected inner area of the house.

Die Zeichnungen veranschaulichen, wie Sonnenlicht und Konvektionsströme im Haus genutzt werden. Oben der geschütztere innere Bereich des Hauses.

Les dessins montrent comment la lumière solaire et la convexion des flux d'air sont mises à profit par l'architecte. Ci-dessus, la partie intérieure protégée de la maison.

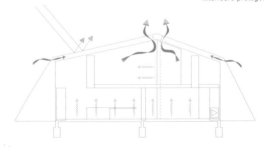

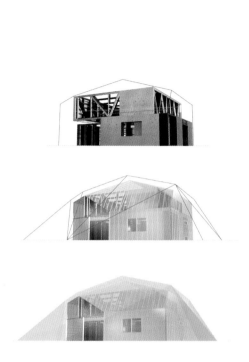

Drawings above show the three-layer concept of the architecture, while photos show the white sail-like awnings that protect the exterior.

Die Zeichnungen oben veranschaulichen das Drei-Lagen-Konzept der Architektur, während Fotos die weißen, segelähnlichen Markisen zeigen, die den Außenbau schützen.

Les dessins ci-dessus illustrent le concept de l'architecture en trois strates. En photo, les auvents en forme de voile qui protègent les façades extérieures.

TERUNOBU FUJIMORI

Terunobu Fujimori
Professor, Institute of Industrial Science, University of Tokyo
4–6–1 Komaba / Meguro-ku
Tokyo 153–8505
Japan

Tel: +81 3 5452 6370
Fax: +81 3 5452 6371
E-mail: fujimori@iis.u-tokyo.ac.jp

Born in Chino City, Nagano, Japan, in 1946, **TERUNOBU FUJIMORI** attended Tohoku University (1965–71) in Sendai, before receiving his Ph.D. in Architecture from the University of Tokyo (1971–78). He is currently a Professor at the University of Tokyo's Institute of Industrial Science. Although research on often long-forgotten Western-style buildings in Japan from the Meiji period onwards remains his main activity, he is also a practicing architect. "I didn't start designing buildings until my forties, so the condition I set for myself is that I shouldn't just repeat the same things that my colleagues or professors were doing," he has stated. His first built work was the Jinchokan Moriya Historical Museum (Chino City, Nagano, 1990–91), which won mixed praise for the use of local materials over a reinforced-concrete structure. Other completed projects include the Akino Fuku Art Museum (Hamamatsu, Shizuoka, 1995–97); the Nira House (Leek House, Machida City, Tokyo, 1995–97); the Student Dormitory for Kumamoto Agricultural College (Koshi City, Kumamoto, 1998–2000); the Ichiya-tei (One Night Teahouse, Ashigarashimo, Kanagawa, 2003); the Takasugi-an (Too-High Teahouse, Chino City, Nagano, 2004), set six meters above the ground like a tree house; the Chashitsu Tetsu (Teahouse Tetsu, Kiyoharu Shirakaba Museum, Nakamaru, Hokuto City, Yamanashi, 2005); and the Charred Cedar House (Nagano City, Nagano, 2006–07, published here), all in Japan. He won the Japan Art Grand Prix (1997) for the Nira House, and the Architectural Institute of Japan Prize for Design (2001) for the Student Dormitory for Kumamoto Agricultural College.

TERUNOBU FUJIMORI wurde 1946 in Chino in der Präfektur Nagano, Japan, geboren und studierte an der Tohoku-Universität in Sendai (1965–71), bevor er an der Universität Tokio in Architektur promovierte (1971–78). Gegenwärtig ist er Professor am Institut für Industriewissenschaften an der Universität Tokio. Obwohl er sich hauptsächlich der Erforschung lang vergessener westlicher Bauten in Japan seit der Meiji-Zeit widmet, praktiziert er auch als Architekt. „Mit dem Entwerfen von Bauten habe ich erst angefangen, als ich über 40 war, und so nahm ich mir vor, nicht einfach das zu wiederholen, was meine Kollegen oder Professoren taten", erklärt Fujimori. Sein erster realisierter Bau war das Historische Museum Jinchokan Moriya (Chino, Nagano, 1990–91), das wegen der Verwendung regionaler Materialien über einer Stahlbetonkonstruktion gemischte Reaktionen hervorrief. Weitere gebaute Projekte sind u. a. das Kunstmuseum Akino Fuku (Hamamatsu, Shizuoka, 1995–97), das Nira House (Lauchhaus, Machida, Tokio, 1995–97), ein Studentenwohnheim für die Landwirtschaftliche Hochschule Kumamoto (Koshi, Kumamoto, 1998–2000), das Ichiya-tei (Teehaus für eine Nacht, Ashigarashimo, Kanagawa, 2003), das wie ein Baumhaus 6 m über der Erde schwebende Teehaus Takasugi-an (Chino, Nagano, 2004), das Chashitsu Tetsu (Teehaus Tetsu, Museum Kiyoharu Shirakaba, Nakamaru, Hokuto, Yamanashi, 2005) sowie das Charred Cedar House (Nagano, Nagano, 2006–07, hier vorgestellt), alle in Japan. Fujimori erhielt den Japan Art Grand Prix (1997) für sein Nira House sowie den Designpreis des Architekturinstituts von Japan (2001) für das Studentenwohnheim der Landwirtschaftlichen Hochschule Kumamoto.

Né à Chino City, Nagano (Japon), en 1946, **TERUNOBU FUJIMORI** a fait ses études à l'université Tohoku (1965–71) à Sendai. Il est docteur en architecture de l'université de Tokyo (1971–78) et enseigne actuellement à l'institut des sciences et techniques de cette université. Si ses recherches sur les réalisations de style occidental au Japon datant de l'ère Meiji, et souvent oubliées, restent sa principale activité, il pratique également l'architecture : « Je n'ai pas commencé à concevoir de construction avant la quarantine, aussi me suis-je donné comme condition de ne pas répéter ce que mes confrères ou professeurs faisaient. » Son premier projet réalisé a été le musée historique Jinchokan Moriya (Chino, Nagano, 1990–91), diversement apprécié pour son recours à des matériaux locaux sur une structure en béton armé. Parmi ses autres réalisations : le musée d'Art Akino Fuku (Hamamatsu, Shizuoka, 1995–97) ; la maison Nira (Leek House, Machida City, Tokyo, 1995–97) ; un dortoir pour le collège d'agriculture de Kumamoto (Koshi, Kumamoto, 1998–2000) ; Ichiya-tei (maison de thé pour une nuit, Ashigarashimo, Kanagawa, 2003) ; Takasugi-an (maison de thé Too-High, Chino City, Nagano 2004), installé à six mètres au-dessus du sol, telle une maison dans un arbre; la Chashitsu Tetsu (maison de thé Tetsu, musée Kiyoharu Shirakaba, Nakamaru, Hokuto, Yamanashi, 2005) et la Charred Cedar House (Nagano, 2006–07, publiée ici), toutes au Japon. Il a remporté le Grand Prix d'art du Japon (1997) pour la maison Nira et le prix de Conception de l'Institut d'architecture du Japon (2001) pour le dortoir du collège agricole de Kumamoto.

CHARRED CEDAR HOUSE

Nagano City, Nagano, Japan, 2006–07

Floor area: 167 m². Client: Keiji Kobayashi.
Cost: not disclosed. Collaborator: Keiichi Kawakami

This house is located in a residential area 10 minutes' walk from the Nagano railway station, on the estate of the Kobayashi family, local 'squires.' The clients had lived in an old house on the estate, but decided after seeing work by Fujimori to call on him to design a new house that remains respectful of Japanese traditions. Curiously, the architect says he was inspired by the caves at Lascaux in France—he compares the inside of the Charred Cedar House to a cave. He chose Japanese chestnut wood for the construction, because it is "strong but tender." Formerly used for inexpensive thatched roof houses, Japanese cedar is no longer a popular wood for construction. Fujimori explains that he likes using wood because "it allows for sloped roofs and gives the impression of lightness." Within the house, chairs, tables and the fireplace were all designed by the architect. Visitors are greeted by a prayer space containing a thin wooden sculpture of Buddha. The use of charred cedar on the exterior of the house is a device seen in Japanese architecture, originally intended to make the wood safe from pests. Here the device is aesthetic and intentionally links the structure to the past without overt historicism. Three *hiroki* cypress trunks from the architect's hometown pierce the roof of the house and emerge as trees without leaves. At one end of the roof, a tiny tearoom is perched in a style that is reminiscent of a number of Fujimori's designs for the tea ceremony.

Das Haus liegt in einem Wohnviertel etwa zehn Minuten vom Bahnhof Nagano entfernt auf dem Anwesen der Familie Kobayashi, einer ortsansässigen Gutsbesitzerfamilie. Die Auftraggeber hatten in einem alten Haus auf dem Grundstück gelebt, sich jedoch entschieden, Fujimori zu beauftragen, ein neues Haus zu entwerfen, das die alten japanischen Traditionen wahrt, nachdem sie sein Werk gesehen hatten. Erstaunlicherweise gibt der Architekt an, von den Höhlen in Lascaux inspiriert gewesen zu sein, und vergleicht das Innere des Hauses mit einer Höhle. Für die Konstruktion wählte er japanisches Kastanienholz, weil es „stark und doch zart" ist. Japanisches Zedernholz, das früher für einfache Häuser mit Schilfdach genutzt wurde, wird heute nicht mehr gern als Baumaterial verwendet. Fujimori erklärt, dass er gern mit Holz arbeitet, weil sich mit ihm „geneigte Dächer bauen lassen und es Leichtigkeit ausstrahlt". Stühle, Tische und Kamin im Haus wurden vom Architekten selbst entworfen. Besucher werden von einer Gebetsnische mit einer schmalen Buddhafigur aus Holz empfangen. Der Einsatz von rußgeschwärztem Zedernholz am Außenbau ist ein typisch japanisches Architekturelement, das ursprünglich dazu diente, das Holz vor Schädlingen zu schützen. Hier hat das Element rein ästhetische Funktion und knüpft bewusst an die Vergangenheit an, ohne in aufdringlichen Historizismus zu verfallen. Drei Hiroki-Zypressenstämme aus der Heimat des Architekten stoßen durch das Dach des Hauses und treten wie laublose Bäume hervor. Am äußersten Ende des Dachs „hockt" ein winziges Teehaus, das an Fujimoris zahlreiche Entwürfe für die Teezeremonie denken lässt.

Cette maison se trouve dans un quartier résidentiel à dix minutes à pied de la gare de Nagano, dans le domaine de la famille Kobayashi, les « seigneurs » locaux. Les clients vivaient dans une vieille maison à proximité mais décidèrent, après avoir vu ses réalisations, de faire appel à Fujimori pour concevoir une maison nouvelle, mais dans le respect des anciennes traditions japonaises. Curieusement, l'architecte a déclaré qu'il avait été inspiré par les grottes de Lascaux en France et compare l'intérieur de cette maison à une caverne. Il a choisi le châtaigner du Japon pour la construction, car c'est un bois « résistant mais tendre ». Jadis utilisé pour les maisons pauvres à toit de chaume, le cèdre du Japon n'est plus utilisé comme matériau de construction. Fujimori explique qu'il « aime se servir du bois parce qu'il lui permet d'édifier des toits très inclinés et de donner une impression de légèreté ». À l'intérieur, les sièges, les tables et la cheminée ont été dessinés par l'architecte. Les visiteurs sont accueillis dans un espace de prière contenant une sculpture en bois de Bouddha. L'utilisation de cèdre carbonisé à l'extérieur est un procédé fréquent dans l'architecture japonaise, utilisé à l'origine pour protéger le bois des maladies. Ici, le procédé est détourné dans un sens esthétique et relie la maison au passé sans références historicistes trop flagrantes. Trois troncs de cyprès *hiroki*, apportés de la ville natale de l'architecte, transpercent la toiture et émergent au-dessus d'elle comme des arbres dénudés. À une extrémité du toit est perchée une petite maison de thé dans un style qui rappelle un certain nombre de projets similaires de Fujimori.

Fujimori plays both on traditional Japanese architecture and on a certain sense of humor – cantilevering a small space for the tea ceremony over the house.

Fujimori spielt mit der japanischen Architekturtradition sowie mit einem gewissen Humor – indem er einen kleinen Raum für die Teezeremonie aus dem Haus herausragen lässt.

Fujimori se sert de l'architecture japonaise traditionnelle et d'un certain humour, comme l'illustre ce petit volume en porte-à-faux prévu pour la cérémonie du thé.

The interior, also inspired by Japanese tradition, exudes a quirkiness and a modernity in such features as the suspended chimney.

Auch das Interieur ist von japanischer Tradition inspiriert. Nichtsdestotrotz ist es ungewöhnlich und modern, wie der hängende Kamin.

L'intérieur est également inspiré de la tradition japonaise et d'un goût pour le bizarre et la modernité, comme l'illustre cette cheminée suspendue.

SOU FUJIMOTO ARCHITECTS

Sou Fujimoto Architects
10–3 Ichikawa-Seihon Building 6F
Higashi-Enoki-Cho Shinjuku
Tokyo 162–0807
Japan

Tel: +81 3 3513 5401
Fax: +81 3 3513 5402
E-mail: sosuke@tka.att.ne.jp
Web: www.sou-fujimoto.com

Suo Fujimoto was born in 1971. He received a B.Arch degree from the University of Tokyo, Faculty of Engineering, Department of Architecture (1990–94). He established his own firm, **SOU FUJIMOTO ARCHITECTS**, in 2000. He is considered one of the most interesting rising Japanese architects, and his forms usually evade easy classification. He has been a lecturer at Kyoto University (2007–), Tokyo University (2004) and the Tokyo University of Science (2001–). His work includes the Industrial Training Facilities for the Mentally Handicapped (Hokkaido, 2003); the Environment Art Forum for Annaka (Gunma, 2003–06); the Final Wooden House in Kumamoto (Kumamoto, 2006–07); the Treatment Center for Mentally Disturbed Children (Hokkaido, 2006); a Tokyo Apartment (Tokyo, 2006–07); and the House O (Chiba, 2007, published here), all in Japan.

Suo Fujimoto wurde 1971 geboren. Sein Architekturstudium an der Fakultät für Bauingenieurwesen der Universität Tokio schloss er mit einem B.Arch. ab (1990–94). Sein eigenes Büro, **SOU FUJIMOTO ARCHITECTS**, gründete er 2000. Er gilt als einer der interessantesten jungen Architekten Japans, seine Formensprache entzieht sich einfachen Zuordnungen. Als Dozent lehrt er an den Universitäten von Kioto (2007–) und Tokio (2004) sowie an der Tokioter Universität der Wissenschaften (2001–). Zu seinen Projekten zählen Ausbildungsstätten für geistig Behinderte (Hokkaido, 2003), das Umwelt-Kunst-Forum in Annaka (Gunma, 2003–06), das Final Wooden House in Kumamoto (Kumamoto, 2006–07), ein Behandlungszentrum für psychisch erkrankte Kinder (Hokkaido, 2006), ein Apartment in Tokio (Tokio, 2006–07) sowie das Haus O (Chiba, 2007, hier vorgestellt), alle in Japan.

Suo Fujimoto, né en 1971, est B.Arch de l'université de Tokyo (faculté d'ingénierie, département d'architecture, 1990–94). Il crée sa propre agence, **SOU FUJI-MOTO ARCHITECTS**, en 2000. On le considère comme l'un des plus intéressants jeunes architectes japonais apparus récemment, et son vocabulaire formel échappe à toutes classifications aisées. Il a été assistant à l'université de Kyoto (2007–), à l'université de Tokyo (2004) et à l'université des sciences de Tokyo (2001–). Parmi ses réalisations : des installations de formation pour handicapés mentaux (Hokkaido, 2003) ; l'Environment Art Forum pour Annaka (Gunma, 2003–06) ; la Final Wooden House à Kumamoto (2006–07) ; un centre de traitement pour les enfants souffrant de troubles mentaux (Hokkaido, 2006) ; un appartement à Tokyo (Tokyo, 2006–07) et la maison O (Chiba, 2007, publiée ici), le tout au Japon.

HOUSE O

Chiba, Japan, 2007

Site area: 656 m². Floor area: 129 m². Client: Dr. O.
Cost: not disclosed. Collaborator: Yumiko Nogiri

This is a single story weekend house for a couple set on a rocky Pacific Ocean coastline about two hours drive from Tokyo. The couple intends to retire to the residence, which was imagined as a continuous room inspired by the branches of a tree. All of the functions of the house, including the entrance, living area, dining space, bedroom, "Japanese style" room, study, and bath are part of this continuous use of space. The client requested that the house have the "feeling of the ocean nearby." Fujimoto explains, that "responding to this image, I thought of creating various oceans—a panoramic view of the ocean, the ocean seen from recesses of a cave, an enclosed ocean and a place that seems projected above the ocean. Oriented in different directions, one can find various views of the ocean walking throughout the house. Living area, bedroom and bathroom each has its unique relation to the ocean. One could say the house is akin to a walking trail along a coast: one could happen by a panoramic view, sometimes feel the ocean at the back, or find the ocean through a small gap." The idea of the basic undivided space relates to Fujimoto's desire to create something "primitive, in between natural and man-made."

Das einstöckige Wochenendhaus für ein Paar liegt an einer felsigen Küste am Pazifik etwa zwei Autostunden außerhalb von Tokio. Die beiden planen, im Ruhestand ganz in das Haus zu ziehen, das inspiriert von den Ästen eines Baums als durchgängiger großer Raum entworfen wurde. Sämtliche Funktionen des Hauses, einschließlich Eingangs-, Wohn-, Essbereich und Schlafzimmer, einem „japanischen Zimmer", Arbeitszimmer und Bad sind Teil dieses Raumkontinuums. Der Bauherr wünschte sich, „das nahe Meer spüren" zu können. Fujimoto erklärt, dass er, „angeregt von diesem Bild, die Idee hatte, verschiedene Meere zu schaffen – einen Panoramablick auf das Meer, das Meer aus der Perspektive einer Höhle, ein umbautes Meer und schließlich einen scheinbar über dem Meer schwebenden Raum. Durch die unterschiedliche Orientierung bieten sich die verschiedensten Ausblicke beim Gang durch das Haus. Ob Wohnraum, Schlafzimmer oder Bad, jeder Raum hat seine eigene unverwechselbare Beziehung zum Meer. Man könnte das Haus mit einem Weg am Meer vergleichen, bei dem sich hier ein Panoramablick ausbreitet, man dort den Ozean im Rücken spürt oder das Meer durch einen schmalen Spalt entdeckt". Die Idee, einen einfachen, ungeteilten Raum zu kreieren, steht in Zusammenhang mit Fujimotos Wunsch, etwas „Primitives, halb Natürliches und halb Künstliches zu schaffen".

Cette maison de week-end sur un seul niveau a été conçue pour un couple. Elle se trouve sur la côte rocheuse du Pacifique, à deux heures environ de voiture de Tokyo. Les propriétaires souhaitent prendre leur retraite dans cette maison qui a été imaginée comme une pièce en continu, inspirée par les branches d'un arbre. Toutes les fonctions, y compris l'entrée, le séjour, l'aire des repas, la chambre, la pièce « de style japonais », le bureau et la salle de bains sont intégrées dans ce continuum spatial. Le client souhaitait que la maison donne le « sentiment de la proche présence de l'océan ». Fujimoto explique que « pour répondre à cette image, j'ai pensé créer divers océans… une vue panoramique de l'océan, l'océan vu du fond d'une caverne, un océan fermé et un lieu qui semble se projeter au-dessus de l'océan ». Grâce à ses diverses orientations, en se promenant dans l'ensemble de la maison, on peut découvrir des vues variées de l'océan. « Le séjour, la chambre et la salle de bains développent chacun une relation unique avec l'océan. On pourrait dire que cette maison est semblable à un chemin de promenade côtier, grâce auquel on peut obtenir brusquement une vision panoramique, avoir parfois la sensation de la présence de l'océan derrière soi, ou le retrouver à travers une petite échappée. » L'idée de cet espace sans division renvoie au désir de Fujimoto de créer quelque chose de « primitif, entre le naturel et ce qui est fait de la main de l'homme ».

The angular articulation of the concrete and glass boxes that make up the house does not really make it fit into the natural setting as such, instead it imposes itself in a manner that establishes a dialectic relationship with the shoreline.

Durch die Kantigkeit der Beton- und Glaskuben integriert sich das Haus nicht gerade in sein natürliches Umfeld, dennoch behauptet es sich auf eine Weise, die von einem dialektischen Verhältnis zur Küstenlandschaft zeugt.

L'articulation anguleuse des boîtes de béton et de verre qui constituent la maison ne l'intègre pas réellement à son cadre naturel, mais l'impose plutôt en créant, à sa manière, un dialogue avec la côte.

With this simply furnished and rather austere looking house, Fujimoto makes it clear that he is an architect to be reckoned with, creating multiple effects with a basically strict geometric vocabulary.

Durch das schlicht möblierte und eher nüchterne Haus macht Fujimoto klar, dass er ein Architekt ist, mit dem zu rechnen ist. Ihm gelingt es, mit einem streng geometrischen Vokabular vielschichtige Effekte zu erzielen.

Par cette maison simplement meublée et à l'aspect plutôt austère, qui multiplie les effets à partir d'un strict vocabulaire géométrique, Fujimoto montre qu'il est un architecte avec lequel il faut maintenant compter.

ANTÓN GARCÍA-ABRIL & ENSAMBLE STUDIO

Antón García-Abril & Ensamble Studio Spain
C/Cabo Candelaria 9B
28290 Las Rozas de Madrid
Spain

Tel: +34 91 17 30 166
E-mail: anton@ensamble.info / Web: www.ensamble.info

ANTÓN GARCÍA-ABRIL was born in Madrid in 1969. He graduated from the ETSA of Madrid (ETSAM) in Architecture and Urbanism in 1995 and went on to receive a doctorate from the same institution in 2000. He is currently a Professor of Architectural Projects at the ETSAM and a visiting critic at Cornell University. García-Abril worked in the office of Santiago Calatrava (1992) and in that of Alberto Campo Baeza (1990–94). He created his first firm in 1995, and his present one, **ENSAMBLE STUDIO**, in 2000. He explains that the name of his firm is derived from a term used in architecture, "assemble," and the musical term "ensemble." "This team," he says, "develops a multidisciplinary working scheme… to carry out the intervention of the architect in the whole process that leads to the artistic work, from the conceptual abstraction to the construction detail." Essentially this means that he has created an in-house contracting firm. His completed projects include: the Musical Studies Center (Santiago de Compostela, 2002); the Concert Hall and Music School (Medina del Campo, 2003); the Valdés Studio (Madrid, 2004); and the Martemar House (Málaga, 2003–05), all in Spain. Amongst his more recent projects: La Casa del Lector Library (Madrid, 2006); the SGAE Central Office (Santiago de Compostela, 2005–07); the Hemeroscopium House (Las Rozas, Madrid, 2007–08, published here); the Berklee SGAE Tower of Music, a vertical campus for contemporary international music education (Valencia, 2008); and the Museum of America (Salamanca, 2008), all in Spain.

ANTÓN GARCÍA-ABRIL, geboren 1969 in Madrid, absolvierte sein Studium im Bereich Architektur und Urbanistik an der Escuela técnica superior de architectura de Madrid (ETSAM), an der er später auch promoviert wurde. Derzeit ist er Dozent am Departamento de proyectos arquitectónicos der ETSAM und Gastdozent an der Cornell University. Von 1990 bis 1994 arbeitete er im Büro von Alberto Campo Baeza und 1992 für Santiago Calatrava. Seine erste eigene Firma gründete er 1995. Den Namen seiner jetzigen, im Jahr 2000 gegründeten Firma **ENSAMBLE STUDIO** erklärt García-Abril als eine Kombination aus dem in der Architektur gebräuchlichen Begriff „assemble" und dem musikalischen „Ensemble". „Das Team", so García-Abril, „entwickelt einen multidisziplinären Arbeitsplan […], der sämtliche Planungen des Architekten umsetzt, aus denen schließlich das fertige Werk hervorgeht, vom abstrakten Konzept bis hin zum einzelnen Baudetail." Im Prinzip hat García-Abril damit also ein hausinternes Vertragsunternehmen geschaffen. Zu den von Ensamble realisierten Projekten gehören die Musikakademie in Santiago de Compostela (2002), die Konzerthalle und Musikschule in Medina del Campo (2003), das Atelier Valdés in Madrid (2004) und die Casa Martemar in Málaga (2003–05). In jüngerer Zeit entstanden die Bibliothek der Casa del Lector (Madrid, 2006), die Zentrale der Sociedad General de Autores y Editores (SGAE) in Santiago de Compostela (2005–07), die Casa Hemeroscopium (Las Rozas, Madrid, 2007–08, hier vorgestellt), die Berklee SGAE Torre de la Música in Valencia (ein Ableger des Berklee College of Music in Boston, 2008) und das Museo de América in Salamanca (2008), alle in Spanien.

ANTÓN GARCÍA-ABRIL, né à Madrid en 1969, est diplômé en architecture et urbanisme de l'ETSA de Madrid (1995) dont il est également docteur (2000). Il est actuellement professeur en projets architecturaux à l'ETSAM et critique invité à Cornell University. García-Abril a travaillé dans l'agence de Santiago Calatrava (1992) et celle d'Alberto Campo Baeza (1990–94). Il a créé sa première agence en 1995, et l'actuel **ENSAMBLE STUDIO** en 2000. Ce nom vient de la contraction du terme architectural « assembler » et du terme musical « ensemble ». « Cette équipe, dit-il, travaille dans un esprit multidisciplinaire… pour que l'intervention de l'architecte soit menée à bien au cours du processus tout entier qui conduit à une création artistique, de l'abstraction conceptuelle au détail constructif. » Il a donc créé une agence à services intégrés. Parmi ses réalisations achevées : un conservatoire de musique (Saint-Jacques-de-Compostelle, 2002) ; une salle de concert et école de musique (Medina del Campo, 2003) ; le studio Valdés (Madrid, 2004) et la maison Martemar (Málaga, 2003–05), toutes en Espagne. Parmi ses plus récents projets : la bibliothèque de la Casa del Lector (Madrid, 2006) ; le siège de la SGAE (Saint-Jacques-de-Compostelle, 2005–07) ; la maison Hemeroscopium (Las Rozas, Madrid, 2007–08, publiée ici) ; la Torre de la Musica Berklee SGAE (un campus pour l'enseignement de la musique contemporaine internationale, Valence, 2008) et le musée d'Amérique (Salamanque, 2008).

HEMEROSCOPIUM HOUSE

Las Rozas, Madrid, Spain, 2007–08

Floor area: 300 m². Client: Hemeroscopium S.L. Cost: not disclosed.
Team: Elena Pérez (Associate Architect), Javier Cuesta (Quantity Surveyor)

The Hemeroscopium House is made up of a series of architectural or engineering challenges, including its stacked beam design and the massive block of stone that tops this assemblage.

Das Hemeroscopium House entstand aus der Bewältigung verschiedener architektonischer und statischer Herausforderungen, wie etwa die gestapelten Träger und der massive Steinblock beweisen, der oben auf der Gesamtkomposition ruht.

La maison Hemoroscopium accumule les défis architecturaux ou techniques, comme le montre son empilement de poutres énormes et le bloc de pierre massif qui le couronne.

The name "Hemeroscopium" is Greek for the place where the sun sets, "An allusion to a place that exists only in our mind, in our senses. It is constantly moving and mutable, but is nonetheless real. It is enclosed, delimited and suggested by the horizon, though it is defined by light and only takes place in a precise moment of time." The architect has placed the beams in an ascendant spiral of seven heavy structural elements that grows lighter as it rises. The juncture of these beams made of a combination of reinforced precast and cast-in-place concrete appears to be simple but demanded complex engineering calculations. "It took us a year to figure out the way to make the equilibrium between elements possible and only seven days to build the structure," says the architect. In rather poetic terms, García-Abril explains, "Thus, an astonishing new language is invented where form disappears and naked space is created. Space, its nudity and emptiness, is framed by a solid and dense structure. The Hemeroscopium House materializes equilibrium with what we ironically call the G point, a 20-ton granite stone, the expression of the force of gravity, a counterweight to the whole structure's mass." Indeed, the enormous block of granite the architect refers to sits on top of the house, a reminder of the forces at play.

Der aus dem Griechischen stammende Begriff Hemeroscopium bezeichnet den Ort, an dem die Sonne untergeht, „eine Anspielung auf einen Ort, der nur in unserem Kopf, in unserer Vorstellung existiert. Er ist unablässig in Bewegung, im Wandel und dennoch real. Er ist umschlossen, umgrenzt und angedeutet durch den Horizont, obwohl er nur vom Licht definiert wird und sich zu einem ganz bestimmten Zeitpunkt ereignet." Der Architekt positionierte die Träger aus sieben schweren Konstruktionselementen zu einer aufsteigenden Spirale, die mit zunehmender Höhe lichter wird. Die Verbindung dieser Träger, teils aus vorgefertigten Stahlbetonelementen und teils aus Ortbeton gegossen, wirkt einfach, erforderte jedoch komplexe statische Berechnungen. „Wir brauchten ein Jahr, um das Gleichgewicht zwischen den Elementen zu berechnen und nur sieben Tage, um die Konstruktion zu errichten", berichtet der Architekt. Auf recht poetische Weise erklärt García-Abril: „Und so erfanden wir eine erstaunliche neue Sprache, in der die Form schwindet und bloßer Raum entsteht. Der Raum, in all seiner Nacktheit und Leere, wird von einer massiven und dichten Struktur umschlossen. Die Villa Hemeroscopium erreicht ihr Gleichgewicht durch einen 20 t schweren Granitblock, den wir ironisch den G-Punkt nennen, ein Ausdruck der Schwerkraft, ein Gegengewicht zur Masse der Gesamtkonstruktion." Und tatsächlich liegt der gewaltige Granitblock, den der Architekt erwähnt, oben auf dem Haus, eine mahnende Erinnerung an die Kräfte, die hier im Spiel sind.

Le mot « Hemeroscopium », issu du grec, signifie « lieu où se couche le soleil », « C'est une allusion à un lieu qui n'existe que dans nos têtes et nos sens. Il se déplace et se transforme constamment, mais n'en est pas moins réel. C'est un lieu clos, délimité et suggéré par l'horizon, bien qu'il soit défini par la lumière et n'apparaisse qu'à un moment précis de la journée. » L'architecte a disposé les poutres en spirale ascendante composée de sept lourds éléments structuraux qui s'allègent peu à peu. La jonction entre ces poutres et le béton armé préfabriqué ou coulé sur place semble simple, mais a demandé des calculs d'ingénierie très complexes. « Il nous a fallu un an pour trouver l'équilibre entre ces éléments, mais sept jours seulement pour le monter », précise l'architecte. En termes assez poétiques, Garcia-Abril explique que « ... ainsi s'est élaboré un étonnant nouveau langage dans lequel la forme disparaît et un espace nu se crée. L'espace – sa nudité et son vide – est cadré par une structure dense et massive. La maison Hemeroscopium matérialise un équilibre avec ce que nous appelons ironiquement le point G, qui est un rocher de granit de 20 tonnes exprimant la force de gravité et faisant contrepoids à toute la structure ». Cet énorme bloc de granit, posé en partie supérieure de la maison, rappelle en effet les forces en jeu.

The volumes formed by the stacked elements of the house are simple and modern in appearance, even if the weightiness of the beams sometimes gives an impression of a careful balance that goes beyond the call of solidity.

Die von den gestapelten Elementen definierten Räume sind schlicht und modern. Dennoch lässt die Schwere der Träger vermuten, dass es beim sorgsamen Austarieren der Konstruktion vielleicht um mehr als das reine Erzielen von Stabilität ging.

Les volumes qui constituent l'empilement d'éléments architecturaux sont d'aspect simple et moderne, même si la lourdeur des poutres donne parfois l'impression d'un équilibre calculé qui dépasse les simples nécessités de la solidité.

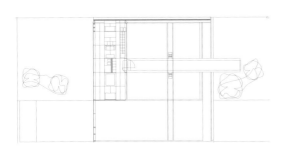

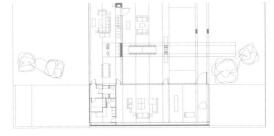

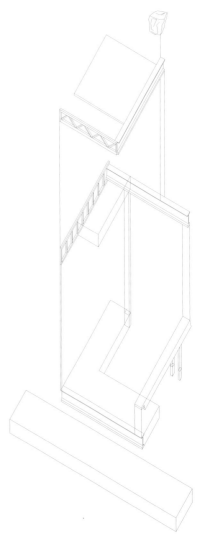

With a plan that is rigorously geometric, and essentially square, the architect nonetheless creates a series of unremitting surprises in his search for excessive dimensions.

Trotz des streng geometrischen, im Grunde quadratischen Grundrisses, gelingt es dem Architekten bei seinem Streben nach exzessiven Dimensionen immer wieder zu überraschen.

Dans ce plan rigoureusement géométrique de forme essentiellement carrée, l'architecte réussit à multiplier les surprises dans sa recherche de dimensionnements extravagants.

SEAN GODSELL

Sean Godsell Architects
Level 1, 49 Exhibition Street
Melbourne, Victoria 3000
Australia

Tel: +61 3 9654 2677
Fax: +61 3 9654 3877
E-mail: godsell@netspace.net.au
Web: www.seangodsell.com

SEAN GODSELL was born in Melbourne in 1960. He graduated from the University of Melbourne in 1984 and worked from 1986 to 1988 in London with Sir Denys Lasdun. He created Sean Godsell Architects in 1994 and received an M.Arch degree from the Royal Melbourne Institute of Technology (RMIT) in 1999. He was assigned the RAIA Award of Merit for new residential work for the Carter/Tucker House in 2000. He taught in the RMIT Department of Architecture from 1986 to 1997. His work has been shown in exhibitions in New York, Paris, London, and Mendrisio (Switzerland). It includes the Carter/Tucker House (Breamlea, Victoria, 1999–2000); the Peninsula House (Victoria, 2001–02; ar+d Prizewinner 2002; RAIA Architecture Award 2003); the Woodleigh School Science Faculty (Baxter, Victoria, 2002; RAIA William Wardell Award 2003); the Lewis House (Dunkeld, Victoria, 2003); the Westwood House (Sydney, NSW, 2003); and the St. Andrews Beach House (Mornington Peninsula, Victoria, 2003–05; RAIA Robin Boyd Award 2006), all in Australia. He has also worked on the CIPEA Housing Project (Nanjing, China, 2003–); La Nada Retreat (Arizona, 2004); and in Australia, the Tanderra House (Rosebud, Victoria, 2006); and the Glenburn House (Glenburn, Victoria, 2004–07, published here). Current projects include the new postgraduate School of Design for RMIT (2007–12).

SEAN GODSELL wurde 1960 in Melbourne geboren. Sein Studium schloss er 1984 an der University of Melbourne ab und arbeitete von 1986 bis 1988 in London für Sir Denys Lasdun. Sein Büro Sean Godsell Architects gründete er 1994. 1999 absolvierte er seinen M.Arch. am Royal Melbourne Institute of Technology (RMIT). Für das Carter/Tucker House erhielt er 2000 den RAIA Award of Merit für neue Wohnbauten. Zwischen 1986 und 1997 lehrte er Architektur am RMIT. Seine Projekte waren in Ausstellungen in New York, Paris, London und Mendrisio (Schweiz) zu sehen. Zu seinen Arbeiten zählen u. a. das Carter/Tucker House (Breamlea, Victoria, 1999–2000), das Peninsula House (Victoria, 2001–02, ar+d Prize 2002, RAIA Architecture Award 2003), die Naturwissenschaftliche Fakultät der Woodleigh School (Baxter, Victoria, 2002, RAIA William Wardell Award 2003), das Lewis House (Dunkeld, Victoria, 2003), das Westwood House (Sydney, NSW, 2003) sowie das St. Andrews Beach House (Mornington Peninsula, Victoria, 2003–05, RAIA Robin Boyd Award 2006), alle in Australien. Darüber hinaus war er am CIPEA Housing Project beteiligt (Nanjing, China, 2003–) und arbeitete am La Nada Retreat (Arizona, 2004) sowie in Australien am Tanderra House (Rosebud, Victoria, 2006) und dem Glenburn House (Glenburn, Victoria, 2004–07, hier vorgestellt). Zu den aktuellen Projekten zählt die neue Postgraduate School of Design des RMIT (2007–12).

SEAN GODSELL, né à Melbourne en 1960, est diplômé d'architecture de l'université de cette même ville (1984). Il a travaillé de 1986 à 1988 à Londres pour Sir Denys Lasdun. Il a créé l'agence Sean Godsell Architects en 1994, et a passé son M.Arch au Royal Melbourne Institute of Technology (RMIT) en 1999. Sa Carter/Tucker House a reçu le RAIA Award of Merit pour une réalisation résidentielle nouvelle en 2000. Il a enseigné au département d'architecture du RMIT de 1986 à 1997. Son œuvre a fait l'objet d'expositions à New York, Paris, Londres, et Mendrisio (Suisse). Parmi ses réalisations : la Carter/Tucker House (Breamlea, Victoria, 1999–2000) ; la Peninsula House (Victoria, 2001–02; ar+d Prize 2002 et RAIA Architecture Award 2003) ; la faculté des sciences de Woodleigh (Baxter, Victoria, 2002; William Wardell RAIA Award 2003) ; la Lewis House (Dunkeld, Victoria, 2003) ; la Westwood House (Sydney, NSW, 2003) ; et la St. Andrews Beach House (Mornington Peninsula, Victoria, 2003–05; RAIA Robin Boyd Award 2006) ; l'immeuble de logements CIPEA (Nanjing, Chine, 2003–) ; la Nada Retreat (Arizona, 2004) et, en Australie, la Tanderra House (Rosebud, Victoria, 2006) et la Glenburn House (Glenburn, Victoria, 2004–07, publiée ici). Il travaille actuellement sur le projet de l'École d'études supérieures de design du RMIT (2007–12).

GLENBURN HOUSE

Glenburn, Victoria, Australia, 2004–07

Floor area: 300 m². Client: not disclosed. Cost: not disclosed.
Project Team: Sean Godsell, Hayley Franklin

Nestled into its site, the Glenburn
House might in some respects recall
the appearance of farm architecture,
but a closer look shows that it is a
much more sophisticated enterprise.

Eingebettet in seine Umgebung mag
das Glenburn House in gewisser Hinsicht an Farmbauten erinnern, doch
bei genauerem Hinsehen zeigt sich,
dass es sich hier um etwas weitaus
Komplexeres handelt.

Nichée dans son cadre, la maison
Glenburn rappelle à certains égards
l'architecture de ferme, même si un
examen rapproché révèle une sophis-
tication beaucoup plus importante.

Glenburn is located an hour and a half's drive north east of Melbourne in the foothills of the Yarra Valley. The site is at the top of a hill with panoramic views on 20 hectares of farmland with a national forest to the north. In order to protect the occupants from heat and winds, the house is partly embedded into the hilltop. Double glazing, solar collectors for power and hot water, rainwater harvesting and digital power management meet the clients' desire for a sustainable design and confirm the architect's own interest in this area. Sean Godsell writes, "The plan extends our research into the notion of 'abstract verandah' to include a barcode motif in the plan. A series of discrete spaces, organized in a way to suit the client's particular requirements, results in a coded arrangement that is unique to them—a tectonic thumbprint for living."

Glenburn liegt etwa anderthalb Autostunden nordöstlich von Melbourne in den Ausläufern des Yarra Valley. Das Grundstück liegt auf der Kuppe eines Hügels und bietet Panoramablicke auf 20 ha landwirtschaftlich genutztes Land und den National Forest im Norden. Um die Bewohner vor Hitze und Wind zu schützen, wurde das Haus teilweise in den Hügel versenkt. Doppelverglasung, Sonnenkollektoren für Strom und Warmwasser, Regenwassergewinnung und digitale Steuerung des Energieverbrauchs kommen dem Wunsch des Bauherrn nach umweltfreundlicher Planung entgegen und stellen zugleich das Interesse des Architekten auf diesem Gebiet unter Beweis. Sean Godsell schreibt: „Der Grundriss bekräftigt unsere Beschäftigung mit dem Konzept einer ‚abstrakten Veranda', wir integrierten ein Barcode-Motiv in den Grundriss. Eine Abfolge separater Räume, die so organisiert wurden, das sie den spezifischen Bedürfnissen des Auftraggebers entsprechen, ergibt eine kodifizierte Anordnung, die einzigartig ist – ein tektonischer Fingerabruck zum Bewohnen."

Glenburn se trouve à une heure et demie de voiture au nord-est de Melbourne, dans les collines de la Yarra Valley. Implantée au sommet d'une éminence, la maison bénéficie d'une vue panoramique sur 20 hectares de terres agricoles et, au nord, sur une forêt domaniale. Pour protéger ses occupants de la chaleur et des vents, elle est en partie enterrée. Le double vitrage, les panneaux solaires pour la production d'énergie et d'eau chaude, la récupération des eaux de pluie et la gestion informatisée de l'ensemble répondent à la demande d'une conception écologique de la part du propriétaire et à l'intérêt de l'architecte pour ces technologies. Sean Godsell explique : « Le plan est un développement de nos recherches sur le concept de »véranda abstraite« et inclut un motif de code-barres. Une succession de volumes discrets, organisés en réponse aux attentes particulières du client, aboutit à une disposition codée spécifique, une sorte d'empreinte tectonique du style de vie des occupants. »

Stepping down into the house, the visitor is greeted by a decided contrast between an opacity generated by wooden slats and large openings.

Betritt der Besucher von oben das Haus, sieht er sich mit einem auffallenden Kontrast konfrontiert: der Opazität der Holzlamellen und den großflächigen Fensteröffnungen.

En descendant les quelques marches qui mènent à l'entrée, le visiteur ressent un contraste marqué entre l'opacité créée par le lattis de bois et les vastes ouvertures.

The very basic rectangular plan of
the house, as well as its insertion
into the site, allows for a protected
feeling inside.

Der sehr einfache rechteckige Grundriss und die Einbettung des Hauses in
das Gelände vermitteln im Innern des
Baus das Gefühl von Sicherheit.

Le plan rectangulaire très basique
de la maison, ainsi que son insertion
dans le site, génèrent à l'intérieur
un sentiment de protection.

Full glazing in a bedroom allows the owners open views onto the natural setting that might not be expected from certain angles.

Die raumhohe Verglasung in einem der Schlafzimmer erlaubt den Besitzern landschaftliche Ausblicke, die man aus manchen Blickwinkeln sicher nicht erwartet hätte.

La baie vitrée toute hauteur de cette chambre offre au propriétaire des perspectives sur l'environnement naturel sous des angles inattendus.

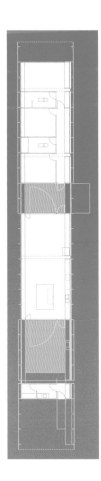

JORGE HERNÁNDEZ DE LA GARZA

JHG Jorge Hernández de la Garza
Alvaro Obregon #278 int. 2.2
Col. Hipódromo Condesa Delegacion Cuauhtemoc, CP 06100
Mexico City
Mexico

Tel: +52 55 5211 0045
E-mail: jorge@hernandezdelagarza.com
Web: www.hernandezdelagarza.com

JORGE HERNÁNDEZ DE LA GARZA was born in Mexico City in 1977. He graduated from La Salle University (Mexico, 1995–2000). Later he studied design at the Architectural Association (London, 2002). In 2007 he was selected as one of the 44 international firms for the "Young Architects Annual Event" in Spain. In the same year he was selected as one the "101 Most Exciting New Architects of the World" in London. He participated in architectural competitions for the Great Grand Plaza (Caracas, Venezuela, 2004) and the Gyeonggi-Do Jeongok Prehistory Museum (South Korea, 2006). His projects include the Vladimir Kaspé Cultural Center (Mexico City, 2006); Los Amates House (Morelos, 2006); the Suntro House (Oaxtepec, 2006–07, published here); the Plaka Comex Pavilion (Mexico City, 2007); and the Smooth Building (Monterrey, 2008), all in Mexico.

JORGE HERNÁNDEZ DE LA GARZA wurde 1977 in Mexiko-Stadt geboren. Im Anschluss an sein Studium an der Universidad La Salle (Mexiko-Stadt, 1995–2000). studierte er Design an der Architectural Association in London (2002). 2007 wurde er als einer von 44 internationalen Architekten für den „Young Architects Annual Event" in Spanien ausgewählt. Im selben Jahr wurde er in London zu einem der „101 aufregendsten neuen Architekten weltweit" erklärt. Er beteiligte sich an Wettbewerben für die Great Grand Plaza (Caracas, Venezuela, 2004) und das Gyeonggi-Do Jeongok Museum für Urgeschichte (Südkorea, 2006). Zu seinen Projekten zählen das Vladimir-Kaspé-Kulturzentrum (Mexiko-Stadt, 2006), die Casa Los Amates (Morelos, 2006), die Casa Suntro (Oaxtepec, 2006–07, hier vorgestellt), der Plaka-Comex-Pavillon (Mexiko-Stadt, 2007) sowie das Smooth Building (Monterrey, 2008), alle in Mexiko.

JORGE HERNÁNDEZ DE LA GARZA, né à Mexico en 1977 et diplômé de l'université La Salle (Mexico, 1995–2000), a étudié à l'Architectural Association (Londres, 2002). En 2007, il a été sélectionné comme l'une des 44 agences internationales à participer à la manifestation « Young Architects Annual Event » en Espagne. La même année, il a été désigné l'un des « 101 Most Exciting New Architects in the World » à Londres. Il a participé aux concours pour la Great Grand Plaza (Caracas, Venezuela, 2004) et le musée de préhistoire Gyeonggi-Do Jeongok (Corée du Sud, 2006). Parmi ses réalisations, toutes au Mexique : le Centre culturel Vladimir Kaspé (Mexico, 2006) ; la maison Los Amates (Morelos, 2006) ; la maison Suntro (Oaxtepec, 2006–07, publiée ici) ; le pavillon Plaka Comex (Mexico, 2007) et l'immeuble Smooth (Monterrey, 2008).

SUNTRO HOUSE

Oaxtepec, Mexico, 2006–07

Floor area: 254 m². Client: Grupo Suntro.
Cost: $200 000

Located in the attractive residential area of Oaxtepec, the Suntro House has a view toward the Tepozteco Mountain. The folded plane design specifically takes into account the hot climate, allowing wind to circulate in a cooling pattern. Thin columns support the overhanging folds of the house with considerable elegance. Public and recreation areas are located on the ground floor with the bedrooms above. An outdoor swimming pool is slightly elevated above the level of the ground floor of the house with its broadly glazed and open façade. White dominates both the simply furnished interior and the exterior as well. The basic rectangular-plan house, which combines lightness and carefully crafted sheltering elements, is surrounded by vegetation, including trees saved during construction.

Das in einer attraktiven Wohngegend von Oaxtepec gelegene Haus Suntro bietet einen Ausblick auf den Berg Tepozteco. Der auf gefalteten Ebenen basierende Entwurf berücksichtigt insbesondere das heiße Klima und lässt den Wind kühlend zirkulieren. Schlanke Stützen tragen die auskragenden Falten des Hauses mit erstaunlicher Eleganz. Gemeinschafts- und Freizeitbereiche verteilen sich über das Erdgeschoss, die Schlafzimmer liegen darüber. Ein Außenpool wurde leicht über Erdgeschossniveau des großzügig verglasten Hauses mit seiner offenen Fassade erhöht. Weiß dominiert sowohl im schlicht möblierten Innenraum als auch am Außenbau. Das auf einem einfachen rechteckigen Grundriss errichtete Haus – eine Kombination aus Leichtigkeit und sorgfältigst durchgearbeiteten, Geborgenheit vermittelnden Elementen – liegt mitten im Grünen, zwischen Bäumen, die beim Bau erhalten wurden.

Située dans le superbe quartier résidentiel d'Oaxtepec, la maison Suntro bénéficie de vues sur la montagne de Tepozteco. Sa forme repliée sur elle-même prend spécifiquement en compte la chaleur du climat puisqu'elle facilite la circulation des vents rafraîchissants. De fines colonnes soutiennent les auvents avec beaucoup d'élégance. Les zones de réception et de détente, largement vitrées et ouvertes, se trouvent au rez-de-chaussée. La couleur blanche domine à l'extérieur comme à l'intérieur, qui est meublé avec simplicité. Construite sur un plan rectangulaire qui combine la légèreté et des éléments de protection soigneusement mis en œuvre, la maison est noyée dans la végétation et les arbres qui ont été préservés pendant le chantier.

The Suntro House is essentially a
wrapped form surrounding the living
spaces – and, above, the broadly
glazed living room facing the pool.

Das Haus Suntro besteht im Grunde
aus einer gefalteten Form, die die
Wohnräume – einschließlich des großzügig verglasten Wohnzimmers mit
Blick auf den Pool (oben) – umfängt.

La maison Suntro est essentiellement
une enveloppe posée sur un espace
de vie – et ci-dessus, le séjour
illuminé face à la piscine.

The architect uses lighting to give the house a marked presence at night, in many ways revealing its wrapping structure, as in the images above and opposite.

Der Architekt setzt die nächtliche Beleuchtung so ein, dass das Haus und vor allem seine „gefaltete" Struktur in Szene gesetzt werden, wie oben und links im Bild zu sehen.

L'architecte a travaillé l'éclairage nocturne pour renforcer la présence de la maison, ce qui met en valeur sa structure enveloppante (ci-dessus et à gauche).

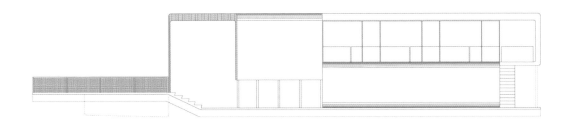

The living space opens out entirely in the direction of the slightly raised swimming pool. The furniture is relatively simple and angular like the architecture.

Der Wohnraum öffnet sich ganz zum leicht erhöhten Pool hin. Das Mobiliar ist vergleichsweise schlicht gehalten und geradlinig wie die Architektur selbst.

Le volume du séjour s'ouvre entiè-rement vers la piscine légèrement surélevée. Comme l'architecture, le mobilier est relativement simple et de formes anguleuses.

Left, a covered passage near the dining area. Below, two plans show the simple rectangular design of the whole, augmented by the outlying exterior walls that "wrap" the whole.

Links ein umbauter Durchgang, der am Essbereich vorbeiführt. Die beiden Grundrisse unten veranschaulichen den schlichten rechteckigen Entwurf, der durch die frei liegenden Außenwände, die das Ganze „ummanteln", zusätzlich betont wird.

À gauche, un passage couvert le long de la salle à manger. Ci-dessus, deux plans montrant la forme rectangulaire et simple à laquelle viennent s'ajouter les murs extérieurs qui « enveloppent » l'ensemble.

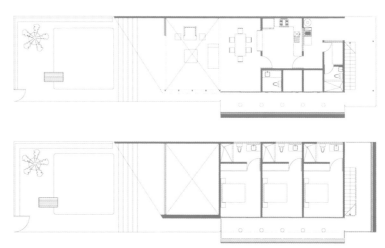

JACKSON CLEMENTS BURROWS

Jackson Clements Burrows Pty Ltd Architects
One Harwood Place
Melbourne, Victoria 3000
Australia

Tel: +61 3 9654 6227
Fax: +61 3 9654 6195
E-mail: jacksonclementsburrows@jcba.com.au
Web: www.jcba.com.au

Tim Jackson was born in San Francisco, USA, in 1964. He worked in the office of Denton Corker Marshall before joining his own father's practice (Daryl Jackson Architects), and running his own firm between 1993 and 1998. He was the project director for the Abito Apartments (Fitzroy, Victoria) that won the 2007 RAIA Architecture Award for Multi-Residential Housing. He also worked on the Kew House (Kew, Victoria, 2004; RAIA Award for residential architecture). Jonathan Clements was born in 1971 in Melbourne. He received his B.Arch degree from Deakin University and worked prior to the formation of **JACKSON CLEMENTS BURROWS** in 1998 with Daryl Jackson. Projects he has been involved with at Jackson Clements Burrows include the Old House (Richmond, Victoria, 2006); the Applecross Residence (Applecross, Western Australia, 2007; RAIA George Temple Poole Award); and the Pier Point Apartments (Geelong, Victoria, 2006–). He also worked on the Cape Schanck House published here (Cape Schanck, Victoria, 2006). Graham Burrows was born in 1971 in Johannesburg, South Africa. He studied at the University of Melbourne and was employed prior to 1998 in the office of Daryl Jackson. Projects he has run for Jackson Clements Burrows include the Separation Creek Residence (Separation Creek, Victoria, 2007); and the Saint Kilda Foreshore Promenade Development in Melbourne (2008). Other work by Jackson Clements Burrows includes the Hue Apartments, a multi-residential project with 29 apartments (Richmond, Melbourne, 2007).

Tim Jackson wurde 1964 in San Francisco, USA, geboren. Er arbeitete zunächst für Denton Corker Marshall, bevor er sich dem Büro seines Vaters anschloss (Daryl Jackson Architects) und schließlich zwischen 1993 und 1998 sein eigenes Büro leitete. Als Projektleiter betreute er die Abito Apartments (Fitzroy, Victoria), die 2007 mit dem RAIA-Architekturpreis für Mehrfamilienhäuser ausgezeichnet wurden. Auch am Kew House war er beteiligt (Kew, Victoria, 2004, RAIA-Preis für Wohnbauten). Jonathan Clements wurde 1971 in Melbourne, Australien, geboren. Er erhielt seinen B.Arch. an der Deakin University und war für Daryl Jackson tätig, bevor er zusammen mit seinen Partnern 1998 **JACKSON CLEMENTS BURROWS** gründete. Dort arbeitete er u. a. an folgenden Projekten: dem Old House (Richmond, Victoria, 2006), der Applecross Residence (Applecross, Westaustralien, 2007, RAIA George Temple Poole Award) sowie den Pier Point Apartments (Geelong, Victoria, 2006–). Beteiligt war er auch am hier vorgestellten Cape Schanck House (Cape Schanck, Victoria, 2006). Graham Burrows wurde 1971 in Johannesburg, Südafrika, geboren. Er studierte an der University of Melbourne und war bis 1998 bei Daryl Jackson tätig. Für Jackson Clements Burrows verantwortete er u. a. folgende Projekte: die Separation Creek Residence (Separation Creek, Victoria, 2007) sowie die Entwicklung der Saint Kilda Foreshore Promenade in Melbourne (2008). Weitere Projekte von Jackson Clements Burrows sind u. a. die Hue Apartments mit 29 Wohnungen (Richmond, Melbourne, 2007).

Tim Jackson, né à San Francisco, États-Unis, en 1964, a travaillé chez Denton Corker Marshall, avant de rejoindre l'agence de son père (Daryl Jackson Architects) et de diriger sa propre structure de 1993 à 1998. Il a été directeur de projet pour les Abito Apartments (Fitzroy, Victoria) qui ont remporté le 2007 RAIA Architecture Award pour logements collectifs. Il a également travaillé sur le projet de la Kew House (Kew, Victoria, 2004 ; RAIA Award pour architecture résidentielle). Jonathan Clements, né en 1971 à Melbourne, est B.Arch de Deakin University et a collaboré avec Daryl Jackson, avant la fondation de **JACKSON CLEMENTS BURROWS** en 1998. Parmi les projets sur lesquels il est intervenu chez Jackson Clements Burrows : la Old House (Richmond, Victoria, 2006) ; l'Applecross Residence (Applecross, Australie occidentale, 2007 ; RAIA George Temple Poole Award) et les Pier Point Apartments (Geelong, Victoria, 2006–). Il a également travaillé sur le projet de la maison Cape Schanck publiée ici (Cape Schanck, Victoria, 2006). Graham Burrows, né en 1971 à Johannesburg, Afrique du Sud, a fait ses études à l'université de Melbourne et a été employé avant 1998 par Daryl Jackson. Parmi ses projets pour Jackson Clements Burrows : la Separation Creek Residence (Separation Creek, Victoria, 2007) et la rénovation de la Saint Kilda Foreshore Promenade à Melbourne (2008). Les autres réalisations de Jackson Clements Burrows comprennent les appartements Hue, un projet de 29 appartements (Richmond, Melbourne, 2007).

CAPE SCHANCK HOUSE

Cape Schanck, Victoria, Australia, 2006

Floor area: 350 m². Client: not disclosed. Cost: not disclosed.
Project Team: Jon Clements, Tim Jackson, Graham Burrows, Kim Stapleton, George Fortey, Brett Nixon

The area in which this house is located is characterized by grass-covered dunes and dense brush. The architects found a hollowed and burned log on the site on the occasion of their first visit and used the metaphor of the log for their design. They compare the base of the house to the surrounding dunes—views of the house are concealed by a wall or screen fence on approach, allowing a broad vision of the surrounding countryside over the deck and pool only from the point of entry. The upper level, inspired by the log, contains a kitchen, dining and living areas, a garage, and laundry room. Another upper level area contains the master bedroom and a study. These main areas are finished in black-stained spotted gum hardwood cladding, confirming the burnt log analogy. Interiors for this house, destined for a retired couple and their extended family, were also designed by the architects. Considerable attention was paid to passive energy strategies including the orientation of the house and shading. Well water is used for the swimming pool and rainwater for household use.

Die Gegend, in der das Haus liegt, wird von grasbewachsenen Dünen und dichtem Buschland dominiert. Bei ihrem ersten Besuch fanden die Architekten einen ausgehöhlten, verkohlten Holzstumpf auf dem Grundstück, den sie als Metapher in ihren Entwurf einfließen ließen. Sie vergleichen das Fundament des Hauses mit den Dünen – der Blick auf das Haus selbst wird bei der Anfahrt durch eine Mauer bzw. einen Zaun verstellt, ein Panoramablick auf die landschaftliche Umgebung über die Terrasse und den Pool hinweg ist nur vom Eingangsbereich aus möglich. In der oberen, vom Holzstumpf inspirierten Ebene des Hauses befinden sich Küche, Ess- und Wohnbereiche, eine Garage und ein Hauswirtschaftsraum. Ein weiteres Obergeschoss beherbergt das Hauptschlafzimmer und ein Arbeitszimmer. Diese Hauptbereiche sind mit Spotted-Gum-Hartholz (einer Eukalyptusart) vertäfelt, was die Analogie zum verkohlten Holzstumpf unterstreicht. Auch die Inneneinrichtung dieses Domizils für ein pensioniertes Paar und seine große Familie wurde von den Architekten entworfen. Besonderen Wert legte man auf einen passiven Energiehaushalt, der u. a. durch die Orientierung des Hauses und Sonnenschutzstrategien erreicht wurde. Quellwasser speist den Pool, für den Hausverbrauch wird Regenwasser gesammelt.

L'environnement de cette maison se caractérise par des dunes couvertes d'herbes et de buissons. Lors de leur première visite, les architectes avaient trouvé sur le terrain une bûche creuse et calcinée et en ont utilisé la métaphore dans leur projet. Ils assimilent la base de la maison aux dunes environnantes. La vue sur la maison est dissimulée aux passants par un mur ou un écran, qui ne permet de découvrir la campagne environnante, par-delà la terrasse et la piscine, que de l'entrée. Le niveau supérieur, qui rappelle une bûche, contient la cuisine, les zones de séjour et de repas, un garage et une lingerie. L'autre niveau supérieur regroupe la chambre principale et un bureau. Ces parties principales sont parées de bois dur (gommier tacheté) teint en noir, ce qui renforce l'analogie avec la bûche. L'intérieur de cette maison, destinée à un couple de retraités et à leur famille élargie, a également été conçu par l'agence. Une attention considérable a été portée aux stratégies d'utilisation de l'énergie passive comme l'orientation de la maison et la protection solaire. L'eau d'un puits sert à alimenter la piscine, et la pluie est récupérée pour les usages domestiques.

With its dramatic cantilevered form and one box-like volume set up on stilts, the Cape Schanck House has an immediately recognizable profile.

Mit seinem dramatisch auskragenden Baukörper und einem auf Stelzen schwebenden kubischen Volumen hat das Cape Schanck House ein unverwechselbares Profil.

Le volume en porte-à-faux et la boîte sur pilotis assurent à la maison de Cape Schanck un profil immédiatement identifiable.

The kitchen (above) is designed in
black and white in cut-out forms that
recall the architecture of the house.
Below, plans for the two levels.

Die Küche (oben) ist schwarz-weiß gehalten, wirkt wie ausgeschnitten und
greift die Architektur des Hauses auf.
Unten die Grundrisse zweier Ebenen.

La cuisine (ci-dessus) se compose de
volumes découpés en noir et blanc qui
rappellent l'architecture de la maison.
Ci-dessous, plans des deux niveaux.

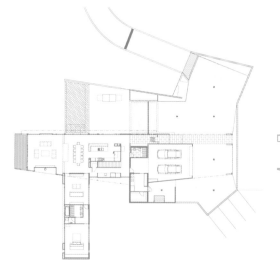

A section of the house shows its overhang on the sloped site. The projecting volumes allow for spectacular views on the neighboring area.

Ein Aufriss des Hauses veranschaulicht den Überhang über das abschüssige Grundstück. Dank der auskragenden Volumina bieten sich spektakuläre Ausblicke.

La coupe de la maison montre un important porte-à-faux au-dessus de la pente du terrain. Les volumes en projection offrent des vues spectaculaires sur la nature avoisinante.

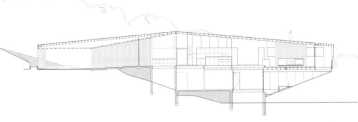

JARMUND/VIGSNÆS

Jarmund/Vigsnæs AS Arkitekter MNAL
Hausmannsgate 6
0186 Oslo
Norway

Tel: +47 22 99 43 43
Fax: +47 22 99 43 53
E-mail: jva@jva.no
Web: www.jva.no

JARMUND/VIGSNÆS often works on projects "related to nature and preferably in strong natural settings with a harsh climate." The principals of the office are Einar Jarmund, Håkon Vigsnæs, and Alessandra Kosberg. Jarmund and Vigsnæs were born in 1962 in Oslo and graduated from the Oslo School of Architecture in 1987 and 1989. Vigsnæs spent one year at the Architectural Association (AA) in London, and Jarmund received a Master's degree from the University of Washington in Seattle. Håkon Vigsnæs worked with Sverre Fehn, while Einar Jarmund taught and worked in Seattle. Both were Visiting Professors at Washington University in St. Louis in 2004 and at the University of Arizona, Tucson, in 2005. Jarmund/Vigsnæs was established in 1995 after teaching and independent practice for both partners. Alessandra Kosberg, born in 1967, graduated from the Oslo School of Architecture in 1995, and started working with Jarmund/Vigsnæs in 1997. In 2004, she became their third partner. The office today employs 18 architects. Their work includes the Red House (Oslo, 2001–02); the Turtagrø Hotel (Jotunheimen, 2002); an apartment for the Crown Prince of Norway (2003); and the Svalbard Science Center (Longyearbyen, Spitsbergen, 2005); the White House (Strand, 2005–06, published here); the Triangle House (Nesodden, 2005–06, also published here); the Norwegian Ministry of Defense (Akershus Fortress, Oslo, 2006); and a high-rise hotel (Fornebu, 2006), all in Norway. In addition, the firm has built 16 one-family houses and vacation homes.

Das Büro **JARMUND/VIGSNÆS** arbeitet oft an Projekten „mit einem Bezug zur Natur und am liebsten in beeindruckender Landschaft mit rauem Klima". Leitende Partner sind Einar Jarmund, Håkon Vigsnæs und Alessandra Kosberg. Jarmund und Vigsnæs wurden beide 1962 in Oslo geboren und beendeten ihr Studium an der Osloer Hochschule für Architektur 1987 bzw. 1989. Vigsnæs verbrachte ein Jahr an der Architectural Association (AA) in London, Jarmund erhielt seinen Mastertitel an der University of Washington in Seattle. Während Håkon Vigsnæs bei Sverre Fehn beschäftigt war, lehrte und arbeitete Jarmund in Seattle. Beide waren 2004 als Gastprofessoren an der Washington University in St. Louis sowie 2005 an der University of Arizona, Tucson, tätig. 1995, nach einer Zeit des Lehrens und freiberuflicher Tätigkeit, gründeten die beiden ihr Büro Jarmund/Vigsnæs. Alessandra Kosberg wurde 1967 geboren, schloss 1995 ihr Studium an der Osloer Hochschule für Architektur ab und ist seit 1997 für Jarmund/Vigsnæs tätig. 2004 wurde sie dritte Partnerin. Gegenwärtig beschäftigt das Büro 18 Architekten. Projekte sind u. a. das Red House (Oslo, 2001–02), das Turtagrø Hotel (Jotunheimen, 2002), ein Apartment für den norwegischen Kronprinzen (2003), das Svalbard Science Center (Longyearbyen, Spitsbergen, 2005), das White House (Strand, 2005–06, hier vorgestellt), das Triangle House (Nesodden, 2005–06, ebenfalls hier vorgestellt), das norwegische Verteidigungsministerium (Festung Akershus, Oslo, 2006) sowie ein Hotelhochhaus (Fornebu, 2006), alle in Norwegen. Darüber hinaus hat das Büro 16 Einfamilienhäuser und Ferienhäuser realisiert.

JARMUND/VIGSNÆS intervient souvent sur des projets « liés à la nature et de préférence dans des conditions climatiques difficiles ». Les dirigeants de l'agence sont Einar Jarmund, Håkon Vigsnæs et Alessandra Kosberg. Jarmund et Vigsnæs, nés en 1962 à Oslo, sont diplômés de l'école d'architecture d'Oslo (1987 et 1989). Vigsnæs a passé une année à l'Architectural Association (AA) de Londres, et Jarmund a reçu son mastère de la Washington University à Seattle. Håkon Vigsnæs a collaboré avec Sverre Fehn, tandis qu'Einar Jarmund enseignait et travaillait à Seattle. Tous deux ont été professeurs invités à la Washington University (St. Louis) en 2004 et à l'université de l'Arizona (Tucson) en 2005. L'agence Jarmund/Vigsnæs a été créée en 1995, après que les deux associés eurent enseigné et travaillé indépendamment. Alessandra Kosberg, née en 1967 et diplômée de l'école d'architecture d'Oslo en 1995, a commencé à travailler pour Jarmund/Vigsnæs en 1997. En 2004, elle est devenue leur troisième associée. L'agence emploie aujourd'hui 18 architectes. Parmi leurs réalisations : la maison Rouge (Oslo, 2001–02) ; l'hôtel Turtagrø (Jotunheimen, 2002) ; un appartement pour le prince héritier de Norvège (2003) et le Centre des sciences Svalbard (Longyearbyen, Spitsbergen, 2005) ; la maison Blanche (Strand, 2005–06, publiée ici) ; la maison Triangle (Nesodden, 2005–06, également publiée ici) ; le ministère norvégien de la Défense (Forteresse d'Akershus, Oslo, 2006) et une tour-hôtel (Fornebu, 2006), tous en Norvège. Par ailleurs, l'agence a construit 16 résidences et maisons de vacances.

WHITE HOUSE

Strand, Norway, 2005–06

Floor area: 205 m². Client: Baard Jessen. Cost: not disclosed.
Team: Einar Jarmund, Håkon Vigsnæs, Alessandra Kosberg, Stian Schjelderup, Roar Lund-Johnsen

Continuing along the lines of the architects' powerful Red House (Oslo, 2001–02), the White House offers a powerful form, though in this case in a rather dense urban setting. The architects explain, "The house twists dynamically between sheltering for privacy and opening up for angles of vistas. The central space of the house stretches between the morning light between the pines towards the east, and the western horizon of the Oslo fjord." Painted wood panels are used for cladding both on the inside of the house and for the exterior. The floors and walls on ground level are made of exposed, cast-in-place concrete, while walls and ceiling on the upper floor are finished in oak.

Stilistisch anknüpfend an das eindrucksvolle Red House des Büros (Oslo, 2001–02), präsentiert sich auch das White House als bemerkenswerte Form, wenn auch in diesem Fall in einem recht dicht besiedelten Umfeld. Die Architekten erklären: „Das Haus ist zwischen dem Streben nach Schutz und Privatsphäre und dem Sichöffnen für Blickachsen dynamisch verkantet. Der zentrale Raum des Hauses erstreckt sich vom Morgenlicht zwischen den Kiefern im Osten und dem Oslofjord am westlichen Horizont." Eine gestrichene Holzvertäfelung zieht sich sowohl durch das Innere des Hauses als auch über den Außenbau. Böden und Wände im Erdgeschoss sind aus Sichtbeton, während Wände und Decken der oberen Etage mit Eichenholz vertäfelt wurden.

Dans la ligne de leur précédente réalisation, la maison Rouge (Oslo, 2001–02), la maison Blanche présente également une forme puissante, bien que cette fois dans un cadre urbain assez dense. Selon ses auteurs : « La maison subit une torsion dynamique entre la protection de l'intimité et l'ouverture vers les vues. L'espace central se dilate entre la lumière matinale qui filtre entre les pins et l'horizon du fjord d'Oslo à l'ouest. » Des panneaux de bois peint habillent à la fois l'intérieur et l'extérieur de la maison. Les sols et les murs du rez-de-chaussée sont en béton coulé sur place et laissés nus, tandis que les murs et le plafond de l'étage supérieur sont parés de chêne.

The White House, like the same architects' Red House before it, has stunning angles and a sharp cut-out forming a terrace with an overhanging roof.

Das White House zeichnet sich, wie schon das Red House vom selben Architektenteam, durch stumpfe Winkel und eine scharf gezeichnete Aussparung aus, die eine Terrasse mit überhängendem Dach bildet.

Comme la maison Rouge du même architecte construite précédemment, la maison Blanche est caractérisée par d'étonnants pans inclinés et un volume découpé qui forme une terrasse sous le toit suspendu.

The house sits nestled into its slightly hilly site, opening to offer broad views on the area and ample light within.

Das Haus schmiegt sich an das leicht hügelige Terrain, bietet großzügige Ausblicke in die Umgebung und ist innen besonders hell.

La maison est nichée dans un terrain légèrement vallonné. Ses grandes ouvertures offrent de vastes perspectives sur le paysage et laissent généreusement pénétrer la lumière naturelle.

The slightly angled plan departs from a pure rectangle as it responds to the topography of the site. Within, shimmering white is the rule, contrasting with wooden floors and sometimes darker furniture.

Der leicht winklige Grundriss löst sich von der einfachen Rechteckform und passt sich an die Topografie des Geländes an. Im Innern dominiert schimmerndes Weiß, ein Kontrast zu den Holzböden und der hier und da dunkleren Möblierung.

La forme pure du rectangle initial du plan se déforme légèrement pour s'adapter à la topographie. À l'intérieur, le blanc qui prend la lumière est de règle, et contraste avec les sols en bois et des meubles de teinte parfois plus sombre.

TRIANGLE HOUSE

Nesodden, Norway, 2005–06

Floor area: 275 m². Clients: Heidi Gaupseth and Geir Kløver. Cost: not disclosed.
Team: Einar Jarmund, Håkon Vigsnæs, Alessandra Kosberg, Stian Schjelderup, Roar Lund-Johnsen

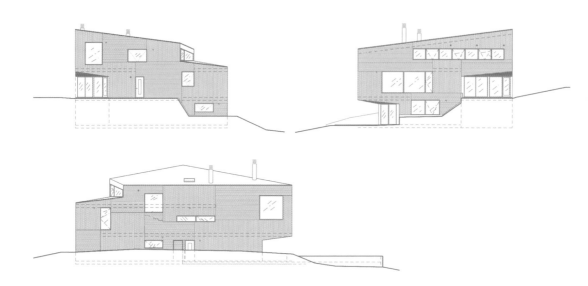

Local zoning restrictions determined both the plan and the height of this house, which offers views toward the sea through a surrounding pine forest. The architects explain their project in the following terms, "While the exterior views are singularly framed by the window openings, closely related to individual spaces, the interior is treated in a more fluent way with overlapping sequences of space and light in section and plan. This duality of focal and flow is the theme of the building." Interior floors are made with cast-in-place concrete partially covered by sisal mats. The interior is clad in OSB (oriented strand boards—an engineered wood product formed by layering strands or flakes of wood in specific orientations), while the bathrooms are clad in brushed aluminum panels. The substantial book collection of the owners gives it a real personality and, as the architects point out, softens the acoustics. "The owners claim that they sleep very well in this house," they conclude.

Die lokalen Bauvorschriften bestimmten Grundriss und Höhe des Hauses, das durch den Kiefernwald der Umgebung hindurch Sicht auf das Meer hat. Die Architekten erklären ihr Vorgehen wie folgt: „Während die verschiedenen Außenansichten des Baus individuell durch die Fensteröffnungen geprägt werden und spezifischen Räumen zugeordnet sind, wurde der Innenraum fließender gestaltet, hier überschneiden sich Raum- und Lichtverläufe im Aufriss ebenso wie im Grundriss. Diese Dualität von Blickpunkt und Fluss ist das zentrale Thema dieses Gebäudes." Die Böden im Innern wurden aus Ortbeton gegossen und hier und da mit Sisalteppichen belegt. Der gesamte Innenraum wurde mit OSB-Platten (oriented strand boards – industriell gefertigte Mehrschichtplatten aus ausgerichteten Grobspänen) vertäfelt, während die Bäder mit gebürsteten Aluminiumplatten verkleidet wurden. Die umfangreiche Bibliothek der Besitzer verleiht dem Haus Persönlichkeit und wirkt den Architekten zufolge außerdem dämpfend auf die Akustik. Zusammenfassend bemerken sie: „Die Bewohner schlafen nach eigener Aussage sehr gut in diesem Haus."

La règlementation locale de zonage a déterminé à la fois le plan et la hauteur de cette maison qui regarde vers la mer à travers une forêt de pins. Les architectes expliquent ainsi leur projet : « Alors que chaque vue sur l'extérieur est cadrée par les fenêtres en rapport avec chaque espace, l'intérieur est traité de façon plus fluide par des séquences superposées d'espace et de lumière, en coupe comme en plan. Cette dualité de focalisation et de flux est le thème principal de cette construction. » Les sols intérieurs sont en béton coulé en place, en partie recouvert de tapis de sisal. L'intérieur est habillé d'OSB (*oriented strand boards*, panneaux en lamelles minces orientées de fabrication industrielle), et les salles de bains sont lambrissées de panneaux d'aluminium. L'importante collection de livres des propriétaires donne aux lieux une réelle personnalité et, comme le font remarquer les architectes, atténue la réverbération sonore. « Les propriétaires affirment qu'ils dorment très bien dans cette maison », concluent-ils.

The Triangle House also responds to its site, stepping down a slope. Its exterior forms surprise in part because of the alternation of horizontal and vertical bands of wood.

Auch das Triangle House passt sich dem Terrain an und folgt stufenförmig dem abschüssigen Hang. Der Außenbau überrascht wegen des Wechsels von horizontaler und vertikaler Holzverkleidung.

La maison Triangle, disposée en escalier le long d'une pente, dialogue avec son site. Sa forme extérieure surprend en partie par la composition alternée des lattes de bois verticales et horizontales sur ses façades.

With its triangular plan, the house nonetheless manages to sit comfortably in the hilly, wooded terrain.

Dank seines dreieckigen Grundrisses fügt sich das Haus ideal in die hügelige, bewaldete Gegend ein.

De plan triangulaire, la maison ne s'inscrit pas moins confortablement dans son terrain vallonné et boisé.

With its sharp angles generated by the triangular plan, the house is dotted with rectangular windows set at unexpected locations or intervals.

Das Haus, dessen spitze Winkel sich aus dem dreieckigen Grundriss ergeben, wird von rechteckigen Fensteröffnungen durchsetzt, deren Anordnung und Abstände überraschen.

Définie par un plan de forme triangulaire à angles vifs, la maison est dotée de fenêtres rectangulaires réparties selon des implantations ou des intervalles inattendus.

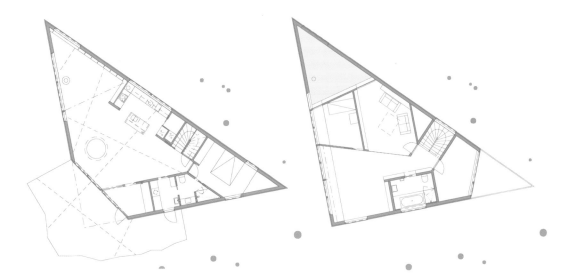

With windows all around its surface, the house is bright inside, and it would appear, too, that the architects have intentionally framed certain views, such as that in the stairway above.

Durch Fensteröffnungen zu allen Seiten ist das Innere des Hauses hell. Fast scheint es, als hätten die Architekten bewusst bestimmte Ausblicke einrahmen wollen, wie oben an der Treppe.

Percée de multiples fenêtres, la maison est très lumineuse à l'intérieur, et les architectes ont sans doute cadré intentionnellement certaines vues, comme celle que l'on perçoit de l'escalier (ci-dessus).

Book shelves hang above the sparsely furnished living area, and wood is the rule for wall and even ceiling surfaces.

Bücherregale schweben über dem sparsam möblierten Wohnraum. Holz dominiert die Wand- und sogar die Deckenflächen.

Des rayonnages de livres dominent le séjour meublé avec parcimonie ; le bois est le matériau privilégié pour les murs et même les plafonds.

CARLOS JIMÉNEZ

Carlos Jiménez Studio
1116 Willard Street
Houston, TX 77006
USA

Tel: +1 713 520 7248
Fax: +1 713 520 1186
E-mail: office@carlosjimenezstudio.com
Web: www.carlosjimenezstudio.com

CARLOS JIMÉNEZ was born in San José, Costa Rica, in 1959 and moved to the United States in 1974. He graduated from the University of Houston School of Architecture in 1981, and established his own office in Houston in 1982. He has served as a Visiting Professor at Rice University, Texas A&M University, SCI-Arc, UCLA, the University of Texas at Arlington, the University of Navarra (Pamplona, Spain), Harvard GSD, Tulane University, UC Berkeley, and at the University of Oregon. He is a tenured Professor at Rice University School of Architecture (2000). He served as a jury member of the Pritzker Architecture Prize (2000–08). His projects include the Jiménez Studio (Houston, Texas, 1983–2007); the Houston Fine Art Press (Houston, Texas, 1985–87); the Central Administration and Junior School, Museum of Fine Arts Houston (Houston, Texas, 1991–94); the Spencer Art Studio Building, Williams College (Williamstown, Massachusetts, 1994); the Peeler Art Center, Depauw University (Greencastle, Indiana, 1997–2002); the Whatley Library (Austin, Texas, 1999–2002); the Crowley House (Marfa, Texas, 2002–04, published here); the Rice University Library Service Center (2002–05) and Data Center (Houston, Texas, 2006–07); the Jiménez House (Houston, Texas, 1994–2007); the Tyler School of Art, Temple University (Philadelphia, Pennsylvania, 2004–08), all in the USA, and, in France, the Evry Housing Tower (Evry, 2006–09).

CARLOS JIMÉNEZ wurde 1959 in San José, Costa Rica, geboren und siedelte 1974 in die USA über. Sein Architekturstudium an der University of Houston schloss er 1981 ab und gründete 1982 sein eigenes Büro in Houston. Jiménez war Gastprofessor an folgenden Institutionen: Rice University, Texas A&M University, SCI-Arc, UCLA, University of Texas in Arlington, Universidad de Navarra (Pamplona, Spanien), Harvard GSD, Tulane University, UC Berkeley sowie University of Oregon. Er ist ordentlicher Professor für Architektur an der Rice University (2000). Darüber hinaus war er Mitglied der Jury für den Pritzker-Preis (2000–08). Zu seinen Projekten zählen sein eigenes Büro (Houston, Texas, 1983–2007), die Houston Fine Art Press (Houston, Texas, 1985–87), die Verwaltungszentrale und Junior School des Museum of Fine Arts Houston (Houston, Texas, 1991–94), das Spencer Art Studio Building am Williams College (Williamstown, Massachusetts, 1994), das Peeler Art Center der Depauw University (Greencastle, Indiana, 1997–2002), die Whatley Library (Austin, Texas, 1999–2002), das Crowley House (Marfa, Texas, 2002–04, hier vorgestellt), das Library Service Center (2002–05), das Data Center (Houston, Texas, 2006–07) an der Rice University, das Jiménez House (Houston, Texas, 1994–2007), die Tyler School of Art der Temple University (Philadelphia, Pennsylvania, 2004–08), alle in den USA, sowie das Apartmenthochhaus Evry (Evry, 2006–09) in Frankreich.

CARLOS JIMÉNEZ, né à San José, Costa Rica, en 1959, s'est installé aux États-Unis en 1974. Diplômé de l'école d'architecture de l'université de Houston en 1981, il a créé son agence dans cette ville en 1982. Il a été professeur invité à la Rice University à Houston, la Texas A&M University, au SCI-Arc, à UCLA, à l'université du Texas à Arlington, à l'université de Navarre (Pamplona, Espagne), à Harvard GSD, à l'université Tulane, UC Berkeley, et à l'université de l'Oregon. Il a été professeur titulaire à l'école d'architecture de la Rice University (2000) et membre du jury du Pritzker Prize (2000–08). Parmi ses projets : le studio Jiménez (Houston, Texas, 1983–2007) ; la Houston Fine Art Press (Houston, Texas, 1985–87) ; le bâtiment de l'administration centrale et l'école du Museum of Fine Arts Houston (Houston, Texas, 1991–94) ; le bâtiment du Spencer Art Studio, Williams College (Williamstown, Massachusetts, 1994) ; le Peeler Art Center, DePauw University (Greencastle, Indiana, 1997–2002) ; la bibliothèque Whatley (Austin, Texas, 1999–2002) ; la maison Crowley (Marfa, Texas, 2002–04, publiée ici) ; le Rice University Library Service Center (2002–05) et le Data Center (Houston, Texas, 2006–07) ; la maison Jiménez (Houston, Texas, 1994–2007) ; l'école d'art Tyler, Temple University (Philadelphie, Pennsylvanie, 2004–08), toutes aux États-Unis, et une tour de logements à Evry, en France (Évry, 2006–09).

CROWLEY HOUSE

Marfa, Texas, USA, 2002–04

*Floor area: 790 m². Clients: Lynn and Tim Crowley. Cost: not disclosed.
Team: Carlos Jiménez (Principal), Brian Burke (Associate)*

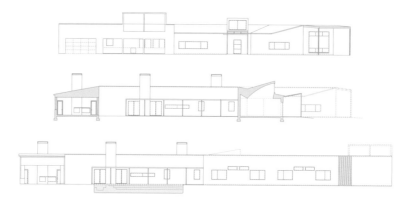

Set on an ample brush-land site, the house adopts something of the austerity of its environment. Its simple clean lines are by no means ostentatious, but a degree of luxury is also apparent.

Das Haus liegt auf einem großen Grundstück im Busch und scheint die Strenge seiner Umgebung teilweise zu übernehmen. Die schlichten klaren Linien sind keinesfalls ostentativ, doch ein gewisser Luxus ist unverkennbar.

Érigée sur un vaste terrain quasi désertique, la maison a en partie adopté l'austérité de son environnement. Ses lignes simples et nettes ne sont pas ostentatoires, mais expriment un certain niveau de luxe.

Located in Marfa, Texas, where the artist Donald Judd established himself, this house is set 10 kilometers from the town center. The sparsely vegetated site measures no less than 809 hectares. As Carlos Jiménez writes, "The sheer exposure and vulnerability of the site inspired an architecture of boundaries and limits, while allowing unobstructed, sweeping views of the surroundings." The one-story structure is laid out in an elongated pattern (one room wide) and has a large area of courtyards and gardens. The main building materials are textured concrete block, stucco, poured-in-place concrete, galvanized steel, and ipe wood decks, all selected to withstand harsh local weather conditions. Carlos Jiménez concludes, "A mixture of native plants and trees complement the house's materiality to blend with the prevailing textures and colors of the high desert. Partially camouflaged amid its setting, the Crowley House asserts its presence without overwhelming the landscape. The house's interior life is greatly enriched by the countless variations of light that charge its ever-changing horizon."

Das in Marfa, Texas, der Wahlheimat von Donald Judd, gelegene Haus befindet sich 10 km außerhalb des Stadtzentrums. Das nur spärlich begrünte Grundstück misst nicht weniger als 809 ha. Carlos Jiménez schreibt: „Die ausgeprägte Exponiertheit und Verletztlichkeit des Grundstücks regten mich zu einer Architektur der Grenzen und Beschränkungen an, die dennoch ungehinderte Panoramablicke in die Umgebung erlaubt." Der eingeschossige Bau ist als lang gestrecktes (nur ein Zimmer breites) Ensemble angelegt und verfügt über großflächige Höfe und Gärten. Gearbeitet wurde in erster Linie mit strukturiertem Betonstein, Gipsputz, Ortbeton, verzinktem Stahl und Terrassen aus Ipéholz – Materialien, die den extremen Witterungsbedingungen standhalten. Carlos Jiménez fasst zusammen: „Eine Mischung aus einheimischen Pflanzen und Bäumen bildet das Pendant zur Materialität des Hauses und lässt es mit den dominierenden Texturen und Farben der Wüste verschmelzen. Das zum Teil in seiner Umgebung verschwindende Crowley House behauptet sich, ohne die Landschaft zu dominieren. Das Innenleben des Hauses profitiert enorm von den zahllosen Lichtvariationen, die den sich unablässig wandelnden Horizont beleben."

Cette maison est située à 10 kilomètres du centre-ville de Marfa, au Texas, où s'était installé l'artiste Donald Judd. Son vaste terrain à la maigre végétation mesure 809 hectares. Comme l'écrit Carlos Jiménez : « L'exposition directe et la vulnérabilité du site ont inspiré une architecture de frontières et de limites, tout en faisant profiter de perspectives sans obstacle qui balayent l'environnement. » La construction d'un seul niveau suit un plan allongé (une pièce de large) et bénéficie de vastes cours et jardins. Les matériaux du bâtiment principal sont les parpaings de béton texturé, le stuc et le béton coulé en place, l'acier galvanisé et l'ipé pour les terrasses, tous choisis pour leur résistance aux conditions climatiques locales difficiles. « Une composition de plantes et d'arbres locaux complète le choix des matériaux de cette demeure pour qu'elle fusionne avec les textures et les couleurs dominantes du désert. Partiellement camouflée dans son cadre, la maison Crowley affirme sa présence sans s'imposer dans le paysage. L'atmosphère intérieure de la maison est fortement enrichie par les variations infinies de la lumière qui animent son horizon en perpétuel changement. »

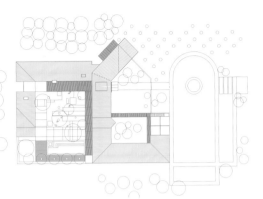

The basic lines of the house are rectilinear, though angles animate the form and covered terraces allow for a more direct contact with the essentially enclosed courtyards.

Die Grundform des Hauses ist rechtwinklig, doch schräge Linien beleben die Struktur. Überdachte Terrassen erlauben direkteren Zugang zu den geschlossenen Innenhöfen.

Si le plan est rectiligne, les angles ont reçu un traitement plus animé, et les terrasses couvertes créent un contraste plus direct, avec des cours à peu près fermées.

JOUIN MANKU

Jouin Manku
8, Passage de la Bonne Graine
75011 Paris
France

Tel: +33 1 55 28 89 20
Fax: +33 1 58 30 60 70
E-mail: agence@jouinmanku.com
Web: www.jouinmanku.com

Born in Nantes, France, in 1967, **PATRICK JOUIN** studied at the École nationale supérieure de création industrielle (ENSCI) in Paris and received his diploma in 1992. He worked in 1992 as a designer at the Compagnie des Wagons-Lits, and for the two following years at Tim Thom, Thomson Multimedia, under Philippe Starck who was then Artistic Director of the brand. From 1995 to 1999, Patrick Jouin was a designer in Philippe Starck's Paris studio. He has designed numerous objects and pieces of furniture, while his architectural work includes: the Alain Ducasse au Plaza Athénée Restaurant (Paris, 2000); the 59 Poincaré Restaurant (Paris, 2000); a Plastic Products Factory (Nantes, 2001); the Plaza Athénée Bar (Paris, 2001); the Spoon Byblos Restaurant (Saint Tropez, 2002); the Chlösterli Restaurants & Club, Spoon des Neiges Restaurant (Gstaad, Switzerland, 2004); Terrasse Montaigne, Plaza Athénée (Paris, 2005); and the Gilt Restaurant and Bar (New York, New York, 2005); all in France unless stated otherwise. **SANJIT MANKU** was born in 1971 in Nairobi, Kenya. He received his B.Arch degree from Carleton University (Ottawa, Canada,1995) and was a designer in the office of Yabu Pushelberg (Toronto,1996–2001). Sanjit Manku joined Patrick Jouin in 2001 and became a partner in 2006. During this period he has worked on interior and architecture projects including the Mix restaurants in New York (2003) and Las Vegas (2004) and private houses in London and Kuala Lumpur (Malaysia, 2004–08, published here), as well as hotels in England and France.

PATRICK JOUIN, 1967 in Nantes, Frankreich, geboren, studierte an der École nationale supérieure de création industrielle (ENSCI) in Paris und erhielt sein Diplom 1992. Im selben Jahr arbeitete er als Designer für die Compagnie des Wagons-Lits, in den folgenden zwei Jahren für Tim Thom, Thomson Multimedia, unter der Leitung von Philippe Starck, der damals Artdirektor der Marke war. Zwischen 1995 und 1999 war Patrick Jouin als Designer in Philippe Starcks Pariser Büro tätig. Er entwarf zahlreiche Objekte und Möbel. Zu seinen architektonischen Arbeiten zählen das Restaurant Alain Ducasse au Plaza Athénée (Paris, 2000), das Restaurant 59 Poincaré (Paris, 2000), eine Kunststofffabrik (Nantes, 2001), die Bar Plaza Athénée (Paris, 2001), das Restaurant Spoon Byblos (Saint-Tropez, 2002), die Restaurants und der Club Chlösterli sowie das Restaurant Spoon des Neiges (Gstaad, Schweiz, 2004), die Terrasse Montaigne, Plaza Athénée (Paris, 2005) sowie Restaurant & Bar Gilt (New York, USA, 2005), alle in Frankreich, sofern nicht anders vermerkt. **SANJIT MANKU** wurde 1971 in Nairobi geboren. Er machte seinen B.Arch an der Carleton University (Ottawa, Canada, 1995) und arbeitete als Designer bei Yabu Pushelberg (Toronto, 1996–2001). 2001 kam er zu Patrick Jouin und wurde 2006 sein Partner. In dieser Zeit arbeitete er an Interieur- und Architekturprojekten wie den Restaurants Mix in New York (2003) und Las Vegas (2004) sowie Häusern in London und Kuala Lumpur (Malaysia, 2004–08, hier vorgestellt) und Hotels in England und Frankreich.

Né à Nantes en 1967, **PATRICK JOUIN** a étudié à l'École nationale supérieure de création industrielle (ENSCI) à Paris, dont il est sorti diplômé en 1992. Il a ensuite travaillé pour la Compagnie des Wagons-Lits, puis les deux années suivantes pour Tim Thom, département de design de Thomson Multimédia, animé par Philippe Starck, alors directeur artistique de la marque. De 1995 à 1999, il a été designer dans le studio parisien de Starck. Il a conçu de nombreux objets et des éléments de mobilier. Ses interventions architecturales comprennent : le restaurant Alain Ducasse du Plaza Athénée (Paris, 2000) ; le restaurant 59 Poincaré (Paris, 2000) ; une usine de produits en plastique (Nantes, 2001) ; le bar du Plaza Athénée (Paris, 2001) ; le restaurant Spoon Byblos (Saint-Tropez, 2002) ; le restaurant et club Chlösterli et le restaurant Spoon des Neiges (Gstaad, Suisse, 2004) ; la Terrasse Montaigne, Plaza Athénée (Paris, 2005) et le Gilt Restaurant and Bar (New York, 2005). **SANJIT MANKU** est né en 1971 à Nairobi, Kenya. Il a reçu son B.Arch à la Carleton University (Ottawa, Canada, 1995) et a été designer dans l'agence de Yabu Pushelberg (Toronto, 1996–2001). Sanjit Manku a rejoint Patrick Jouin en 2001 et est devenu son associé en 2006. Pendant ce temps, il a travaillé sur des projets de construction et d'architecture d'intérieur, tels les restaurants Mix à New York (2003) et Las Vegas (2004), ainsi que sur des maisons à Londres et Kuala Lumpur, Malaisie (2004–08, publiée ici) et des hôtels en Angleterre et en France.

HOUSE

Kuala Lumpur, Malaysia, 2004–08

Floor area: 3000 m². Client: not disclosed. Cost: not disclosed. Team: Yann Brossier (Architect), Richard Perron (Designer), Sophie Agata Ambroise (Garden design), Hervé Descotte/L'Observatoire (Lighting). Architect of Record: Sp. Ytl

As Sanjit Manku explains: "This private residence for a prominent family in Malaysia is one that explores complex relations between new and old cultures. The program given to us was one that could have been written centuries ago: to design a stately home for three current generations of an important family. The home is to be used as a residence but also as a symbol of the family's power in culture, politics, business, civil importance, and, perhaps most importantly, an icon to the family's legacy within a culture." Acting in this instance as an architect, together with his partner Sanjit Manku, and designer, since he is responsible for many aspects of the house interiors, Jouin explains that until a recent date, residences of this nature might have been more likely to be designed in the form of "*faux* Palladian villas next to French chateaux and Spanish villas." His radically modern design thus breaks the mold and marks his emergence as an architect. The house includes nine bedrooms, two suites, two family rooms, a family kitchen and dining room, library, game room, formal dining room, reception room, ballroom, and chapel, as well as two guest suites. The structure is only 5% smaller in surface area than the site, which required the architect to engage in very careful planning, dividing the house into three zones—the family house, public space in the base, and guest area in a sculptural ring-shaped form at ground level. Manku concludes, "For this project we were searching for a spatial and formal language as dramatic as the landscape itself—to create a home that is not a village house, nor a 'traditional tropical house,' yet at the same time was truly based on and almost at times mimicked the particular spatial character of the natural environment. We wished to create a project that rests with ease among the dense tropical flora."

Sanjit Manku führt aus: „Dieser private Wohnsitz für eine prominente Familie in Malaysia geht dem komplexen Verhältnis von neuen zu alten Kulturen auf den Grund. Das gewünschte Programm hätte ebenso gut vor Jahrhunderten formuliert werden können: ein herrschaftliches Anwesen für drei Generationen einer bedeutenden Familie. Das Anwesen wird als Wohnsitz dienen, jedoch ebenso als Symbol für den Einfluss der Familie in Kultur, Politik, Wirtschaft und bürgerschaftlichem Engagement und – vielleicht mehr als alles andere – als Ikone des Vermächtnisses der Familie in einer Kultur." Jouin, der in diesem Fall mit seinem Partner Sanjit Manku sowohl als Architekt als auch als Designer für viele Aspekte der Innengestaltung des Hauses verantwortlich zeichnet, weist darauf hin, dass man Anwesen dieser Art noch bis vor Kurzem eher als „pseudopalladianische Villen, französische Châteaux oder spanische Villen" entworfen hätte. Sein radikal modernes Design bricht mit diesem Muster und ist zugleich sein erster Auftritt als Architekt. Das Haus hat neun Schlafzimmer, zwei Suiten, zwei Wohnzimmer sowie eine Küche und ein Esszimmer für die Familie, eine Bibliothek, ein Spielzimmer, ein offizielles Speisezimmer, einen Empfangsraum, einen Ballsaal, eine Kapelle sowie zwei Gästesuiten. Die Gebäudefläche ist nur 5 % kleiner als das Baugrundstück, was den Architekten zwang, höchst sorgfältig zu planen. Er gliederte das Haus in drei Zonen – den Wohnbereich für die Familie, die öffentlichen Räume in der unteren Ebene und den Bereich für die Gäste als skulpturales, ringförmiges Ensemble zu ebener Erde. Manku fasst zusammen: „Für dieses Projekt haben wir nach einer Raum- und Formensprache gesucht, die ebenso dramatisch ist wie die Landschaft selbst – um ein Heim zu schaffen, das weder ein Landhaus noch ein ‚traditionelles Haus in den Tropen' ist und dennoch zutiefst in der räumlichen Charakteristik seines landschaftlichen Umfelds verwurzelt ist, ja es mitunter sogar imitiert. Wir wollten ein Projekt realisieren, das mühelos inmitten der dichten tropischen Flora ruht."

Comme l'explique Sanjit Manku : « Cette résidence privée construite pour une riche famille malaisienne explore, entre autres, les relations complexes entre des cultures anciennes et nouvelles. Le programme aurait pu être rédigé il y a des siècles : concevoir une demeure de prestige pour trois générations d'une importante famille. La maison est une résidence, mais aussi un symbole de la puissance du rôle de cette famille dans la vie culturelle, politique et économique et peut-être, plus important encore, son rôle d'icône du patrimoine au sein de cette culture. » Intervenant ici comme architecte et designer avec son associé, Sanjit Manku, puisqu'il est également responsable de beaucoup d'aspects des aménagements intérieurs, Jouin précise que, jusqu'à une certaine date, une résidence de cette nature aurait probablement pris la forme d'une « fausse villa palladienne, aux côtés de châteaux français et de villas espagnoles ». Sa conception radicalement moderne en a ainsi brisé le moule et marque son apparition sur la scène de l'architecture. La maison comprend neuf chambres, deux suites, deux séjours, une cuisine et salle à manger, une bibliothèque, une salle de jeux, une salle à manger de réception, un salon de réception, une salle de bal et une chapelle, ainsi que deux suites pour invités. La construction occupe 95% de la surface du terrain, et l'architecte a dû se livrer à un délicat exercice de programmation pour diviser la maison en trois zones – famille, réception, invités – à l'intérieur de l'élément en forme d'anneau sculptural qui couvre le rez-de-chaussée. « Pour ce projet, nous avons recherché un langage spatial et formel aussi spectaculaire que le paysage environnant afin de créer une demeure qui ne soit pas une maison de village, ni une »maison tropicale traditionnelle« , mais qui repose aussi authentiquement et parfois même imite le caractère particulier de cet environnement naturel. Nous avons souhaité créer un projet en harmonie avec la dense flore tropicale. »

The house sits on a hill in the former diplomatic community, occupying 95 % of its site. The drawing, below, shows the overall complexity of the design.

Das Haus liegt auf einem Hügel im ehemaligen Diplomatenviertel und beansprucht 95% der Grundstücksfläche. Die Zeichnung unten illustriert die Komplexität des Entwurfs.

La maison qui se dresse sur une colline dans l'ancien quartier des ambassades occupe 95% de son terrain. Le dessin ci-dessous illustre la complexité d'ensemble du projet.

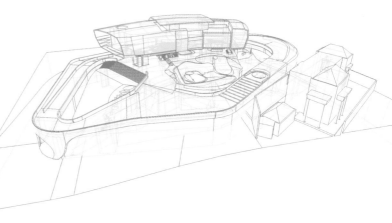

With its views toward the symbolic Petronas Towers in downtown Kuala Lumpur, the house in a sense dominates the city, sitting above its swimming pool, with an open living area located at this main level.

Mit seiner Aussicht auf die Petronas Towers im Zentrum von Kuala Lumpur thront das Haus gewissermaßen über der Stadt. Ihm zu Füßen, auf der Hauptebene des Baus, liegen der Pool und ein offener Wohnbereich.

La maison, d'où l'on aperçoit au loin les tours Petronas du centre de Kuala Lumpur, domine la ville. À son pied, une vaste piscine. Le séjour ouvert se trouve au rez-de-chaussée.

The unusual forms of the house are rendered even more transparent at night. Below, a large ring above the entrance area houses guest rooms, and below left, the 12-car parking garage.

Die ungewöhnliche Form des Hauses wird besonders bei Nacht deutlich. Im großen Ring über der Zufahrt, unten, sind Gästezimmer untergebracht. Unten links die Garage für zwölf Fahrzeuge.

De forme originale, la maison semble encore plus transparente, vue de nuit. Ci-dessous, l'aile incurvée, qui surmonte l'entrée, est réservée aux chambres d'invités. Ci-dessous, à gauche, le garage pour 12 voitures.

Above, the main gate and entrance area of the house. Below, the kitchen and family dining area open to the view of the city at night.

Oben das Haupttor und die Zufahrt zum Haus. Unten Küche und Familienessbereich mit Blick auf die nächtliche Stadt.

Ci-dessus, le portail principal et l'entrée de la maison. Ci-dessous, vue nocturne sur la ville depuis la cuisine et la salle à manger familiale.

The spiral staircase leading to the upper floor bedrooms is one of the main features of the main level. Broad glazing at this level allows ample views and permits direct access to the swimming pool.

Die Wendeltreppe zu den Schlaf-zimmern der oberen Etagen ist zentraler Blickfang der Hauptebene, wo Glasfronten den Panoramablick freigeben und direkten Zugang zum Pool erlauben.

L'escalier en spirale conduisant aux chambres est l'un des éléments les plus spectaculaires du niveau du séjour. La façade entièrement vitrée s'ouvre totalement sur le panorama et permet un accès direct à la piscine.

Right, a specially designed bar located near the main dining room is made of DuPont Corian. The light fixture, also custom designed by Jouin Manku is made of porcelain. A slatted screen protects interior areas from the strong local sun.

Rechts eine speziell entworfene Bar aus DuPont Corian neben dem Hauptspeisezimmer. Der Lüster, ebenfalls ein Spezialentwurf von Jouin Manku, wurde aus Porzellan gefertigt. Jalousien schützen den Innenraum vor der intensiven Sonneneinstrahlung.

À droite, un bar DuPont Corian près de la salle à manger principale. Le lustre en porcelaine a également été dessiné par Jouin Manku. Un écran en lattis protège l'intérieur du soleil tropical.

Above, the upper level library. Right, a solid Carrara marble counter in the kitchen seen from the main level and from above.

Oben die Bibliothek auf der oberen Etage. Rechts ein massiver Tresen aus Carraramarmor in der Küche, von oben und der Hauptebene aus gesehen.

Ci-dessus, la bibliothèque à l'étage. À droite, le comptoir en marbre de Carrare massif de la cuisine, vu de l'étage et de la salle à manger familiale.

Light fixtures were designed by Jouin
Manku, as well as furniture. Below,
left, the family chapel.

Auch die Leuchten sind Entwürfe von
Jouin Manku, ebenso wie die Möbel.
Unten links die Familienkapelle.

Les luminaires et le mobilier ont été
conçus par Jouin Manku. Ci-dessous
à gauche, la chapelle de la famille.

An outdoor garden at the back of the house created by Lugano-based Sophie Agata Ambroise. Stairs are one of the features that have been given considerable attention by Jouin Manku.

Ein Garten hinter dem Haus wurde von Sophie Agata Ambroise aus Lugano gestaltet. Die Treppen sind eines der Elemente, denen Jouin Manku besondere Aufmerksamkeit widmeten.

Le jardin aménagé à l'arrière de la maison a été dessiné par Sophie Agata Ambroise de Lugano. Les escaliers sont des éléments particulièrement soignés par Jouin Manku.

KAMAYACHI + HARIGAI

Seiji Kamayachi Architects
#4A, Nakae-Building, 5–3–14 Hiroo,
Shibuya-ku, Tokyo 150–0012
Japan

Tel + Fax: +81 35 422 9458
E-mail: info@kamayachiseiji.com

Masafumi Harigai
Kengo Kuma & Associates
2–24–8 BY-CUBE 2–4F Minamiaoyama
Minato-ku, Tokyo 107–0062
Japan

Tel: +81 3 3401 7721
Fax: +81 3 3401 7778
E-mail: harigai@kkaa.co.jp

SEIJI KAMAYACHI was born in 1979 in Kanagawa Prefecture, Japan. In 2006, he created his office KIKA with Nagisa Kidosaki, obtaining his M.Arch degree from the Graduate School of Engineering, Department of Architecture at Yokohama National University in 2007. **MASAFUMI HARIGAI** was born in Tochigi Prefecture, Japan, in 1980. He also obtained his M.Arch degree from the same school as Kamayachi in 2007. He began work in the office of Kengo Kuma in 2007, having created a temporary partnership with Kamayachi specifically for the design of the G House (Yokohama, Japan, 2005–07, published here). The two say they may work together again in the future, but for the moment, they have no plans to do so.

SEIJI KAMAYACHI wurde 1979 in der Präfektur Kanagawa, Japan, geboren. 2006 gründete er mit Nagisa Kidosaki sein Büro KIKA. Seinen Masterabschluss am Institut für Bauingenieurwesen und Architektur der Nationaluniversität Yokohama absolvierte er 2007. **MASAFUMI HARIGAI** wurde 1980 in der Präfektur Tochigi, Japan, geboren. Seinen M.Arch. absolvierte er 2007 an derselben Hochschule wie Kamayachi. Seit 2007 arbeitet er für Kengo Kuma, nachdem er für die Gestaltung des G House (Yokohama, Japan, 2005–07, hier vorgestellt) eine zeitweilige Partnerschaft mit Kamayachi begründet hatte. Nach eigener Aussage werden die beiden in Zukunft möglicherweise erneut zusammenarbeiten, planen dies derzeit jedoch nicht konkret.

SEIJI KAMAYACHI, né en 1979 dans la préfecture de Kanagawa au Japon, a fondé en 2006 son agence KIKA avec Nagisa Kidosaki et obtenu son diplôme de M.Arch de l'École supérieure d'ingénierie, département d'architecture de l'université nationale de Yokohama en 2007. **MASAFUMI HARIGAI**, né dans la préfecture de Tochigi au Japon, en 1980, est M.Arch de la même école que Kamayachi (2007). Il a commencé à travailler pour l'agence de Kengo Kuma en 2007 et a créé un partenariat temporaire avec Kamayachi pour le projet de la G House (Yokohama, Japon, 2005–07, publiée ici). Les deux architectes pensent retravailler ensemble dans le futur, mais n'ont pas de projet plus précis pour le moment.

G HOUSE

Yokohama, Japan, 2005–07

*Site area: 309 m². Floor area: 184 m². Client: Noriyoshi Sumiya.
Cost: €307 000. Collaborators: Nagisa Kidosaki (Garden design), Masato Araya (Structure design)*

The architects explain this house in terms of a radical critique of suburban housing developments, "In England, in the USA, but also in Japan, the suburban new town landscapes are planned according to a simple rule: the repetition of a flat site, a private garden, and a pitched roof. The project is situated in a 1970s suburban new town. Each house is built on a flat artificial pedestal, and the repetition of this typology creates a landscape, like shortcakes in a display window. This project takes away one of these shortcakes to propose a building with a new system of values." The first thing the architects did was to remove the pedestal, artificially raised to the level of the street. The concrete wall of the resulting embankment defines the living area. They then created a volume with a pitched roof above the real living space, now apparently below grade, that resembles surrounding residences but contains nothing but a void used as a sort of open family space. A sloping garden relates the street level to that of the "basement" residence. The architects conclude that by using the very rules of the town, they created "a building which has completely different values, and spaces where people can have different kinds of life styles. The town can peacefully make its renewal. The creation of one new residence becomes an opportunity to create a new landscape in the suburbs."

Die Architekten beschreiben das Haus als radikale Kritik an der Planung typischer Vorstadtsiedlungen: „In England, in den USA, aber auch in Japan werden neue Siedlungen in den Vorstädten nach einem schlichten Muster geplant: Wiederholung von flachem Baugrundstück, privatem Garten und Satteldach. Das Projekt liegt in einer in den 1970er-Jahren entstandenen Satellitenstadt. Alle Häuser wurden auf einem flachen, künstlichen Sockel errichtet, und die Wiederholung dieser Typologie schafft eine Landschaft wie Teekuchen in einer Ladenauslage. Dieses Projekt entfernt einen dieser Teekuchen und schlägt stattdessen ein Gebäude vor, das auf einem neuen Wertesystem beruht." Als Erstes ließen die Architekten den Sockel entfernen, den man künstlich auf Straßenniveau angehoben hatte. Die so entstandene Stützmauer aus Beton definiert den Wohnbereich. Schließlich errichtete das Team einen Baukörper mit Satteldach über dem tatsächlichen Wohnraum, der scheinbar im Souterrain zu liegen scheint. Dieser Baukörper ähnelt den Häusern der Nachbarschaft, enthält jedoch nichts weiter als einen Leerraum, der als offener Raum für die Familie dient. Ein schräg abfallender Garten stellt die Verbindung zwischen dem Straßenniveau und dem „Keller"-Haus her. Zusammenfassend bemerken die Architekten, dass sie durch Aufgreifen der bestehenden Regeln des Vororts „ein Gebäude geschaffen haben, das vollkommen andere Werte hat und Räume bietet, in denen Menschen alternative Lebensstile finden können. Die Stadt kann sich friedlich erneuern. Die Schaffung eines neuen Hauses bietet die Gelegenheit, in den Vororten eine neue Landschaft entstehen zu lassen."

Les deux architectes présentent cette maison comme une critique radicale des lotissements de banlieue. « En Angleterre, aux États-Unis, mais aussi au Japon, les paysages des nouvelles villes de banlieue sont établis selon une règle simple : la répétition de trois éléments, terrain plat, jardin privé et toit à pignon. Le projet se situe dans une ville nouvelle édifiée dans les années 1970. Chaque maison est construite sur un socle artificiel plat, et c'est la répétition de cette typologie qui crée le paysage, comme des biscuits alignés dans une vitrine. Ce projet s'empare de l'un de ces »biscuits« pour proposer sa construction dans le cadre d'un nouveau système de valeurs. » La première chose a été de supprimer le socle artificiellement relevé au niveau de la rue. Le mur de béton qui résulte de cet enfoncement définit l'aire de séjour. Ils ont ensuite dessiné un volume surmonté d'une toiture à deux pentes au-dessus du séjour qui ressemble à celle des autres maisons, mais ne contient rien d'autre qu'un vide affecté à l'espace de vie familial. Un jardin en pente relie le niveau de la rue à celui de la résidence en « sous-sol ». Les architectes concluent qu'en utilisant les règles mêmes de la ville ils ont créé un « bâtiment qui répond à des valeurs entièrement différentes et des espaces dans lesquels les occupants peuvent mener des styles de vie entièrement autres. La ville peut ainsi tranquillement entreprendre son renouveau. La création d'une nouvelle maison devient une opportunité de créer un nouveau paysage de banlieue. »

The house appears extremely simple or even "ordinary" from a certain distance, but its apparent austerity is far from banal.

Aus der Distanz wirkt das Haus extrem schlicht, ja fast „gewöhnlich", dabei ist die scheinbare Strenge alles andere als banal.

La maison paraît extrêmement simple, ou même « ordinaire », vue d'une certaine distance, mais son austérité apparente est loin d'être banale.

Elevations of the house show its
shed-like form, while the photo above
reveals the luminous base set in the
excavated bottom of the site.

Aufrisse des Hauses machen die
scheunenartige Form anschaulich,
doch das Foto oben enthüllt das
leuchtende Fundament im ausgeho-
benen Grundstück.

Les élévations montrent une forme
classique de maison à pignon. La
photo ci-dessous met en évidence
la base éclairée, creusée dans le sol.

A site plan shows that the form of the
house is even less differentiated than
that of the neighboring structures
with more complex roofs.

Ein Lageplan verrät, dass die Form
des Hauses noch weniger unterglie-
dert ist, als die Nachbarbauten mit
ihren komplexeren Dächern.

Le plan général de l'implantation
montre que la forme de la maison est
encore plus simple que celle de ses
voisines aux toitures plus complexes.

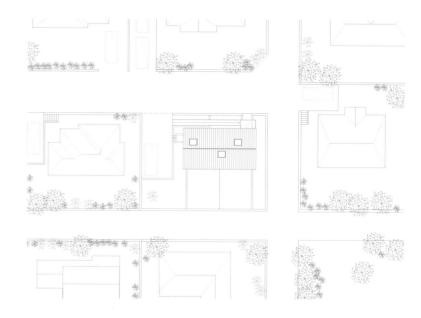

KOTARO IDE

ARTechnic architects
#3, 3-34-1, Kamimeguro
Meguro
153-0051 Tokyo
Japan

Tel: + 81 3 5768 8718
Fax: + 81 3 5768 8738
E-mail: info@artechnic.jp
Web: www.artechnic.jp

KOTARO IDE was born in Tokyo in 1965. He graduated from the Department of Architecture of the College of Art and Design at Musashino Art University (Tokyo, 1989). He worked in the office of Ken Yokogawa Architects & Associates Inc. from 1989 to 1994 and established his own office, ARTechnic architects in 1994. His main works include the SMD House (Zushi, Kanagawa, 1995); the Oak Terrace Apartment Building (Oota, Tokyo, 1997); the YMM House (Suginami, Tokyo, 1999); the MSO House (Shibuya, Tokyo, 2000); the Cherry Terrace Library (Shibuya, Tokyo, 2002); the Manazuru Studio (Manazuru, Kanagawa, 2003); the YMG House (Yokohama, Kanagawa, 2003); the NKM House (Shibuya, Tokyo, 2005) and SHELL (Karuizawa, Nagano, 2008, published here), all in Japan.

KOTARO IDE wurde 1965 in Tokio geboren. Sein Architekturstudium schloss er 1989 am College of Art and Design an der Universität der Künste in Musashino (Tokio) ab. Zwischen 1989 und 1994 arbeitete er im Büro von Ken Yokogawa Architects & Associates Inc., bevor er 1994 sein eigenes Büro, ARTechnic architects, gründete. Zu seinen wichtigsten Projekten zählen das SMD House (Zushi, Kanagawa, 1995), das Apartmenthaus Oak Terrace (Oota, Tokio, 1997), das YMM House (Suginami, Tokio, 1999), das MSO House (Shibuya, Tokio, 2000), die Bibliothek der Cherry Terrace (Shibuya, Tokio, 2002), das Studio Manazuru (Manazuru, Kanagawa, 2003), das YMG House (Yokohama, Kanagawa, 2003), das NKM House (Shibuya, Tokio, 2005) sowie SHELL (Karuizawa, Nagano, 2008, hier vorgestellt), alle in Japan.

KOTARO IDE, né à Tokyo en 1965, est diplômé du département d'architecture du collège d'art et de design de l'université d'art Muashino (Tokyo, 1989). Il a travaillé dans l'agence Ken Yokogawa Architects & Associates Inc. de 1989 à 1994 et a créé sa propre structure, ARTechnic architects en 1994. Parmi ses principales réalisations : la maison SMD (Zushi, Kanagawa, 1995) ; l'immeuble d'appartements Oak Terrace (Oota, Tokyo, 1997) ; la maison YMM (Suginami, Tokyo, 1999) ; la maison MSO (Shibuya, Tokyo, 2000) ; la bibliothèque Cherry Terrace (Shibuya, Tokyo, 2002) ; le studio Manazuru (Manazuru, Kanagawa, 2003) ; la maison YMG (Yokohama, Kanagawa, 2003) ; la maison NKM (Shibuya, Tokyo, 2005) et SHELL (Karuizawa, Nagano, 2008, publiée ici), toutes au Japon.

SHELL

Karuizawa, Kitasaku, Nagano, Japan, 2006–08

Site area: 1711 m². Floor area: 353 m².
Client: Mr. Kunimoto. Cost: not disclosed

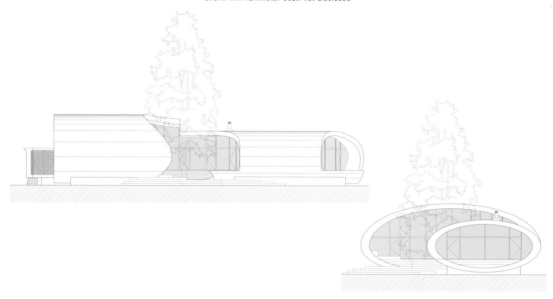

The surprising forms of the shell house are readily understandable through the elevations above and the images to the right.

Die überraschenden Formen des Muschel-Hauses werden anhand der Aufrisse oben und der Bilder rechts nachvollziehbar.

Les formes étonnantes de la maison coquille se comprennent plus aisément sous l'éclairage des élévations ci-dessus et des photos de droite.

Kotaro Ide's description of this house is surprising: "There is a large shell-shaped structure dropped in the woods… We know it is not part of the surrounding nature like a rock or cave. It is not so-called ruins either. It looks like part of a structure built somewhere else for a completely different purpose. This image reminds us of science-fiction films. 'A resident dwells in a space ship that had fallen to the earth. Soon, trees grow around the structure, and, over many years, the ship merges completely into the scenery.'" SHELL is built around an existing fir tree, and is intended as a weekend cottage for a Tokyo resident (one hour and ten minutes away on the Shinkansen rapid train). Urethane foam covered with a synthetic resin is used for interior surfaces. Careful attention was paid to the energy consumption of the structure with a custom-designed warm-air system installed in the floors. A sophisticated biometric system locks and secures the residence.

Kotaro Ides eigene Beschreibung des Hauses ist überraschend: „Es scheint, als sei ein riesiges kapselförmiges Etwas mitten in den Wald gestürzt … Es ist ganz offensichtlich kein Teil der natürlichen Umgebung, ein Felsen etwa oder eine Höhle. Es ist auch keine sogenannte Ruine. Es wirkt, als sei es Teil einer anderen Konstruktion, die irgendwo anders für völlig andere Zwecke gebaut wurde. Das Bild lässt an Science-Fiction-Filme denken. ‚Ein Bewohner hat sich in einem zur Erde gestürzten Raumschiff niedergelassen. Schon bald wachsen Bäume um das Gebilde, und im Lauf vieler Jahre verschmilzt das Raumschiff völlig mit seinem Umfeld.'" SHELL wurde um eine Tanne herum gebaut und ist das Wochenenddomizil für einen Bauherrn aus Tokio (mit dem Schnellzug Shinkansen nur eine Stunde und zehn Minuten entfernt). Für die Oberflächen im Inneren des Baus wurde mit Kunstharz überzogener Urethanschaum eingesetzt. Besonderer Wert wurde auf den Energieverbrauch des Baus gelegt, in dessen Boden ein Warmluftsystem integriert wurde. Eine ausgeklügelte biometrische Anlage verschließt und sichert das Haus.

La description par Kotaro Ide de cette maison est assez surprenante : « C'est une grande structure en forme de coquille qui serait tombée au milieu des bois… Nous savons qu'elle ne fait pas partie de cet environnement à l'instar d'un rocher ou d'une caverne. Ce n'est pas non plus ce que l'on pourrait appeler une ruine. Elle a l'air d'un élément d'une structure construite quelque part ailleurs pour une fonction entièrement différente. Cette image rappelle les films de science-fiction. Quelqu'un s'installe dans un vaisseau spatial tombé sur la terre. Bientôt, des arbres poussent tout autour et, des années plus tard, le vaisseau fusionne entièrement avec le paysage. » Résidence de week-end d'un Tokyoïte, située à une heure et dix minutes de la capitale par le train à grande vitesse, cette coquille est édifiée autour d'un bouleau existant. L'intérieur est en mousse d'uréthane enduite de résine synthétique. Une réelle attention a été portée à la consommation énergétique, ce qui se traduit par la présence d'un système de chauffage à air chaud par le sol, conçu sur mesure. Un système biométrique sophistiqué ferme la maison et assure sa sécurité.

The curves of the house are echoed
throughout its design, as is evident
from the manner in which the roof
and wall form a base for the tree seen
to the right.

Die geschwungenen Linien des Hauses
ziehen sich durch den gesamten
Entwurf. Zu sehen etwa rechts im Bild
an der Art, wie Dach und Wände zur
Säulenbasis für einen Baum werden.

Les courbes sont le principe de base
de ce projet, comme le montre la
façon dont le toit, la terrasse et la
façade entourent cet arbre conservé
(à droite).

The interior design is entirely coherent with the architecture itself, giving rise to furniture in the spirit of the house.

Die Gestaltung des Interieurs knüpft nahtlos an die Architektur an, die Möbel scheinen ganz dem Geist des Hauses zu entspringen.

La conception de l'intérieur est en parfaite cohérence avec l'architecture, comme le souligne le mobilier traité dans l'esprit de la maison.

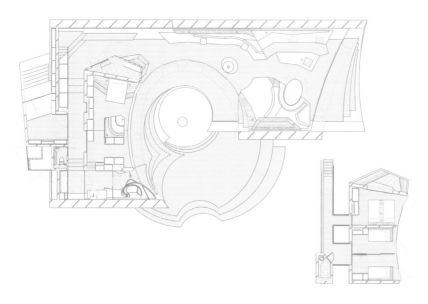

The fundamental continuity of the house is completely original, but might bring to mind such seminal works as Oscar Niemeyer's Canoas House (Rio de Janeiro, Brazil, 1952).

Auch wenn der dem Haus zugrunde liegende kontinuierliche Entwurf ein absolut eigenständiger ist, erinnert er doch an Schlüsselwerke wie Oscar Niemeyers Haus in Canoas (Rio de Janeiro, Brasilien, 1952).

La recherche de continuité qui caractérise cette maison est originale, mais rappelle aussi des œuvres historiques, comme la maison Canoas d'Oscar Niemeyer (Rio de Janeiro, 1952).

KIERANTIMBERLAKE

KieranTimberlake Associates LLP
420 North 20th Street
Philadelphia, PA 19130.3828
USA

Tel: +1 215 922 6600
Fax: +1 215 922 4680
E-mail: kta@kierantimberlake.com
Web: www.kierantimberlake.com

Founded in Philadelphia in 1984 by Stephen Kieran and James Timberlake, **KIERANTIMBERLAKE** is comprised of a staff of 54. Kieran graduated from Yale University and got his M.Arch from the University of Pennsylvania. James Timberlake graduated from the University of Detroit before receiving his M.Arch from the University of Pennsylvania. The firm's projects include programming, planning, and design of all types of new structures and their interiors; and the renovation, reuse, and conservation of existing structures. KieranTimberlake has received over 80 design awards, including the 2008 Architecture Firm Award from the American Institute of Architects. In 2003, the firm developed SmartWrapTM: The Building Envelope of the Future, a mass customizable, high-performance building façade that was initially exhibited at the Smithsonian Institution, Cooper-Hewitt National Design Museum. Structures completed in 2007 include the Sculpture Building Gallery, Yale University (New Haven, Connecticut) and the Suzanne Roberts Theater, Philadelphia Theater Company (Philadelphia, Pennsylvania). Buildings by KieranTimberlake completed in 2008 include the Lower School, Sidwell Friends School (Bethesda, Maryland); and the Multi-Faith Center and Houghton Memorial Chapel Restoration, Wellesley College (Wellesley, Massachusetts). Further projects are the Northwest Campus Student Housing, University of California (Los Angeles, California); the Center City Building, University of North Carolina at Charlotte (Charlotte, North Carolina); and the Morse and Stiles Colleges, Yale University (New Haven, Connecticut), all in the USA.

KIERANTIMBERLAKE wurde 1984 von Stephen Kieran und James Timberlake in Philadelphia gegründet und hat 54 Mitarbeiter. Kieran schloss sein Studium in Yale ab und erhielt seinen M.Arch. an der University of Pennsylvania. James Timberlake machte seinen Abschluss an der University of Detroit und erhielt seinen M.Arch. an der University of Pennsylvania. Das Büro befasst sich mit Programmentwicklung, Planung und Gestaltung von Neubauten aller Art und deren Innenraumgestaltung sowie der Sanierung, Umnutzung und Erhaltung bestehender Bauten. KieranTimberlake erhielt über 80 Designpreise, darunter den Architecture Firm Award 2008 des American Institute of Architects. 2003 entwickelte das Büro SmartWrapTM, die Gebäudehülle der Zukunft, eine technisch ausgeklügelte Gebäudefassade, die sich individualisiert in Massenfertigung herstellen lässt und erstmals im Cooper-Hewitt National Design Museum der Smithsonian Institution präsentiert wurde. Zu den 2007 realisierten Bauten zählen die Sculpture Building Gallery an der Yale University (New Haven, Connecticut) sowie das Suzanne Roberts Theater für die Philadelphia Theater Company (Philadelphia, Pennsylvania). 2008 wurden folgende Bauten fertig: die Lower School an der Sidwell Friends School (Bethesda, Maryland) sowie das Multi-Faith Center und die Sanierung der Houghton Memorial Chapel am Wellesley College (Wellesley, Massachusetts). Weitere Projekte sind ein Studentenwohnheim für den Northwest-Campus der University of California (Los Angeles, Kalifornien), das Center City Building der University of North Carolina (Charlotte, North Carolina) sowie das Morse und das Stiles College, Yale University (New Haven, Connecticut), alle in den USA.

Fondée à Philadelphie en 1984 par Stephen Kieran et James Timberlake, l'agence **KIERANTIMBERLAKE** emploie 54 collaborateurs. Kieran est diplômé de Yale University et M.Arch de l'université de Pennsylvanie. James Timberlake, diplômé de l'université de Detroit, est M.Arch de la même université. L'agence propose des services de programmation, d'urbanisme et de conception de tous types de constructions et de leur intérieur, ainsi que la rénovation, la réutilisation et la préservation de bâtiments existants. KieranTimberlake a reçu plus de 80 distinctions, dont l'Architecture Firm Award 2008 de l'American Institute of Architects. En 2003, l'agence a mis au point le SmartWrapTM : The Building Envelope of the Future, façade adaptable à hautes performances qui a été exposée initialement au Cooper-Hewitt National Design Museum (Smithsonian Institution). Parmi ses réalisations achevées en 2007 : la Sculpture Building Gallery, Yale University (New Haven, Connecticut), et le Suzanne Roberts Theater, compagnie de théâtre de Philadelphie (Philadelphie, Pennsylvanie). En 2008, KieranTimberlake a réalisé les projets suivants : une école primaire, Sidwell Friends School (Bethesda, Maryland), et la restauration du centre œcuménique et de la Houghton Memorial Chapel de Wellesley College (Wellesley, Massachusetts). D'autres projets sont des logements pour étudiants du Northwest Campus, université de Californie (Los Angeles, Californie) ; le Center City Building, université de Caroline du Nord (Charlotte, Caroline du Nord), et les Morse and Stiles Colleges, Yale University (New Haven, Connecticut), tous aux États-Unis.

LOBLOLLY HOUSE

Taylors Island, Maryland, USA, 2007

Floor area: 167 m². Client: Barbara DeGrange. Cost: not disclosed.
Team: Stephen Kieran (Design Partner), James Timberlake (Design Partner), David Riz (Associate in Charge)

Lifted up off the ground, with its irregular cladding, folding shades
and exterior stairway, the Loblolly
House is an original and ecologically
responsible realization.

Über dem Boden aufgeständert, mit
seiner unregelmäßigen Holzverblendung, klappbaren Fensterläden und
einer Außentreppe ist das Loblolly
Haus einmalig und ökologisch verantwortlich zugleich.

Surélevée, marquée par ses pare-
ments irréguliers, ses volets pliants
et son escalier extérieur, la maison
Loblolly est une réalisation originale
et écologiquement responsable.

This house is named for the pines on its Chesapeake Bay site. The architects have sought to form the house in its context of trees, tall grasses, and the sea. Set up on timber piles "it is a house among and within the trees." It was built with off-site fabricated elements in a period of six weeks using an innovative assembly system. The bathroom and mechanical systems were assembled as modules off-site as well and lifted into place. The methods used allow the house to be disassembled using little more than a wrench, in a particularly effective expression of environmental responsibility. The house won a 2008 AIA Honor Award—the citation read: "The Loblolly House, by the 2008 AIA Architecture Firm Award winner KieranTimberlake, draws inspiration and formal cues from the surrounding coastal flora and landscape: loblolly pines and saltmeadow cordgrass. The 1800-square-foot house was modularly constructed with simple tools in only six weeks and is intended to sit lightly on the land." The staggered vertical wood siding of the house gives it an unusual appearance that is far from what one might expect of a residence conceived for easy assembly.

Das Haus, benannt nach den Loblolly-Kiefern auf dem an der Chesapeake Bay gelegenen Grundstück, soll den Architekten zufolge im Kontext der Bäume, Gräser und des Meeres Gestalt annehmen. Auf Kiefernpfählen aufgeständert ist es „ein Haus zwischen und in den Bäumen". Die Montage aus vorgefertigten Bauelementen mithilfe eines innovativen Systems erfolgte in nur sechs Wochen. Die Versorgungsleitungen des Hauses ebenso wie das Bad wurden als Module vorinstalliert und mit einem Kran an Ort und Stelle gehoben. Diese Technik erlaubt zudem, das Haus bei Bedarf mit kaum mehr als einem Schraubenschlüssel zu demontieren, ein besonders überzeugender Beweis für umweltbewusstes Bauen. 2008 wurde das Haus mit einem Sonderpreis der AIA ausgezeichnet, die Begründung lautete: „Das Loblolly House vom Büro KieranTimberlake, das 2008 mit dem AIA Architecture Firm Award geehrt wurde, lässt sich von der Küstenflora und -landschaft seines Umfelds inspirieren und formal anregen: von den Loblolly-Kiefern ebenso wie von den Schlickgräsern. Das 167 m² große Haus wurde mit einfachen Werkzeugen in nur sechs Wochen aus Modulen montiert und soll leicht auf dem Baugrund stehen." Die vertikal gestaffelte Verschalung aus Holzpaneelen verleiht dem Haus eine ganz eigene Optik, die sich erheblich von dem unterscheidet, was man von einem Leichtmontagebau erwarten würde.

Cette maison tire son nom des pins qui occupent ce terrain en bordure de la baie de Chesapeake. Les architectes ont cherché à lui donner une forme répondant à ce contexte d'arbres, d'herbes hautes et d'océan. Surélevée sur des piles de bois, « c'est une maison parmi et dans les arbres ». Elle a été construite à partir d'éléments préfabriqués en six semaines grâce à un tout nouveau système d'assemblage. La salle de bains et les installations techniques ont été préalablement assemblées en modules et mis en place. Ces méthodes permettent de démonter la maison avec guère plus qu'une clé à pipes, illustration particulièrement efficace de la responsabilité environnementale. La maison a remporté un AIA Honor Award en 2008 avec le commentaire suivant : « La maison Loblolly de l'agence KieranTimberlake tire son inspiration et ses exemples formels de la flore et du paysage côtier environnant : les pins loblolly et les *spartina* des prés salés. D'une surface de 167 m², elle a été construite selon un principe de modularité et de montage original en six semaines seulement, à l'aide d'outils simples, et n'exerce qu'un impact léger au sol. » Les décalages dans le parement de bois donne à la maison un aspect curieux, différent de ce que l'on pouvait attendre d'une résidence d'assemblage aussi facile.

The irregularity of the cladding of the house makes it blend into the trees that surround it, while allowing those within to fully profit from the view.

Die unregelmäßige Holzverblendung lässt das Haus mit den Bäumen verschmelzen; von innen erlaubt sie, die Aussicht maximal zu genießen.

La composition irrégulière de l'habillage des façades les intègre aux arbres qui l'entourent, tout en laissant ses occupants bénéficier pleinement de la vue.

The house's interior is warm, yet open to views of the water, not at all in the minimalist atmosphere that other architects might have proposed. Right, the window shades fold up to become canopies.

Das Interieur des Hauses ist warm und so offen, dass Ausblick aufs Wasser möglich ist, und doch keineswegs minimalistisch geprägt, wie es andere Architekten vielleicht vorgeschlagen hätten. Rechts die aufgeklappten Fensterläden.

L'intérieur de la maison, chaleureux tout en restant ouvert sur l'océan, est très différent de l'atmosphère minimaliste que d'autres architectes auraient pu proposer. À droite, les volets-écrans transformés en auvents.

MATHIAS KLOTZ

Mathias Klotz
Los Colonos 0411
Providencia, Santiago
Chile

Tel:+56 2 233 6613
Fax: +56 2 232 2479
E-mail: estudio@mathiasklotz.com
Web: www.mathiasklotz.com

MATHIAS KLOTZ was born in 1965 in Viña del Mar, Chile. He received his architecture degree from the Pontificia Universidad Católica de Chile in 1991. He created his own office in Santiago the same year. He has taught at several Chilean universities and was Director of the School of Architecture of the Universidad Diego Portales in Santiago (2001–03). His work has been exhibited at the GA Gallery in Tokyo (Japan); at MoMA in New York, where he was a finalist for the 1998 Mies van der Rohe Prize; and at Archilab (Orleans, France, 2000). He participated in the Chinese International Practical Exhibition of Architecture in Nanjing in 2004, together with such architects as David Adjaye, Odile Decq, Arata Isozaki, and Kazuyo Sejima. Further work includes the Casa Viejo (Santiago, 2001); the Smol Building (Concepción, 2001); the Faculty of Health, Universidad Diego Portales (Santiago, 2004); the remodeling of the Cerro San Luis House (Santiago, 2004); the Ocho al Cubo House (Marbella, Zapallar, 2005); the Techos House (Nahuel Huapi Lake, Patagonia, Argentina, 2006–07, published here); the 11 Mujeres House (Cachagua, 2007, also published here); 20 one-family houses in La Dehesa (Santiago); and the Buildings Department San Isidro (Buenos Aires, Argentina), all in Chile unless stated otherwise.

MATHIAS KLOTZ wurde 1965 in Viña del Mar, Chile, geboren. Er schloss sein Architekturstudium 1991 an der Pontificia Universidad Católica de Chile ab. Sein eigenes Büro gründete er im gleichen Jahr in Santiago. Klotz hat an verschiedenen Universitäten in Chile gelehrt und war Direktor der Architekturfakultät der Universidad Diego Portales in Santiago (2001–03). Sein Werk wurde bereits in der GA Gallery in Tokio (Japan) präsentiert, im MoMA in New York, wo er 1998 Finalist für den Mies-van-der-Rohe-Preis war, und schließlich bei Archilab (Orléans, Frankreich, 2000). 2004 nahm er an der Chinese International Practical Exhibition of Architecture (CIPEA) in Nanjing teil, neben Architekten wie David Adjaye, Odile Decq, Arata Isozaki und Kazuyo Sejima. Zu seinen weiteren Projekten zählen u. a. die Casa Viejo (Santiago, 2001), das Geschäftszentrum Smol (Concepción, 2001), die Fakultät für Medizin an der Universidad Diego Portales (Santiago, 2004), die Umgestaltung der Casa Cerro San Luis (Santiago, 2004), die Casa Ocho al Cubo (Marbella, Zapallar, 2005), die Casa Techos (Nahuel-Huapi-See, Patagonien, Argentinien, 2006–07, hier vorgestellt), die Casa 11 Mujeres (Cachagua, 2007, ebenfalls hier vorgestellt), 20 Einfamilienhäuser in La Dehesa (Santiago) sowie die Baubehörde in San Isidro (Buenos Aires, Argentinien), alle in Chile, sofern nicht anders vermerkt.

MATHIAS KLOTZ, né en 1965 à Viña del Mar, au Chili, est architecte diplômé de la Pontificia Universidad Católica du Chili (1991). Il a fondé son agence à Santiago du Chili la même année. L'architecte a enseigné dans plusieurs universités chiliennes et a été directeur de l'école d'architecture de l'Universidad Diego Portales à Santiago (2001–03). Son travail a été présenté à la Galerie GA à Tokyo (Japon), au MoMA à New York, lorsqu'il était finaliste du Prix Mies van der Rohe 1998, et à Archilab (Orléans, France, 2000). Il a participé à la Chinese International Practical Exhibition of Architecture (CIPEA) à Nankin en 2004, en compagnie d'autres architectes comme David Adjaye, Odile Decq, Arata Isozaki et Kazuyo Sejima. Autres projets : la Casa Viejo (Santiago du Chili, Chili, 2001) ; l'immeuble Smol (Concepción, Chili, 2001) ; la faculté de médecine, Universidad Diego Portales (Santiago du Chili, Chili, 2004) ; le remodelage de la maison Cerro San Luis (Santiago du Chili, Chili, 2004), la maison Ocho al Cubo (Marbella, Zapallar, Chili, 2005) ; la maison Techos (Lac Nahuel Huapi, Patagonie, Argentine, 2006–07, publiée ici) ; la maison des 11 Mujeres (Cachagua, Chili, 2007, également publiée ici) ; 20 maisons monofamiliales à La Dehesa (Santiago du Chili, Chili) et des immeubles du service d'urbanisme à San Isidro (Buenos Aires, Argentine).

TECHOS HOUSE

Nahuel Huapi Lake, Patagonia, Argentina, 2006–07

Site area: 2200 m². Floor area: 600 m². Client: not disclosed.
Cost: $1.5 million. Collaborator: Alejandro Beals

This is a vacation house built on the north shore of Nahuel Huapi Lake in the northern part of Patagonia. The main views from the house are quite naturally turned toward the water. Public and family spaces are located on the larger access level, while guest and service areas are on the lower floor together with a swimming pool that opens out onto the garden. Building regulations in the area require the use of a slightly pitched roof, and it was decided with the client to insert windows in the north facing side of the copper roof. Terraces and patios increase the usable areas of the residence and, as the architect writes, "along with the roof windows, they generate different kinds of relations with the natural surroundings and between the different programmatic elements of the house."

Das Ferienhaus liegt am nördlichen Ufer des Nahuel-Huapi-Sees im Norden Patagoniens. Die Blickrichtung des Hauses geht naturgemäß in Richtung Wasser. Gemeinschafts- und Familienbereiche liegen auf der größer angelegten Zugangsebene des Hauses, während sich Gäste- und Versorgungsbereiche sowie der Pool, der sich zum Garten hin öffnet, auf der unteren Ebene befinden. Die örtlichen Bauvorschriften erforderten ein leicht geneigtes Dach, und so entschied man gemeinsam mit dem Auftraggeber, mehrere Sheddachfenster in das Kupferdach zu integrieren. Terrassen und Veranden erweitern die Nutzfläche des Hauses und, wie der Architekt formuliert, „schaffen ebenso wie die Dachfenster verschiedene Bezüge zur landschaftlichen Umgebung und zwischen den verschiedenen Elementen des Hausprogramms".

Il s'agit d'une maison de vacances construite sur la rive nord du Lac Nahuel Huapi, dans le nord de la Patagonie. Les vues principales de la maison sont naturellement dirigées vers le plan d'eau. Les espaces familiaux et de réception sont situés au niveau de l'entrée, le plus vaste, tandis que les chambres d'amis et pièces de service se trouvent au niveau inférieur, donnant sur la piscine et le jardin. La réglementation régionale de la construction exige des toits légèrement inclinés, et il a été décidé avec le client d'ouvrir des fenêtres sur la face nord de la toiture en cuivre. Les terrasses et les patios démultiplient les zones à vivre et, comme l'écrit l'architecte, « avec les fenêtres en toiture, elles génèrent différents types de relations avec l'environnement naturel et entre les divers composants programmatiques de la maison ».

The Techos House appears as two superimposed bands with ample glazing and contrasting materials facing the garden.

Die Casa Techos wirkt wie zwei großzügig verglaste, übereinanderliegende Bänder aus kontrastierenden Materialien, die sich zum Garten hin orientieren.

La maison Techos se présente sous forme de deux éléments horizontaux superposés, amplement vitrés, et habillés de matériaux contrastés côté jardin.

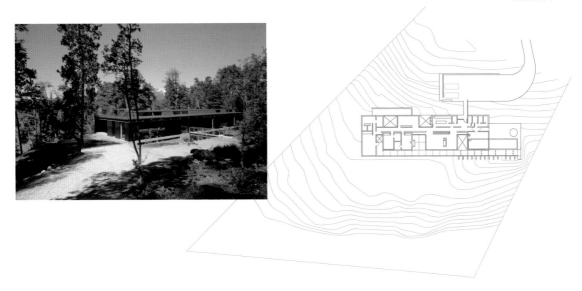

A topographic map of the site shows the way the largely rectangular volume sits on the curving slope.

Eine topografische Karte des Grundstücks veranschaulicht die Hanglage des weitgehend rechteckigen Baukörpers.

Le plan topographique du terrain montre comment la maison de forme essentiellement rectangulaire prend sa place dans la pente.

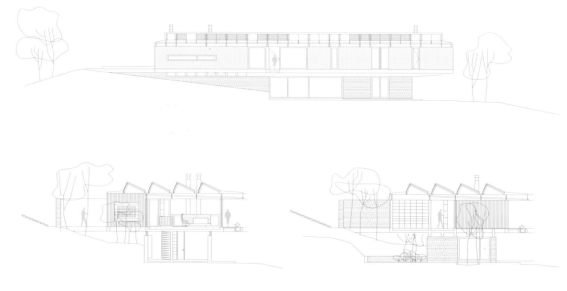

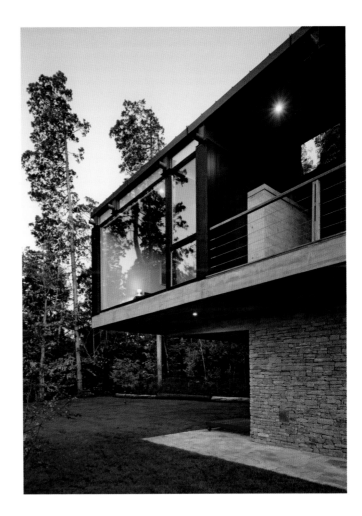

Served by an entrance bridge on the
higher side of the slope, the house
opens below to the garden, where the
hill is lower.

Am oberen Ende des Hangs führt
eine Brücke zum Eingang des Hauses,
nach unten hin öffnet sich der Bau
zum Garten, wo das Grundstück
abfällt.

Desservie par une passerelle partant
du sommet de la pente, la maison
s'ouvre en partie inférieure sur
le jardin.

With its sliding glass doors and
partitions, the house readily opens
out into its natural setting, a design
facilitated of course by the local
climate.

Mit Glasschiebetüren und -trennwän-
den öffnet sich das Haus großzügig
zur Umgebung, ein Konzept, das
natürlich durch das örtliche Klima
begünstigt wird.

Grâce à ses portes et cloisons coulissantes, la maison s'ouvre aisément
sur son cadre naturel, un concept
bien adapté au climat local.

An indoor pool can be opened with sliding glass doors that lead outside.

Das Schwimmbad lässt sich durch Schiebetüren nach außen öffnen.

La piscine intérieure peut s'ouvrir sur le jardin par ses portes coulissantes.

From the bedroom to the living spaces, the house has floor-to-ceiling glazing that permits a veritable interpenetration of the natural setting with the carefully designed and essentially rectilinear architecture.

Vom Schlafzimmer bis zu den Wohnräumen ist das gesamte Haus mit raumhohen Fenstern ausgestattet, sodass die Landschaft den einfühlsam gestalteten und geradlinigen Bau geradezu durchdringen kann.

De la chambre au séjour, la façade est vitrée sur toute sa hauteur, ce qui permet une véritable interpénétration du cadre naturel et de l'architecture de formes rectilignes très soigneusement dessinées.

11 MUJERES HOUSE

Cachagua, Chile, 2007

Floor area: 700 m². Client: Radovan Kegevic.
Cost: $2 million. Collaborator: Baltazar Sanchez

Jutting out from a steep slope above the ocean, the house, like other work by Mathias Klotz, is based on an architecture of right angles composed of rectangles.

Se projetant d'une pente escarpée au-dessus de l'océan, la maison, comme d'autres réalisations de Mathias Klotz, reprend un principe d'architecture orthogonale composée d'éléments rectangulaires.

Das Haus ragt über einen steilen Abhang am Meer hinaus und ist, wie andere Projekte von Mathias Klotz, Architektur, die auf orthogonal angeordneten Rechtecken basiert.

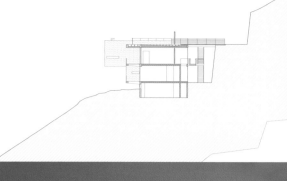

This "house of eleven women" is a vacation residence set on a steeply sloping site that leads down to the Cachagua beach and the Pacific Ocean. It is 140 kilometers north of Santiago, the capital of Chile. The clients have eleven daughters, whence the name of the residence, and the brief called for space for all of them, as well as a master bedroom and spaces for entertaining and guests. The base of the house includes game and TV rooms. The intermediate level contains the bedrooms for the eleven daughters. Since they ranged in age from four to twenty at the time the house was completed, there are two living rooms for the daughters, according to their ages. The upper level of the house has the master bedroom, living, family and dining areas, as well as service spaces. Built essentially of concrete with travertine marble floors, the house adapts to the contours of the site to offer the best possible views from each room. Large terraces encourage outdoor life, while hinged shutters protect the interiors from the sun on the west.

Das „Haus der elf Frauen" ist ein Ferienhaus und liegt auf einem steil abfallenden Grundstück, das zum Cachagua-Strand am Pazifik hinunterführt, 140 km nördlich der chilenischen Hauptstadt Santiago. Die Auftraggeber haben elf Töchter, die dem Haus seinen Namen gaben. Der Auftrag sah Raum für sie alle vor, ebenso Platz für ein Hauptschlafzimmer und Räume für Feste und Gäste. Im untersten Geschoss befinden sich u. a. ein Spiel- und ein Fernsehzimmer. Auf der mittlere Ebene liegen die Schlafzimmer der elf Töchter. Da sie zur Zeit der Fertigstellung des Baus zwischen vier und 20 Jahre alt waren, gibt es ihrem Alter entsprechend auch zwei Wohnzimmer für die Töchter. In der obersten Etage liegen das Hauptschlafzimmer, Wohn-, Familien- und Essbereiche sowie die Versorgungsräume. Das überwiegend aus Beton gebaute Haus mit Böden aus Travertin folgt den Konturen des Baugrunds, um optimale Aussicht für alle Räume zu erhalten. Große Terrassen laden ein, Zeit im Freien zu verbringen, während Fensterläden auf der Westseite das Innere des Hauses vor Sonne schützen.

Cette « Maison des onze femmes » est une résidence de vacances implantée sur un terrain escarpé qui descend vers la plage de Cachagua et l'océan Pacifique, à 140 kilomètres au nord de Santiago du Chili, la capitale du Chili. Les clients ont onze filles, d'où le nom de la maison. Le programme prévoyait une chambre pour chacune d'entre elles, une chambre principale, des pièces de réception et des chambres d'amis. La base de la maison comprend des salles de télévision et de jeux. Le niveau intermédiaire contient les chambres des onze jeunes filles. Comme leur âge allait de 4 à 20 ans au moment de l'achèvement du chantier, deux salles de séjour ont été prévues à ce niveau, en fonction de l'âge des enfants. Le niveau supérieur regroupe la chambre principale, les zones de séjour et de repas ainsi que celles réservées à la vie familiale et au service. Essentiellement construite en béton et travertin pour les sols, la maison s'adapte au profil du terrain pour offrir de chaque pièce la meilleure vue possible. De vastes terrasses incitent à vivre à l'extérieur et des volets articulés protègent l'intérieur du soleil couchant.

Given the nature of the site, the house must be entered through a set of steps and a bridge that approach it from roof level. Right, a topographic site plan showing the slope down to the water.

Bedingt durch die Lage des Grundstücks wird das Haus über Treppen und eine Brücke erschlossen, die auf das Dach des Baus führen. Der topografische Lageplan rechts illustriert die Neigung des Geländes zum Wasser hin.

Étant donné la nature du site, la maison n'est accessible que par une volée de marches et une passerelle au niveau du toit. À droite, plan topographique montrant la pente par rapport à l'océan.

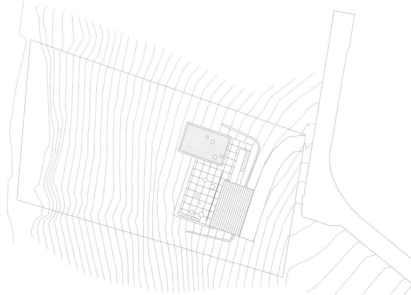

Views from the roof or the inside of
the house are spectacular, but the architect also provides the owners with
more intimate, enclosed spaces.

Der Ausblick vom Dach oder aus
dem Haus ist spektakulär, dennoch
bietet der Architekt den Besitzern
auch intimere, abgeschirmte Räume
an.

Les vues du toit ou de l'intérieur
de la maison sont spectaculaires,
mais l'architecte a également prévu
des espaces plus clos et intimes.

The horizontal bands that shape the
house are relieved by a cantilevered
volume. The house is complemented
by a pool located on the slope above
the beach.

Die horizontalen Bänder, aus denen
das Haus aufgebaut ist, werden vom
auskragenden Volumen aufgelockert.
Ergänzt wird das Haus um einen Pool
auf dem Abhang über dem Strand.

Les éléments horizontaux qui donnent
à la maison sa forme sont mis en
valeur par le volume en porte-à-faux.
La maison se complète d'une piscine
nichée dans la pente au-dessus de
la plage.

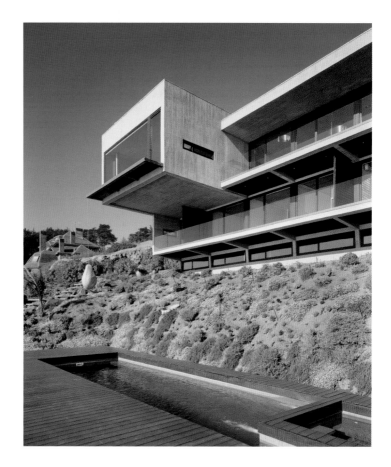

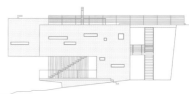

Floor-to-ceiling sliding glass windows
provide uninterrupted views of the
ocean, while interior spaces like the
kitchen or bathroom are shielded
from the bright open vistas present
elsewhere in the house.

Raumhohe Glasschiebetüren bieten
ungestörte Aussicht auf das Meer.
Die im Innern gelegenen Räume hingegen, etwa Küche und Bad, wurden
von den hellen offenen Sichtachsen
im übrigen Haus abgeschirmt.

Les multiples baies coulissantes
toute hauteur offrent des vues illimi-
tées sur l'océan, sauf dans certains
espaces intérieurs comme la cuisine
ou la salle de bains.

KENGO KUMA

Kengo Kuma & Associates
2–24–8 BY-CUBE 2F Minamiaoyama
Minato-ku
Tokyo 107–0062
Japan

Tel: +81 3 3401 7721 / Fax: +81 3 3401 7778
E-mail: kuma@ba2.so-net.ne.jp / Web: www.kkaa.co.jp

Born in 1954 in Kanagawa, Japan, **KENGO KUMA** graduated in 1979 from the University of Tokyo with an M.Arch degree. In 1985–86, he received an Asian Cultural Council Fellowship Grant and was a Visiting Scholar at Columbia University. In 1987, he established the Spatial Design Studio, and in 1991, he created Kengo Kuma & Associates. His work includes the Gunma Toyota Car Show Room (Maebashi, 1989); the Maiton Resort Complex (Phuket, Thailand); Rustic, Office Building (Tokyo); Doric, Office Building (Tokyo); M2, Headquarters for Mazda New Design Team (Tokyo), all in 1991; the Kinjo Golf Club, Club House (Okayama, 1992); the Karuizawa Resort Hotel (Karuizawa, 1993); the Kiro-san Observatory (Ehime, 1994); the Atami Guest House, Guest House for Bandai Corp (Atami, 1992–95); the Japanese Pavilion for the Venice Biennale (Venice, Italy, 1995); the Tomioka Lakewood Golf Club House (Tomioka, 1993–96); and the Toyoma Noh-Theater (Miyagi, 1995–96). He has also completed the Stone Museum (Nasu, Tochigi, 2000); a Museum of Ando Hiroshige (Batou, Nasu-gun, Tochigi, 2000); the Great (Bamboo) Wall Guest House (Beijing, China, 2002); One Omotesando (Tokyo, 2003); LVMH Osaka (Osaka, 2004); the Nagasaki Prefecture Art Museum (Nagasaki, 2005); the Fukusaki Hanging Garden (Osaka, 2005); and the Zhongtai Box, Z58 Building (Shanghai, China, 2003–06), all in Japan unless stated otherwise. Recent work includes the Suntory Museum of Art (Tokyo Midtown, Minato-ku, Tokyo, 2004–07); the Tobata C Block Project (Kitakyushu, Fukuoka, 2005–07); Yien East (Kyoto, 2006–07); and the Steel House (Bunkyo-ku, Tokyo, 2006–07, published here), all in Japan.

KENGO KUMA, 1954 im japanischen Kanagawa geboren, schloss sein Studium an der Universität Tokio 1979 mit einem M.Arch. ab. Von 1985 bis 1986 besuchte er mit einem Stipendium des Asian Cultural Council als Gastwissenschaftler die Columbia University. 1987 gründete er das Büro Spatial Design Studio und 1991 Kengo Kuma & Associates. Sein Werk umfasst den Showroom für Toyota in der Präfektur Gunma (Maebashi, 1989), die Hotelanlage Maiton (Phuket, Thailand), ein Bürogebäude für Rustic (Tokio), ein Bürogebäude für Doric (Tokio), M2, die Zentrale für das neue Mazda-Designteam (Tokio), alle 1991, ein Klubhaus für den Kinjo Golf Club (Okayama, 1992), das Hotel Karuizawa (Karuizawa, 1993), das Obervatorium Kiro-san (Ehime, 1994), das Atami-Gästehaus für Bandai (Atami, 1992–95), den japanischen Pavillon für die Biennale in Venedig (Venedig, Italien, 1995), das Klubhaus des Lakewood Golf Club in Tomioka (Tomioka, 1993–96) sowie das No-Theater in Toyoma (Miyagi, 1995–96). Darüber hinaus realisierte er das Steinmuseum in Nasu (Tochigi, 2000), ein Ando-Hiroshige-Museum (Batou, Nasu-gun, Tochigi, 2000), das Great (Bamboo) Wall Guest House (Peking, China, 2002), One Omotesando (Tokio, 2003), LVMH Osaka (Osaka, 2004), das Kunstmuseum der Präfektur Nagasaki (Nagasaki, 2005), die Hängenden Gärten von Fukusaki (Osaka, 2005) sowie die Zhongtai-Box, Z58 (Shanghai, China, 2003–06), alle in Japan, sofern nicht anders vermerkt. Jüngere Projekte sind u. a. das Suntory-Kunstmuseum (Minato-ku, Tokio, 2004–07), der Tobata C Block (Kitakyushu, Fukuoka, 2005–07), Yien East (Kioto, 2006–07) sowie das Stahlhaus (Bunkyo-ku, Tokio, 2006–07, hier vorgestellt), alle in Japan.

Né en 1954 à Kanagawa, Japon, **KENGO KUMA** est diplômé de l'université de Tokyo (1979). En 1985–86, il bénéficie d'une bourse de l'Asian Cultural Council et devient chercheur invité à Columbia University. En 1987, il crée le Spatial Design Studio, et en 1991, Kengo Kuma & Associates. Parmi ses réalisations : le Car Show Room Toyota de Gunma (Maebashi, 1989) ; le complexe Maiton Resort (Phuket, Thaïlande, 1991) ; l'immeuble de bureaux Rustic (Tokyo, 1991) ; l'immeuble de bureaux Doric (Tokyo, 1991) ; M2, le siège du département de design de Mazda (Tokyo, 1991) ; le club house du Kinjo Golf Club (Okayama, 1992) ; le Karuizawa Resort Hotel (Karuisawa, 1993) ; l'observatoire Kiro-san (Ehime, 1994) ; l'Atami Guest House pour Bandaï Corp. (Atami, 1992–95) ; le Pavillon japonais pour la Biennale de Venise (1995) ; le club house du Tomioka Lakewood Golf Club (Tomioka, 1993–96) et le théâtre Nô Toyoma (Miyagi, 1995–96). Il a également réalisé le musée de la Pierre (Nasu, Togishi, 2000) ; un musée consacré à Ando Hiroshige (Batou, Nasu-gun, Tochigi, 2000) ; la Great (Bamboo) Wall Guest House (Pékin, Chine, 2002) ; l'immeuble One Omotesando (Tokyo, 2003) ; l'immeuble LVMH Osaka (2004) ; le Musée d'art de la préfecture de Nagasaki (2005) ; le jardin suspendu de Fukusaki (Osaka, 2005) et la Zhongtai Box, immeuble Z58 (Shanghai, Chine, 2003–06). Plus récemment se sont ajoutés le Musée d'art Suntory (Centre de Tokyo, Minato-ku, Tokyo, 2004–07) ; le projet Tobata C Block (Kitakyushu, Fukuoka, 2005–07) ; Yien East (Kyoto, 2006–07) et la maison Steel (Bunkyo-ku, Tokyo, 2005–07, publiée ici).

STEEL HOUSE
Bunkyo-ku, Tokyo, Japan, 2006–07

Floor area: 265 m². Client: Professor Hirose. Cost: not disclosed.
Structural design: Ejiri Structural Engineers. Construction: Eiger Co. Ltd.

This monocoque design resembling a "freight car," because the client is interested in trains, was made of 3.2-millimeter-thick corrugated steel plates, without any beams or columns. Obviating the need for traditional structure, the steel skin becomes the load-bearing element. The two-story residence is fitted into an L-shaped site. The architect explains that "the basic idea of the architectural structure is to bend the steel plates to gain strength." Kengo Kuma points out that if the steel is not bent, but is painted, it would look like any other material—plaster boards or concrete for example. "The detail created by bending the steel," he states, "establishes communication between the steel and us. Based on these ideas, we have also been creating architecture from materials such as stone and wood." In this instance, the unpainted and bent, or rather folded steel assumes its industrial appearance and stands out in its densely built Tokyo residential neighborhood. The client proudly displays his collection of toy trains within.

Der Schalenbau, der an einen „Güterwaggon" erinnert – der Bauherr ist Eisenbahnliebhaber – wurde ohne jegliche Träger oder Stützen aus 3,2 mm starken Wellblechplatten gefertigt. Die Stahlhaut selbst wird zum tragenden Element und macht ein traditionelles Tragwerk verzichtbar. Das zweistöckige Haus wurde in ein L-förmiges Grundstück eingepasst. Der Architekt erläutert: „Es ist die Grundidee dieser architektonischen Konstruktion, die Stahlplatten zu biegen, um sie tragfähig zu machen." Kengo Kuma weist darauf hin, dass der Stahl, falls er nicht gebogen, sondern nur gestrichen wäre, wie jedes beliebige andere Baumaterial wirken würde – wie Leichtbauplatten etwa oder Beton. „Das Detail, das sich ergibt, wenn man den Stahl biegt", betont er, „schafft eine Verbindung zwischen dem Stahl und uns. Ausgehend von dieser Idee haben wir auch Konstruktionen aus Baumaterialien wie Stein und Holz realisiert." In diesem Fall gewinnt der ungestrichene und gebogene oder vielmehr gefaltete Stahl eine industrielle Anmutung und beginnt, inmitten der dichtbesiedelten Wohngegend Tokios aufzufallen. In den Innenräumen präsentiert der Bauherr stolz seine Modelleisenbahnsammlung.

Ce projet monocoque, qui évoque un « wagon de fret », car le client s'intéresse aux trains, est en tôle d'acier ondulé de 3,2 mm d'épaisseur, sans poutres ni colonnes. Contournant la nécessité d'une structure de soutien, la peau d'acier devient ainsi l'élément porteur. Le plan de cette maison sur deux niveaux est adapté au terrain en forme de « L ». L'architecte explique que « l'idée de base de la structure architecturale est de plier les tôles pour gagner en résistance ». Kuma fait également remarquer que, si l'acier n'était pas plié et peint, il ressemblerait à n'importe quel autre matériau, des panneaux de plâtre ou de béton par exemple. « La forme, créée par le pliage de l'acier, établit une communication entre l'acier et nous. À partir de ces idées, nous avons également créé des architectures sur des matériaux comme la pierre et le bois. » Ici, l'acier brut courbé, ou plutôt plié, assume son aspect industriel et attire le regard dans ce quartier résidentiel dense de Tokyo. Le client peut y présenter fièrement sa collection de trains miniatures.

Kengo Kuma uses corrugated steel, a material that might seem rather "industrial", in a sophisticated way, giving this house an undeniable presence in a crowded residential area of Tokyo.

Kengo Kuma arbeitet mit Wellblech, einem Material, das auf anspruchsvolle Weise „industriell" wirkt und dem Haus in der dicht besiedelten Wohngegend Tokios zweifellos Präsenz verleiht.

Kengo Kuma s'est servi de tôle d'acier ondulée – un matériau qui peut sembler assez « industriel » – mais de façon sophistiquée, qui confère à la maison une présence indéniable dans ce quartier résidentiel surpeuplé de Tokyo.

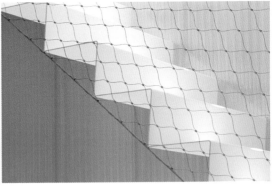

The architect continues the rather industrial vocabulary of the house inside, using chain-link fencing material near the stairway.

Im Innern des Hauses führt der Architekt die industrielle Formensprache fort, etwa indem er an der Treppe mit Maschendraht arbeitet.

L'architecte emploie le même vocabulaire industriel à l'intérieur de la maison, avec, par exemple, le garde-corps en grillage de l'escalier.

Largely closed in on itself, the house nonetheless makes subtle use of natural light throughout. A long curtain covers a wall (right), and a more traditional tea ceremony space is included (below).

Das überwiegend geschlossene Haus nutzt dennoch auf subtile Weise im gesamten Bau Tageslicht. Ein bodenlanger Vorhang kaschiert eine Wand (rechts), auch ein Raum für die Teezeremonie fehlt nicht (unten).

Refermée sur elle-même, la maison n'en utilise pas moins avec subtilité la lumière naturelle dans tous ses volumes. Un long rideau recouvre un mur (à droite), et un espace plus traditionnel pour la cérémonie du thé a été prévu (ci-dessous).

ANDREW MAYNARD ARCHITECTS

Andrew Maynard Architects pty ltd
551 Brunswick Street
North Fitzroy, Melbourne
Victoria 3068
Australia

Tel: +61 3 9481 5110
Fax: +61 3 8640 0439
E-mail: info@maynardarchitects.com
Web: www.maynardarchitects.com

ANDREW MAYNARD was born in Tasmania, Australia, in 1974. He received a B. A. in Environmental Design from the University of Tasmania in 1996. He received his B.Arch degree from the same university in 1998. Following his graduation in 1998 he traveled throughout the United States and England. Upon returning to Australia he was employed by Woods Bagot in Melbourne until early 2000, when he began working for Six Degrees Architects. In 2000 Andrew Maynard won both the Australia/New Zealand regional award and the overall Grand Prize in the Asia Pacific Design Awards for the Design Pod. He created his own firm in 2002. His work includes the Essex Street House (Brunswick, Victoria, 2005); the Skene House (Fitzroy North, Victoria, 2006); the Tattoo House (Fitzroy North, Victoria, 2007, published here); and CV08 (2008, unbuilt), all in Australia.

ANDREW MAYNARD wurde 1974 in Tasmanien, Australien, geboren. Er machte seinen Bachelor in Umweltdesign 1996 an der University of Tasmania, wo er 1998 auch seinen B.Arch. erwarb. Im Anschluss an seinen Studienabschluss 1998 reiste er durch die USA und England. Nach seiner Rückkehr nach Australien war er bei Woods Bagot in Melbourne beschäftigt, bis er Anfang 2000 begann, für Six Degrees Architects zu arbeiten. Für seinen Design Pod gewann Maynard 2000 sowohl den australischen und neuseeländischen Regionalpreis als auch den Großen Preis der Asia Pacific Design Awards. Sein eigenes Büro gründete er 2002. Zu seinen Projekten zählen das Essex Street House (Brunswick, Victoria, 2005), das Skene House (Fitzroy North, Victoria, 2006), das Tattoo House (Fitzroy North, Victoria, 2007, hier vorgestellt) sowie CV08 (2008, nicht realisiert), alle in Australien.

ANDREW MAYNARD, né en 1974 en Tasmanie, Australie, est B. A. en conception environnementale de l'université de Tasmanie (1996) et B.Arch de la même université en 1998. Il a ensuite beaucoup voyagé aux États-Unis et en Grande-Bretagne. À son retour en Australie, il a été employé par l'agence Woods Bagot à Melbourne jusqu'au début de 2000, où il a commencé à travailler pour Six Degrees Architects. En 2000, il a remporté à la fois le prix régional Australie/Nouvelle Zélande et le Grand Prix des Asia Pacific Design Awards pour le Design Pod. Il a créé sa propre agence en 2002. Parmi ses réalisations : la Essex Street House (Brunswick, Victoria, 2005) ; la Skene House (Fitzroy North, Victoria, 2006) ; la Tattoo House (Fitzroy North, Victoria, 2007, publiée ici) et CV08 (2008, non construit).

TATTOO HOUSE

Fitzroy North, Victoria, Australia, 2007

Floor area: 30 m². Client: Stepping Stone Relocations.
Cost: $300 000

This project was essentially a glass box addition to a 19th-century house—with the particularity of the use of tree graphics on the glass. The architect explains that one goal of the project was to make "the design as green as you can make a glass box." Light from the north (Southern Hemisphere) is controlled with horizontal slot windows, while double glazing is employed on the entire southern façade. Efficient seals were employed for all doors and windows, while windows and vents create a "chimney" effect that leads heat out of the structure. High value insulation materials were used for the walls and roof. The graphics on the glass created with UV stable stickers helped to meet local regulations requiring 75% opacity to second-story windows, and also reduced glare. The desire of the client and the architect was to make this small extension to an older and rather closed three-bedroom house as open as possible. Clearly, the Tattoo House meets those requirements in a cheerful way.

Das Projekt ist im Grunde ein kastenförmiger Glasanbau an ein Gebäude aus dem 19. Jahrhundert – die Besonderheit sind die Baumgrafiken auf dem Glas. Dem Architekten zufolge war es Ziel des Projekts, „den Entwurf für einen Glaskasten so grün wie nur möglich" zu gestalten. Der Lichteinfall aus Norden (südliche Hemisphäre) wird durch horizontale Fensterschlitze reguliert, die gesamte Südfassade wurde doppelverglast. Alle Türen und Fenster wurden effizient abgedichtet, Fenster und Lüftungsauslässe erzeugen eine „Kaminwirkung", die die Wärme aus dem Bau entweichen lässt. An Wänden und Dach kamen hochwertige Isoliermaterialien zum Einsatz. Die Grafiken auf den Glasflächen wurden mithilfe von UV-beständigen Klebefolien aufgebracht und entsprechen den örtlichen Baubestimmungen, denen zufolge Fenster im zweiten Stock 75 % Opazität aufweisen müssen. Darüber hinaus reduzieren sie das Blendlicht. Wunsch des Auftraggebers und des Architekten war es, den Anbau an ein älteres und vergleichsweise geschlossenes Haus mit drei Schlafzimmern so offen wie nur möglich zu gestalten. Ganz offensichtlich entspricht das Tattoo House diesem Wunsch auf besonders heitere Art.

Ce projet est essentiellement l'extension vitrée d'une maison du XIXᵉ siècle, dont la particularité est d'utiliser des visuels graphiques d'arbres sur sa façade en verre. Les architectes expliquent que l'un des objectifs du projet était de rendre « *le design* aussi écologique que possible avec une boîte de verre ». La lumière du nord (nous sommes dans l'hémisphère sud) est contrôlée par de minces fenêtres en bandeaux horizontales, tandis que la façade sud est entièrement en double vitrage. Des joints de scellement efficaces ont été utilisés pour les portes et fenêtres tandis que les fenêtre et les grilles d'aération créent un effet de cheminée qui évacue la chaleur de la maison. Des matériaux à très haut pouvoir d'isolation ont été utilisés pour les murs et le toit. La composition graphique sur le verre est en vitrophanie résistante aux UV qui a permis de répondre à la réglementation locale exigeant une opacité de 75% pour les fenêtres de l'étage et de réduire le gain solaire. Le désir du client, mais aussi de l'architecte, était de rendre aussi ouverte que possible cette petite extension d'une maison ancienne de quatre pièces assez fermée. La maison « tatouée » répond d'une heureuse façon à cette demande.

This tiny extension to an existing house is surprising in its transparency and use of façade graphics.

Dieser kleine Anbau an ein bestehendes Haus überrascht mit Transparenz und Fassadengrafiken.

Cette petite extension d'une maison existante surprend par sa transparence et sa façade « illustrée ».

Below, the simple folded design of the volume seen in successive drawings.

Eine Reihe von Zeichnungen illustrieren das einfache Faltprinzip des Entwurfs (unten).

Ci-dessous, illustration en déroulé du concept de pli qui a donné naissance au plan de la maison.

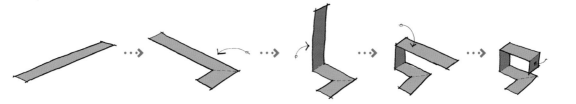

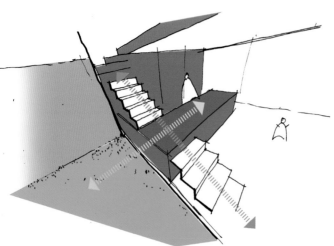

The folding glass façade makes it possible to open the entire ground floor of the house to the exterior. Steps lead to a more private mezzanine.

Die auffaltbare Glasfassade erlaubt, das gesamte Erdgeschoss nach außen zu öffnen. Stufen führen zu einem privateren Zwischengeschoss.

La façade de panneaux de verre repliables permet d'ouvrir entièrement le rez-de-chaussée de la maison sur l'extérieur. Quelques marches mènent à une mezzanine plus privative.

Inside, the graphics might well give the impression of real shadows. They provide some privacy and protection from the sun.

Im Innern des Baus wirken die Grafi-ken fast wie echte Schatten. Zugleich bieten sie Privatsphäre und Schutz vor der Sonne.

À l'intérieur, le traitement graphique des baies produit de véritables ombres. Il apporte une certaine intimité et protège du soleil.

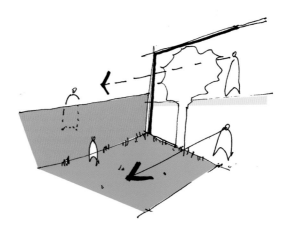

Floating House

MOS

MOS
226 West 135th Street
New York, NY 10030
USA

Tel: +1 646 797 3046
Fax: +1 866 431 3928
E-mail: info@mos-office.net
Web: www.mos-office.net

Michael Meredith was born in New York in 1971. He received his B.Arch degree from Syracuse University (1989–94) and his M.Arch from the Harvard University Graduate School of Design (1998–2000). He completed a residency at the Chinati Foundation (Marfa, Texas) in 2000. He is presently an Assistant Professor of Architecture at the Harvard GSD. Hilary Sample was born in Pennsylvania in 1971 and also attended Syracuse University (B.Arch), receiving her M.Arch from Princeton (2003). She worked in the offices of Skidmore, Owings & Merrill in New York (1997–99); and at OMA in Rotterdam (2000–02) as a project architect. She is an Assistant Professor at the Yale University School of Architecture. Michael Meredith and Hilary Sample created their present firm, **MOS**, in 2003. Their projects include the Hill House (Rochester, New York, 2003); the Huyghe + Le Corbusier Puppet Theater, Harvard University Art Museums (Cambridge, Massachusetts, 2004); the Floating House (Lake Huron, Ontario, Canada, 2006–07, published here); and the Winters Studio (Columbia County, New York, 2007, also published here), all in the USA unless stated otherwise.

Michael Meredith wurde 1971 in New York geboren. Er machte seinen B.Arch. an der Syracuse University (1989–94) und seinen M.Arch. an der Harvard University Graduate School of Design (1998–2000). 2000 folgte ein Gastaufenthalt an der Chinati Foundation (Marfa, Texas). Gegenwärtig ist Meredith Juniorprofessor für Architektur an der Harvard GSD. Hilary Sample wurde 1971 in Pennsylvania geboren und studierte ebenfalls an der Syracuse University (B.Arch.), ihren M.Arch. erhielt sie in Princeton (2003). Sie arbeitete für Skidmore, Owings & Merrill in New York (1997–99) sowie als Projektarchitektin für OMA in Rotterdam (2000–02). Sie ist Juniorprofessorin an der Architekturfakultät in Yale. Michael Meredith und Hilary Sample gründeten 2003 ihr Büro **MOS**. Zu ihren Projekten zählen u. a. das Hill House (Rochester, New York, 2003), das Huyghe + Le Corbusier Puppentheater, die Harvard University Art Museums (Cambridge, Massachusetts, 2004), das Floating House (Huronsee, Ontario, Kanada, 2006–07, hier vorgestellt) sowie das Studio Winters (Columbia County, New York, 2007, ebenfalls hier vorgestellt), alle in den USA, sofern nicht anders vermerkt.

Michael Meredith, né à New York en 1971, est B.Arch de Syracuse University (1989–94) et M.Arch de la Harvard University GSD (1998–2000). Il a bénéficié d'une résidence à la Chinati Foundation (Marfa, Texas) en 2000. Il est actuellement professeur assistant d'architecture à la Harvard GSD. Hilary Sample, née en Pennsylvanie en 1971, a également étudié à Syracuse University (B.Arch) et a passé son M.Arch à Princeton (2003). Elle a travaillé chez Skidmore, Owings & Merrill à New York (1997–99) et à l'OMA à Rotterdam (2000–02) en qualité d'architecte de projet. Elle est professeur assistant à l'école d'architecture de Yale University. Michael Meredith et Hilary Sample ont créé leur agence actuelle, **MOS**, en 2003. Parmi leurs réalisations : la maison Hill (Rochester, New York, 2003) ; le théâtre de marionnettes Huyghe + Le Corbusier, Harvard University Art Museums (Cambridge, Massachusetts, 2004) ; la Floating House (Lac Huron, Ontario, Canada, 2006–07, publiée ici) et le Winters Studio (comté de Columbia, New York, 2007, également publié ici).

FLOATING HOUSE

Lake Huron, Pointe du Baril, Ontario, Canada, 2006–07

Floor area: 204 m². Client: Doug Worple. Cost: $350 000

The architects intentionally used a "vernacular house typology" with cedar siding for an unusual site, an island on Lake Huron. Since the water levels of the lake vary considerably from season to season, the house is set up on steel pontoons that allow it to move up or down with the water level. The most was made of water transport, given the remote location of the site. Thus the steel platform with its pontoons attached was towed to the lake outside the builder's workshop. The house was then brought to the site and anchored—causing it to be moved a total of 80 kilometers on the water. The architects explain that "a 'rainscreen' envelope of cedar strips condense to shelter interior space and expand to either filter light entering interior spaces or screen and enclose exterior spaces giving a modulated yet singular character to the house, while performing pragmatically in reducing wind load and heat gain." The house includes a small boat dock and an upper-floor bridge linking it to the rocky coast.

Die Architekten entschieden sich bei diesem ungewöhnlichen Grundstück, einer Insel im Huronsee, ganz bewusst für ein mit Zedernholz verblendetes „regionaltypisches Haus". Da der Wasserstand des Sees je nach Jahreszeit stark wechselt, wurde das Haus auf Stahlpontons installiert, die sich dem Wasserstand anpassen. Angesichts der abgelegenen Lage profitierte man so weit wie möglich vom Wasser als potenziellem Transportweg. So wurde die auf den Pontons montierte Stahlplattform über den See geschleppt. Schließlich wurde das Haus vor Ort gebracht und dort verankert – zu diesem Zeitpunkt hatte es bereits 80 km auf dem Wasser zurückgelegt. Die Architekten beschreiben, dass sich die „hinterlüftete Fassade aus Zedernholzlatten verdichtet, um den Innenraum zu schützen und sich öffnet, um den Lichteinfall nach innen zu regulieren. Sie dient auch zur Abschirmung bzw. Einfriedung der Außenbereiche, wodurch das Haus einen ebenso modulierten wie unverwechselbaren Charakter gewinnt und zugleich ganz pragmatisch Windlasten und Wärme reduziert." Zum Haus gehören ein kleiner Bootsanleger und eine Brücke, die die obere Etage mit der felsigen Küste verbindet.

Les architectes ont intentionnellement fait appel à une « typologie de maison vernaculaire » qu'ils ont habillée de cèdre pour ce terrain très inhabituel, une île sur le lac Huron. Comme le niveau des eaux varie considérablement d'une saison à l'autre, la maison repose sur des pontons en acier qui lui permettent de suivre ces variations. Le transport par eau a été beaucoup utilisé pour ce site reculé. La plate-forme en acier et ses pontons ont été remorqués sur le lac à partir des ateliers du constructeur. La maison a ensuite été amenée *in situ* et ancrée après un parcours lacustre de 80 kilomètres. Les architectes expliquent qu'« une enveloppe »écran de pluie« en lattes de cèdre protège le volume intérieur, et se dilate pour filtrer la lumière ou enclore et protéger les espaces extérieurs, ce qui confère à la maison un caractère modulaire mais singulier, tout en permettant de réduire concrètement la pression des vents et le gain solaire ». La maison intègre un petit ponton pour un bateau et une passerelle supérieure qui la relie à la côte rocheuse.

As its name implies, the Floating House which was brought by water to its remote site, could rather easily be moved somewhere else. It is set on pontoons to compensate for varying lake levels.

Wie schon der Name sagt, wurde das Floating House auf dem Wasserweg an seinen entlegenen Standort gebracht und ließe sich ebenso problemlos an einen anderen Ort transportieren. Wegen des variierenden Wasserpegels schwimmt das Haus auf Pontons.

Comme son nom l'indique, la « maison flottante » a été transportée par voie d'eau jusqu'à son site reculé et pourrait facilement se transférer ailleurs. Elle est posée sur des pontons pour compenser les changements de niveau du lac.

WINTERS STUDIO

Columbia County, New York, USA, 2007

Floor area: 511 m². Client: Terry Winters.
Cost: not disclosed

"This project explores the idea of creating a space for both painting and drawing set against an intense landscape of shale cliffs, forest, and ponds," say the architects. Zinc panels are used for all exterior cladding, with the ends of the structure fully glazed to permit views to the hills of Taconic State Park. An angle in the glass wall allows for a covered exterior porch area. Intended for both painting and drawing, the interior is column free and allows for free movement between the disciplines of the owner. A kitchen, archives, and washroom are contained in a centrally positioned gray box with sliding panels. A concrete floor inside gives way to a ring of shale around the exterior.

Den Architekten zufolge „beschäftigt sich das Projekt mit der Idee, einen Raum zum Malen und Zeichnen zu schaffen, der in ein bemerkenswertes natürliches Umfeld aus Schieferkliffs, Wald und Teichen eingebunden ist". Die Verkleidung des Außenbaus besteht aus Zinkpaneelen, während die Kopfseiten des Baus vollständig verglast sind, um Ausblick auf die Hügellandschaft des Taconic State Park zu ermöglichen. Durch die schräge Positionierung der Glaswand entsteht eine überdachte Veranda. Der sowohl zum Malen als auch Zeichnen vorgesehene Innenraum ist stützenfrei und erlaubt dem Hausherrn, sich frei zwischen den beiden Disziplinen zu bewegen. In einer zentral positionierten grauen „Box" mit Schiebetüren befinden sich Küche, Archiv und ein kleines Bad. Um den Betonfußboden im Inneren des Hauses zieht sich außen ringförmig ein Bodenbelag aus Schiefer.

« Ce projet explore l'idée d'un espace pour peindre et dessiner face à un paysage d'une grande intensité, composé de falaises de schistes, de forêts et d'étangs », expliquent les architectes. L'habillage extérieur est en panneaux de zinc tandis que les extrémités de la structure ont été entièrement vitrées pour dégager des vues sur les collines du parc d'État de Taconic. Le retrait en biais du mur de verre dégage l'emplacement d'un porche. Conçu pour un artiste, l'intérieur de cet atelier sans colonnes permet à son propriétaire d'exercer ses diverses pratiques artistiques. La cuisine, les archives et une salle d'eau occupent une boîte centrale de couleur grise fermée de panneaux coulissants. La transition entre le sol intérieur en béton et l'extérieur se fait par une gouttière de schiste autour de la maison.

The rather simple and slightly asym-
metric volume of the studio does not
suggest a precise function from the
exterior.

Das vergleichsweise schlichte und
leicht asymmetrische Volumen des
Atelierhauses verrät seine genaue
Funktion von außen nicht.

Vu de l'extérieur, le volume assez
simple et légèrement asymétrique
ne suggère aucune fonction précise.

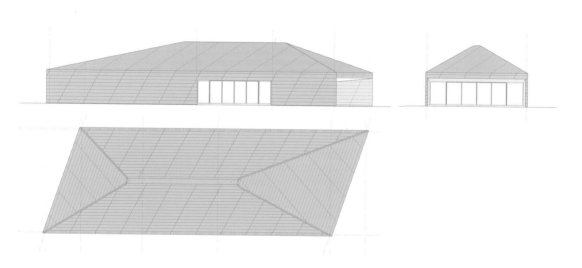

Inside the large open volume,
the artist is free to dispose of his
working environment as he sees fit.
Ceiling lights complement the lateral
natural light.

Im Innern des großen offenen Baus
steht es dem Künstler frei, seinen Arbeitsraum nach Belieben einzuteilen.
Deckenleuchten ergänzen das seitlich
einfallende Tageslicht.

Dans ce vaste volume ouvert, l'artiste
est libre d'organiser son cadre de
travail comme il l'entend. Les spots
complètent l'éclairage naturel.

The gray box (left) contains a washroom, kitchen and archives. Furnish-
ings are kept to a strict minimum
and, in these images, even works of
art are not made readily visible.

In der grauen „Box" (links) sind ein
Bad, eine Küche und ein Archiv untergebracht. Die Möblierung wurde auf
das absolute Minimum reduziert und
selbst Kunstwerke sind auf diesen
Abbildungen kaum zu sehen.

Le bloc de couleur grise vu à gauche
contient une salle d'eau, une cuisine
et des archives. La présence du
mobilier est minimale et, sur ces
images, même les œuvres d'art sont
pratiquement invisibles.

MOUNT FUJI ARCHITECTS STUDIO

Akasaka Heights 501
9–5–26 Akasaka
Minato-ku
Tokyo 107–0052
Japan

Tel: +81 3 3475 1800
Fax: +81 3 3475 0180
E-mail: fuji-s@rmail.plala.or.jp
Web: www14.plala.or.jp/mfas/fuji.htm

Masahiro Harada was born in Yaidu, Shizuoka Prefecture, Japan, in 1973. He graduated with a Master's in Architecture from the Shibaura Institute of Technology, Department of Architecture, in 1997. He worked as an architect in the office of Kengo Kuma in Tokyo (1997–2000), in the office of José Antonio Martinez Lapeña and Elias Torres in Barcelona, Spain (2001–02, Japanese Government Scholarship), and finally in the office of Arata Isozaki in Tokyo as a Project Manager (2003), before establishing **MOUNT FUJI ARCHITECTS STUDIO** in 2004. He has taught since 2007 at the Shibaura Institute of Technology as an associate professor. Harada Mao was born in Sagamihara, Kanagawa Prefecture, Japan, in 1976 and graduated from the Department of Architecture, Faculty of Engineering at the Shibaura Institute of Technology in 1999, before working in the editorial office of the Workshop for Architecture and Urbanism (2000–03) and establishing Mount Fuji Architects Studio with Masahiro Harada. They have worked on the M3/KG Residence (Meguro-ku, Tokyo, 2006); the T House (Chofu-shi, Tokyo, 2006); the Sakura House (Meguro-ku, Tokyo, 2006, published here); the Okinawa Football Stadium (Okinawa Prefecture, 2006–); the E and K Houses (Tokyo, 2007–); and the Clover Building (Yokohama, 2008–), all in Japan.

Masahiro Harada wurde 1973 in Yaidu, Präfektur Shizuoka, Japan, geboren. Sein Architekturstudium schloss er 1997 am Department of Architecture des Shibaura Institute of Technology mit einem Master ab. Als Architekt war er bei Kengo Kuma in Tokio (1997–2000), im Büro von José Antonio Martinez Lapeña und Elias Torres in Barcelona, Spanien (2001–02), und schließlich bei Arata Isozaki in Tokio als Projektmanager tätig (2003), bevor er 2004 **MOUNT FUJI ARCHITECTS STUDIO** gründete. Seit 2007 lehrt er am Shibaura Institute of Technology. Harada Mao wurde 1976 in Sagamihara, Präfektur Kanagawa, Japan, geboren und schloss ihr Architekturstudium 1999 am Shibaura Institute of Technology ab, bevor sie im Verlagsbüro des Workshop for Architecture and Urbanism arbeitete (2000–03) und mit Masahiro Harada das Büro Mount Fuji Architects Studio gründete. Gemeinsam arbeiteten sie an der M3/KG Residence (Meguro-ku, Tokio, 2006), am T House (Chofu-shi, Tokio, 2006), am Sakura House (Meguro-ku, Tokio, 2006, hier vorgestellt), am Fußballstadion von Okinawa (Präfektur Okinawa, 2006–), am E House und am K House (Tokio, 2007–) sowie am Clover Building (Yokohama, 2008–), alle in Japan.

Masahiro Harada est né à Yaidu, préfecture de Shizuoka, Japon, en 1973. Il a obtenu un mastère en architecture au Shibaura Institute of Technology, département d'architecture, en 1997. Il a d'abord travaillé dans l'agence Kengo Kuma à Tokyo (1997–2000), puis chez José Antonio Martinez Lapeña et Elias Torres à Barcelone, Espagne (2001–02, bourse du gouvernement japonais), et finalement chez Arata Isozaki à Tokyo en tant que chef de projets (2003), avant de créer **MOUNT FUJI ARCHI-TECTS STUDIO** en 2004. Il enseigne comme professeur associé depuis 2007 au Shibaura Institute of Technology. Harada Mao, né à Sagamihara, préfecture de Kanagawa, Japon, en 1976, a été diplômé du département d'architecture de la faculté d'ingénierie du Shibaura Institute of Technology en 1999, avant d'entrer dans le bureau d'édition du Workshop for Architecture and Urbanism (2000–03) et de fonder Mount Fuji Architects Studio avec Masahiro Harada. Ils ont réalisé : la résidence M3/KG (Meguro-ku, Tokyo, 2006) ; la maison T (Chofu-shi, Tokyo, 2006) ; la maison Sakura (Meguro-ku, Tokyo, 2006, publiée ici) ; le stade de football d'Okinawa (préfecture d'Okinawa, 2006–) ; les maisons E et K (Tokyo, 2007–) et le Clover Building (Yokohama, 2008–), tous au Japon.

SAKURA HOUSE

Meguro-ku, Tokyo, Japan, 2006

Site area: 131 m². Floor area: 279 m². Client: a couple.
Cost: not disclosed

The annual blossoming of the cherry trees (sakura) remains an important ritual in Japan despite its congested urban environments. This house is largely closed to its environment, though the patterned openings recall cherry blossom time.

Die alljährliche Kirschblüte (sakura) bleibt in Japan trotz der drangvollen Enge der Städte ein entscheidendes Ritual. Die Lochstanzungen dieses Hauses, das sich weitgehend seinem Umfeld verschließt, erinnern an die Kirschblüte.

La floraison annuelle des cerisiers (sakura) reste un rituel important au Japon malgré l'expansion des villes. Autour de cette grande maison très fermée sur elle-même, les perforations rappellent le temps des cerisiers en fleurs.

This four-story home and office has a footprint of 75 square meters and is 8.48 meters high. It is located in one of the most expensive and densely built residential areas of Tokyo. Built with reinforced concrete and a partial steel frame, it makes use of stainless-steel cladding panels on the exterior and chestnut wood flooring within. Masahiro Harada says that he thought of the "classic Glass Houses by Mies (Farnsworth House) and Philip Johnson" in conceiving Sakura (cherry blossom). Since the forested land used by Mies van der Rohe and Johnson was not available, the architect sought to replace nature with a pair of freestanding walls. Respectively 7.5 and 5 meters tall, and made with elaborately pierced 3-millimeter steel plates, these walls "filter light like sunshine through foliage, with holes punched out in a floral pattern depicting cherry blossoms, a traditional Ise paper stencil pattern." The Japanese await the blossoming of the cherry trees with great anticipation and the use of this pattern is thus a symbolic recreation of a natural setting not available in Tokyo.

Das vierstöckige Wohnhaus mit Büro hat eine Grundfläche von 75 m² und ist 8,48 m hoch. Es liegt in einer der teuersten und dichtest besiedelten Gegenden Tokios. Der teils als Stahlbeton- und teils als Stahlrahmenkonstruktion realisierte Bau ist außen mit Stahlplatten verblendet, innen wurden Holzböden aus Kastanie verlegt. Masahiro Harada gibt an, dass er beim Entwurf von Sakura (Kirschblüte) an die „klassischen Glasbauten von Mies (Farnsworth House) und Philip Johnson" dachte. Da ihnen die Waldlandschaften, in denen Mies van der Rohe und Johnson gebaut hatten, nicht zur Verfügung standen, entschieden sich die Architekten, die Natur durch frei stehende Wände zu ersetzen. Die jeweils 7,5 m bzw. 5 m hohen Wände wurden aus 3 mm starken Stahlplatten mit Ausstanzungen gefertigt; die Wände „filtern das Licht wie Sonnenschein, der durch Laub fällt. Die Löcher wurden als florales Muster gestanzt, das Kirschblüten symbolisiert, ein traditionelles Papierschablonenmuster aus Ise." Die Japaner erwarten die Kirschblüte jedes Jahr sehnsüchtig, und so kommt die Wahl dieses Motivs der symbolischen Nachbildung einer natürlichen Umgebung gleich, die es in Tokio nicht gibt.

Cette maison et bureau de quatre niveaux de 8,48 mètres de haut présente une emprise au sol de 75 m². Elle se trouve dans l'un des quartiers résidentiels les plus recherchés et les plus construits de Tokyo. Édifiée en béton armé sur ossature partielle en acier, elle est habillée à l'extérieur d'un parement d'acier inoxydable et ses sols intérieurs sont en châtaignier. Masahiro Harada avoue avoir pensé aux « classiques maisons de verre de Mies (Farnsworth House) et de Philip Johnson » en concevant cette maison Sakura (fleurs de cerisier). Le cadre boisé des réalisations de Mies van der Rohe et de Johnson n'étant pas possible, l'architecte a cherché à remplacer la nature par un couple de murs autoporteurs. Mesurant respectivement 5 et 7,5 mètres de haut, ces murs, en tôle d'acier de 3 millimètres d'épaisseur et percés, « filtrent la lumière comme le feuillage filtre le soleil, leurs perforations reprenant un motif floral de fleurs de cerisiers utilisé dans les pochoirs traditionnels en papier *Ise* ». Les Japonais attendent chaque année fiévreusement l'apparition des fleurs de cerisiers, et l'utilisation de ce motif recrée ainsi symboliquement le cadre naturel qui n'était pas accessible à Tokyo.

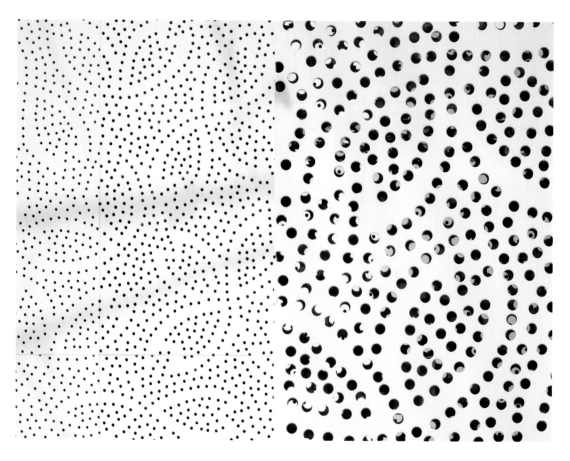

The complex perforation of the screen makes for varied light patterns, while interior spaces are lighter and more open to sky light.

Die komplexe Perforation der Wände erzeugt wandelbare Lichtmuster. Die Innenräume sind heller und lassen Licht von oben ein.

Les perforations complexes de l'écran sont de motifs variés. Les volumes intérieurs sont plus lumineux et plus ouverts vers le ciel.

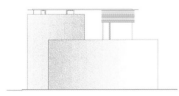

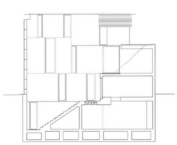

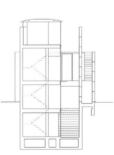

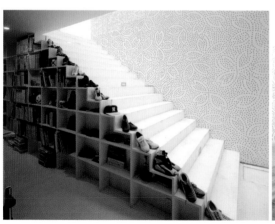

The interior of the house adapts an austere Japanese minimalism in its décor, but light is everywhere present in different forms.

Die Ausstattung der Innenräume orientiert sich am nüchternen japanischen Minimalismus, doch Licht ist überall in verschiedener Form präsent.

Pour son décor, l'intérieur de la maison a adopté un minimalisme austère, très japonais. Sous différentes formes, la lumière reste omniprésente.

Cube House

PLASMA STUDIO

Plasma Studio
Unit 51 – Regents Studios
8 Andrews Road
London E8 4QN
UK

Tel: +44 207 812 9875
Fax: +44 870 486 5563
E-mail: mail@plasmastudio.com
Web: www.plasmastudio.com

PLASMA STUDIO was founded by Eva Castro and Holger Kehne in London in 1999. Eva Castro studied architecture and urbanism at the Universidad Central de Venezuela and subsequently completed the Graduate Design program under Jeff Kipnis at the Architectural Association (AA) in London. She is Director of the AA's M. A. in Landscape Urbanism, and a Unit Master for its Diploma Unit 12. Holger Kehne studied architecture at the University of Applied Sciences in Münster, Germany, and at the University of East London. He is also a Unit Master for Diploma Unit 12 at the AA. The office made its reputation through a number of small residential and refurbishment projects in London. The architects say: "The studio is best known for its architectural use of form and geometry. Shifts, folds and bends create surface continuities that are never arbitrary but part of the spatial and structural organization." They won the Corus/Building Design 'Young Architect of the Year Award' in 2002. They participated in the Hotel Puerta América project with architects such as Jean Nouvel and Zaha Hadid (Madrid, Spain, 2005). Their recent work includes the Esker House (San Candido, 2006); the Strata Hotel (Alto Adige, 2007); the Tetris House, a multi-family residential compound (San Candido, 2007); and the Cube House (Sesto, 2005–08, published here), all in Italy. Since then Plasma has expanded into Europe with a second office location in Sesto near Bolzano, Italy, lead by partner Ulla Hell.

PLASMA STUDIO wurde 1999 von Eva Castro und Holger Kehne in London gegründet. Eva Castro studierte Architektur und Stadtplanung an der Universidad Central de Venezuela und absolvierte danach bei Jeff Kipnis den Aufbaustudiengang Entwurf an der Architectural Association (AA) in London. An der AA leitet sie das Master-Programm Landscape Urbanism und ist Unit Master für den Diplombereich 12. Holger Kehne studierte Architektur an der Fachhochschule Münster sowie an der University of East London. Auch er ist Unit Master für den Diplombereich 12 an der AA. Einen Namen machte sich das Büro durch verschiedene kleinere Wohnbau- und Sanierungsprojekte in London. Die Architekten erklären: „Das Studio ist besonders für seinen architektonischen Umgang mit Formgebung und Geometrie bekannt. Materialverschiebungen, -faltungen und -biegungen schaffen Oberflächenkontinuitäten, die nie zufällig sind, sondern Teil der räumlichen und konstruktiven Organisation." 2002 erhielt das Büro den Corus/Building Design Young Architect of the Year Award. Darüber hinaus waren Castro und Kehne neben Architekten wie Jean Nouvel und Zaha Hadid am Hotel Puerta América beteiligt (Madrid, Spanien, 2005). Zu ihren jüngeren Projekten zählen das Haus Esker (San Candido, 2006), das Hotel Strata (Alto Adige, 2007), das Haus Tetris, ein Mehrfamilienwohnkomplex (San Candido, 2007), sowie das Haus Kubus (Sesto, 2005–08, hier vorgestellt), alle in Italien. Inzwischen hat sich Plasma in Europa vergrößert: Das zweite Büro in Sesto bei Bozen, Italien, wird von Partnerin Ulla Hell geleitet.

L'agence **PLASMA STUDIO** a été fondée par Eva Castro et Holger Kehne à Londres en 1999. Eva Castro a étudié l'architecture et l'urbanisme à l'Universidad Central de Venezuela, puis à l'Architectural Association (AA) à Londres (Graduate Design program sous la direction de Jeff Kipnis). Elle est directrice du mastère d'urbanisme paysager à l'AA, et responsable de l'Unité de diplôme 12. Holger Kehne a étudié l'architecture à l'université des sciences appliquées de Münster, Allemagne, et à l'université de East London. Il est également responsable de l'unité de diplôme 12 à l'AA. Plasma Studio s'est fait remarquer par un certain nombre de petits projets résidentiels et de rénovation à Londres. « L'agence est surtout connue pour l'utilisation architecturale de la forme et de la géométrie. Glissements, plis et courbures créent des continuités de surface qui ne sont jamais arbitraires, mais font partie de l'organisation spatiale et structurelle », précisent les architectes. Ils ont remporté le Corus/Building Design « Young Architect of the Year Award » en 2002 et ont participé au projet de l'hôtel Puerta America en compagnie d'architectes comme Jean Nouvel et Zaha Hadid (Madrid, Espagne, 2005). Parmi leurs réalisations récentes : la maison Esker (San Candido, 2006) ; l'hôtel Strata (Haut-Adige, 2007) ; la maison Tetris, complexe familial résidentiel (San Candido, 2007), et la maison Cube (Sesto, 2005–08, publiée ici), toutes en Italie. Depuis, l'agence Plasma s'est développée en Europe avec l'ouverture d'un second bureau à Sesto, près de Bolzano en Italie, dirigé par une de ses associées, Ulla Hell.

CUBE HOUSE

Sesto, Italy, 2005–08

Floor area: 178 m². Client: Patrick Holzer. Cost: not disclosed.
Team: Eva Castro, Holger Kehne, Ulla Hell

As these three elevations show, the house gives pride of place to its balconies, as might be considered appropriate in this mountain environment. The wood cladding wraps around, leaving generous openings for the glazing.

Wie diese drei Aufrisse zeigen, kommt den Balkonen bei diesem Haus eine Schlüsselrolle zu, was inmitten der Berglandschaft durchaus angemessen scheint. Die Holzverkleidung umfängt den gesamten Bau und lässt Raum für großzügige Verglasung.

Comme le montrent ces trois élévations, la maison laisse la place d'honneur aux balcons en retrait, ce qui est approprié dans cet environnement de montagne. L'habillage de bois contourne les vastes ouvertures vitrées.

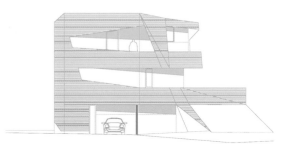

This house was designed for a steep site compressed by neighboring structures, and its angled forms, in both plan and section have a great deal to do with fitting in to the allotted space. A stairway leads up from two covered parking spots at the front of the residence to the main floor living areas, and on to the bedrooms on the second floor. Large balconies and terraces directed to the south, protected by overhanging roofs, give further effective living areas to the house. Its angled, timber-clad surfaces certainly set it apart from neighboring mountain-style architecture, but, perhaps because of its extensive use of wood, the Cube House does not appear to be shocking in its context.

Das Haus wurde für ein steiles und von Nachbarbauten beengtes Grundstück entworfen, und so hat seine winklig-geneigte Formgebung in Grund- und Aufriss viel damit zu tun, den zur Verfügung stehenden Platz zu nutzen. Eine Treppe führt von zwei überdachten Parkplätzen vor dem Haus zu den Hauptwohngeschossen hinauf und weiter zu den Schlafzimmern im zweiten Stock. Großzügige Balkone und Terrassen sind nach Süden orientiert und von überhängenden Dächern geschützt, was dem Haus zusätzliche Wohnbereiche verschafft. Mit seinen winklig-geneigten, holzverkleideten Oberflächen setzt sich das Haus eindeutig von der rustikalen Architektur der umgebenden Bauten ab. Trotzdem wirkt das Haus Kubus in seinem Umfeld nicht schockierend – vielleicht wegen der ausgeprägten Verwendung von Holz.

Cette maison a été conçue pour un terrain en forte pente comprimé entre des constructions voisines. Ses formes inclinées, aussi bien en plan qu'en coupe, s'expliquent en grande partie par l'adaptation nécessaire à l'espace disponible. Un escalier part des deux parkings couverts implantés devant la résidence pour monter au niveau principal et jusqu'aux chambres au second niveau. De vastes balcons et terrasses orientés sud, protégés par le surplomb des toits, apportent des espaces de vie supplémentaires. Les plans inclinés habillés de bois distinguent certainement cette maison de l'architecture de montagne des constructions avoisinantes, mais, par son usage généreux du bois, elle ne semble pas choquante dans ce contexte.

The typology of the house naturally differs from that of neighboring structures, and yet its wood cladding and terraced design show that there are connections between older buildings and this modern interpretation.

Typologisch unterscheidet sich das Haus ganz offensichtlich von seinen Nachbarbauten. Dennoch signalisieren die Holzverkleidung und die Balkone, dass es eine Verbindung zwischen den älteren Häusern und dieser moderneren Interpretation gibt.

Si le style de la maison diffère de celui de ses voisines, l'habillage de bois et la conception en plans et terrasses superposés montrent un lien entre les bâtiments anciens et cette interprétation moderne.

Views of the town are framed by the openings and the house offers protected terrace space all around.

Öffnungen rahmen den Blick auf den Ort. Das Haus ist rundum mit überdachten Balkonen versehen.

Les vues du village sont cadrées par les ouvertures. La maison possède des terrasses protégées dans toutes les directions.

ANTOINE PREDOCK

Antoine Predock Architect PC
300 12th Street NW
Albuquerque, NM 87102
USA

Tel: +1 505 843 7390 / Fax: +1 505 243 6254
E-mail: studio@predock.com / Web: www.predock.com

Born in 1936 in Lebanon, Missouri, **ANTOINE PREDOCK** studied at the University of New Mexico and received his B.Arch from Columbia University in 1962. He has been the principal of Antoine Predock Architect PC since 1967. He was a visiting lecturer at SCI-Arc from 1995 to 2000 and has held teaching positions at Harvard, Clemson and UCLA. In 2006 Antoine Predock received the AIA Gold Medal. His notable buildings include the Zuber House (Phoenix, Arizona, 1989); the Nelson Fine Arts Center, Arizona State University (Tempe, Arizona, 1990); the Hotel Santa Fe, Euro Disney, (Marne-la-Vallée, France, 1992); the Classroom/Laboratory/Administration Building, California Polytechnic State University (Pomona, California 1993); the American Heritage Center and Art Museum (University of Wyoming, Laramie, Wyoming, 1993); the Civic Arts Plaza, Thousand Oaks Performing Arts Center and City Hall (Thousand Oaks, California, 1994); the Ventana Vista Elementary School (Tucson, Arizona, 1994); the Arizona Science Center (Phoenix, Arizona, 1996); the Gateway Center, University of Minnesota (Minneapolis, Minnesota, 2000). Recent work includes the Tacoma Art Museum (Tacoma, Washington, 2003); the Flint RiverQuarium (Albany, Georgia, 2004); the Austin City Hall and Public Plaza (Austin, Texas, 2004); the Student Activity and Recreation Center, Ohio State University (Columbus, Ohio, 2006), the Logjam House (Rio Blanco, Colorado, 2007, published here); the Doudna Fine Arts Center, Eastern Illinois University (Charleston, Illinois, 2007); the Science Canyon, Academy School (Colorado Springs, Colorado, 2008); the Canadian Museum for Human Rights (Winnipeg, Manitoba, Canada, 2010); and the National Palace Museum (Chiayi County, Taiwan, 2011), all in the USA unless stated otherwise.

ANTOINE PREDOCK wurde 1936 in Lebanon, Missouri, geboren und studierte an der University of New Mexico. 1962 erhielt er seinen B.Arch. an der Columbia University. Seit 1967 ist er leitender Partner bei Antoine Predock Architect PC. Zwischen 1995 und 2000 war er Gastdozent an der SCI-Arc und bekleidete verschiedene weitere Positionen als Lehrender in Harvard, Clemson und an der UCLA. 2006 erhielt Antoine Predock die Goldmedaille der AIA. Zu seinen wichtigsten Bauten zählen das Zuber House (Phoenix, Arizona, 1989), das Nelson Fine Arts Center an der Arizona State University (Tempe, Arizona, 1990), das Hotel Santa Fe in Euro Disney (Marne-la-Vallée, Frankreich, 1992), ein Lehrsaal-, Labor- und Verwaltungsgebäude für die California Polytechnic State University (Pomona, Kalifornien, 1993), das American Heritage Center and Art Museum (University of Wyoming, Laramie, Wyoming, 1993), die Civic Arts Plaza am Performing Arts Center und das Rathaus von Thousand Oaks (Thousand Oaks, Kalifornien, 1994), die Ventana Vista Elementary School (Tucson, Arizona, 1994), das Arizona Science Center (Phoenix, Arizona, 1996) und das Gateway Center an der University of Minnesota (Minneapolis, Minnesota, 2000). Jüngere Projekte sind u. a. das Tacoma Art Museum (Tacoma, Washington, 2003), das Flint RiverQuarium (Albany, Georgia, 2004), die Austin City Hall und Public Plaza (Austin, Texas, 2004), das Student Activity and Recreation Center an der Ohio State University (Columbus, Ohio, 2006), das Logjam House (Rio Blanco, Colorado, 2007, hier vorgestellt), das Doudna Fine Arts Center an der Eastern Illinois University (Charleston, Illinois, 2007), der Science Canyon für die Academy School (Colorado Springs, Colorado, 2008), das Canadian Museum for Human Rights (Winnipeg, Manitoba, Kanada, 2010) sowie das National Palace Museum (Chiayi County, Taiwan, 2011), alle in den USA, sofern nicht anders vermerkt.

Né en 1936 à Lebanon, Missouri, **ANTOINE PREDOCK** étudie à l'université du Nouveau-Mexique et devient B.Arch de Columbia University (1962). Il dirige Antoine Predock Architect PC depuis 1967. Il a été professeur invité au SCI-Arc de 1995 à 2000, et a également enseigné ponctuellement à Harvard, Clemson et UCLA. En 2006, il reçoit la AIA Gold Medal. Parmi ses réalisations les plus connues : la maison Zuber (Phoenix, Arizona, 1989) ; le Nelson Fine Arts Center, Arizona State University (Tempe, Arizona, 1990) ; l'hôtel Santa Fe, Euro Disney (Marne-la-Vallée, France, 1992) ; des salles de cours, des laboratoires et l'immeuble de l'administration de la California Polytechnic State University (Pomona, Californie, 1993) ; l'American Heritage Center and Art Museum (université du Wyoming, Laramie, Wyoming, 1993) ; le Civic Arts Plaza, Thousand Oaks Performing Arts Center and City Hall (Thousand Oaks, Californie, 1994) ; l'école élémentaire Ventana Vista (Tucson, Arizona, 1994) ; l'Arizona Science Center (Phoenix, Arizona, 1996) ; le Gateway Center, université du Minnesota (Minneapolis, Minnesota, 2000). Récemment, il a réalisé le Tacoma Art Museum (Tacoma, Washington, 2003) ; le Flint RiverQuarium (Albany, Géorgie, 2004) ; l'hôtel de ville d'Austin et une place publique (Austin, Texas, 2004) ; le Centre pour les activités et loisirs des étudiants, Ohio State University (Columbus, Ohio, 2006); la Logjam House (Rio Blanco, Colorado, 2007, publiée ici) ; le Doudna Fine Arts Center, Eastern Illinois University (Charleston, Illinois, 2007) ; le Science Canyon, Academy School (Colorado Springs, Colorado, 2008) ; le Musée canadien des droits de l'homme (Winnipeg, Manitoba, Canada, 2010) et le Musée national du palais (comté de Chiayi, Taiwan, 2011).

LOGJAM HOUSE

Rio Blanco, Colorado, USA, 2007

Floor area: 269 m². Client: not disclosed.
Cost: not disclosed

The house stands in solitary splendor in the forest, echoing the trees with its main volume, lifted up off the ground on trunk-sized pilotis.

Einsam und stolz steht das Haus mitten im Wald. Aufgeständert auf baumstammähnlichen pilotis erinnert der Hauptbau formal an Bäume.

La maison se dresse, isolée, au milieu d'une forêt ; les pilotis aux proportions de troncs du volume principal rappellent les arbres.

The connection between the house and the forest is affirmed by an unusual use of logs that actually enter the structure.

Unterstrichen wird die Verbindung von Haus und Wald durch den ungewöhnlichen Einsatz von Holzstämmen, die den Bau regelrecht durchstoßen.

La connexion entre la maison et la forêt se renforce par la présence des grumes qui vont jusqu'à pénétrer dans la structure.

This house is located at the northeastern end of the Rio Blanco River Basin in a mountainous area occupied mostly by farms or ranches. The site includes a number of Ponderosa pine trees. The architect imagined that at some future point these pines might be felled, "a symbolic warping of time in which the decomposed grove produces new life" in the form of this house. Large glazed surfaces allow for constant views of the trees, as do large "floating" decks on the southern and eastern sides of the house. Rather than a "formal entry," circulation into the house is through an equipment room where bicycles, skis and so on are displayed. The living spaces are conceived as a continuous high volume with a guest bedroom and workroom looking down into them. A glazed catwalk leads to the private areas, with the master bedroom perched high "as though it were a tree house." Predock's work often has a direct relation to the earth, and in this instance, the Logjam House rises from the trees that surround it.

Das Haus liegt am nordöstlichen Ende des Rio-Blanco-Flussbeckens in einer überwiegend mit Farmen und Ranches besiedelten Berggegend. Auf dem Grundstück stehen einige Gelbkiefern. Der Architekt malte sich aus, dass die Kiefern irgendwann in der Zukunft gefällt werden könnten, „eine symbolische Zeitschleife, in der aus dem verfallenen Wäldchen" in Gestalt des Hauses „neues Leben entsteht". Großzügig verglaste Flächen ebenso wie die „schwebenden" Terrassen an der Süd- und Ostseite des Hauses erlauben den ungehinderten Ausblick in die Bäume. Statt durch einen „offiziellen Eingangsbereich" wird der Besucher durch einen Geräteraum, in dem Fahrräder, Skier usw. untergebracht sind, ins Haus geleitet. Die Wohnbereiche wurden als kontinuierliches hohes Raumvolumen definiert, in die Gästezimmer und Arbeitsraum hinabblicken. Ein verglaster Gang führt zu den Privatbereichen hinauf, wo sich das Hauptschlafzimmer „wie ein Baumhaus" an den Bau zu klammern scheint. Predocks Projekte haben oft einen unmittelbaren Bezug zur Natur – hier erhebt sich das Logjam House aus den Bäumen seiner Umgebung.

Cette maison se trouve à l'extrémité nord-est du bassin du Rio Blanco, dans une zone montagneuse principalement occupée par des fermes ou des ranchs. Le terrain est planté d'un certain nombre de pins de Ponderosa. L'architecte a pensé que, dans un certain laps de temps, ces arbres pourraient être coupés, comme « un glissement symbolique du temps dans lequel la futaie décomposée produit une vie nouvelle » sous la forme de cette maison. Les vastes surfaces vitrées offrent des vues sur les arbres, de même que les grandes terrasses « flottantes » des côtés sud et est. L'entrée ne se fait pas par une pièce formelle, mais par une sorte de vestiaire où sont rangés les vélos, les skis et autres accessoires de sport. Un atelier et une chambre d'amis à l'étage donnent sur les espaces de vie formant un volume continu de grande hauteur. Une coursive vitrée conduit à la partie plus privative. La chambre principale est perchée tout en haut « comme une maison dans les arbres ». Le travail de Predock entretient souvent une relation directe avec la terre. Ici, la maison Logjam semble s'élever naturellement parmi les arbres qui l'entourent.

The logs that are seen to enter the house from the outside penetrate the house and give it a more "rustic" appearance than the clean white walls and sophisticated materials employed elsewhere.

Die Stämme, die das Haus sichtbar von außen durchstoßen, verleihen dem Haus eine rustikalere Atmosphäre als die schlichten weißen Wände und eleganteren Materialien, die sonst am Bau zum Einsatz kommen.

Les grumes que l'on voit pénétrer la maison lui donnent un aspect « rustique » qui ponctue les murs blancs et les matériaux sophistiqués utilisés par ailleurs.

A drawing below shows the pattern akin to felled trees that represents the penetration of the architecture by tree-trunks. From some angles (right) the house appears less intentionally forest-bound.

Die Zeichnung unten visualisiert die Durchstoßpunkte der Stämme durch den Bau, ein Muster das an gefällte Bäume erinnert. Aus bestimmten Blickwinkeln (rechts) scheint das Haus weitaus weniger an die waldige Umgebung gebunden.

Le plan de composition ci-dessous évoque des arbres tombés qui expliquent la pénétration de la maison par les grumes. Sous certains angles (à droite), la maison est moins liée à son environnement.

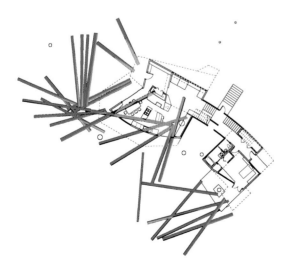

LAURENT SAVIOZ

Laurent Savioz Architecte
Ch. St-Hubert 2
1950 Sion
Switzerland

Tel: +41 27 322 54 91
Fax: +41 27 322 68 83
E-mail: contact@loar.ch
Web: www.loar.ch

LAURENT SAVIOZ was born in 1976 and received his degree in Architecture from the Haute École Spécialisée (HES) of Fribourg (1998). He worked in the office of Bonnard & Woeffray in Monthey, Switzerland (1999–2003), before co-founding Savioz Meyer Fabrizzi in Sion with François Meyer and Claude Fabrizzi in 2004. He carried forward the Roduit House (Chamoson, 2004–05, published here) on his own. Projects he has worked on with Savioz Meyer Fabrizzi include the Hôtel de la Poste (Sierre, 2006–07), a footbridge over the Rhone at Finges (Sierre, 2006–09); the construction supervision of a new building at the mountain Cabane de Moiry (Grimentz, 2006–07); the Iseli House (Venthône, 2007–); and a primary school (Vollèges, 2007–), all in Switzerland.

LAURENT SAVIOZ wurde 1976 geboren und schloss sein Architekturstudium 1998 an der Haute École Spécialisée (HES) in Fribourg ab. Er arbeitete für Bonnard & Woeffray in Monthey, Schweiz (1999–2003), bevor er 2004 mit François Meyer und Claude Fabrizzi das Büro Savioz Meyer Fabrizzi gründete. Das Haus Roduit (Chamoson, 2004–05, hier vorgestellt) realisierte er allein. Zu den gemeinsamen Projekten von Savioz Meyer Fabrizzi zählt das Hôtel de la Poste (Sierre, 2006–07), eine Fußgängerbrücke über die Rhône bei Finges (Sierre, 2006–09) und ein Neubau am Berg Cabane de Moiry (Grimentz, 2006–07). Zudem arbeiten sie am Haus Iseli (Venthône, 2007–) und an einer Grundschule (Vollèges, 2007–), alle in der Schweiz.

LAURENT SAVIOZ, né en 1976, est diplômé d'architecture de la Haute École Spécialisée (HES) de Fribourg (1998). Il a travaillé dans l'agence Bonnard & Woeffray à Monthey, Suisse (1999–2003), avant de cofonder Savioz Meyer Fabrizzi à Sion avec François Meyer et Claude Fabrizzi, en 2004. Il a conçu lui-même la maison Roduit (Chamoson, 2004–05, publiée ici). Parmi ses projets pour Savioz Meyer Fabrizzi, tous en Suisse : l'Hôtel de la Poste (Sierre, 2006–07) ; une passerelle sur le Rhône à Finges (Sierre, 2006–09) ; la supervision de la construction d'un nouveau bâtiment de montagne à la Cabane de Moiry (Grimentz, 2006–07) ; la maison Iseli (Venthône, 2007–) et une école primaire (Vollèges, 2007–).

RODUIT HOUSE

Chamoson, Switzerland, 2004–05

Floor area: 258 m². Clients: Josyane and Michel Roduit.
Cost: not disclosed

Chamoson is located in the mountains above the Rhône Valley in the Canton of the Valais. Set against a soaring cliff face, the town includes a number of old structures such as the 1814 stone and wood structure that Josyane and Michel Roduit asked the young architect Laurent Savioz to renovate in 2003. Owners of a much more traditional wooden vacation house directly adjacent to the older building, the Roduits allowed Savioz a good deal of freedom—which he used to replace the wooden upper section with thick concrete walls, retaining the original natural stone walls at the base. The renovated house contains a living room, kitchen, office, bedroom, and on the lower level a wine cellar, painting studio, and small exhibition gallery for the owner's paintings. Given the rather conservative nature of the township, it was somewhat surprising that they allowed this very modern conversion, insisting nonetheless that openings in the house correspond to the locations of the original windows. Laurent Savioz designed the kitchen for the house as well, and the owners have respected the rather harsh interior concrete surfaces, that seem to be as much inspired by the typical "Swiss box" contemporary architecture as they are by certain modern Japanese dwellings. What sets the Roduit House apart is that it retains its old, natural stone base and original form.

Chamoson liegt in den Bergen über dem Rhônetal im Kanton Wallis. In dem vor einer beeindruckenden Steilwand gelegenen Städtchen stehen auch einige Altbauten wie das Haus aus Stein und Holz von 1814, das Josyane and Michel Roduit 2003 von dem jungen Architekten Laurent Savioz umbauen ließen. Die Roduits, auch Eigentümer eines wesentlich traditionelleren Ferienhauses aus Holz unmittelbar neben dem älteren Gebäude, ließen Savioz viel Freiheit – die er nutzte, um den oberen Bereich des Hauses aus Holz durch massive Betonmauern zu ersetzen, dabei jedoch die Natursteinmauern des Untergeschosses erhielt. Das umgebaute Haus umfasst Wohnzimmer, Küche, Büro, Schlafzimmer sowie im unteren Geschoss einen Weinkeller, ein Maleratelier und eine kleine Galerie für die Bilder des Eigentümers. Angesichts des eher konservativen Umfelds im Ort ist es erstaunlich, dass man diesem sehr modernen Umbau zustimmte. Allerdings beharrte man darauf, dass die Öffnungen des Hauses mit den ursprünglichen Fensteröffnungen übereinzustimmen hätten. Laurent Savioz entwarf auch die Küche des Hauses, und die Auftraggeber akzeptierten die eher strengen Betonoberflächen im Interieur, die ebenso sehr von der typischen zeitgenössischen „Swiss-Box"-Architektur inspiriert zu sein scheinen wie von manchen modernen Wohnbauten in Japan. Was das Haus Roduit zu etwas Besonderem macht, ist die Erhaltung des alten Natursteinsockels und der ursprünglichen Hausform.

Chamoson est une petite ville du canton du Valais, située au-dessus de la vallée du Rhône. Implantée au pied d'une falaise, elle possède un certain nombre de constructions anciennes comme cette maison de pierre et de bois datant de 1814, que Josyane et Michel Roduit ont demandé au jeune architecte Laurent Savioz de rénover en 2003. Propriétaires d'une maison de vacances en bois de facture beaucoup plus traditionnelle directement adjacente à l'ancienne construction, les Roduit ont accordé une grande liberté à Savioz, qu'il a mise à profit pour remplacer la partie supérieure en bois par d'épais murs de béton, tout en conservant les murs de pierre de la base. La maison rénovée contient un séjour, une cuisine, un bureau, une salle de bains et, à l'étage inférieur, une cave à vin, un atelier de peinture et une petite galerie d'exposition pour les peintures du propriétaire. Étant donné la nature assez conservatrice de la ville, on peut être surpris que le permis de construire ait été accordé à une conversion aussi moderne, avec cependant l'obligation pour les ouvertures de se trouver à la même place que les anciennes. Laurent Savioz a également conçu la cuisine, et les propriétaires ont respecté les surfaces de béton assez brutes de l'intérieur, qui semblent être aussi bien inspirées par le concept de la « boîte suisse », typique de l'architecture contemporaine, que par certaines réalisations japonaises. Ce qui caractérise la maison Roduit réside dans le choix d'avoir retenu sa base en vieilles pierres naturelles et conservé sa forme originale.

Although the house is based on existing stone walls, the use of concrete to replace the original timber upper section gives it a strong, contemporary presence.

Zwar ruht das Haus auf seinen alten Steinmauern, doch durch das Ersetzen des oberen hölzernen Fassadenabschnitts durch Beton gewinnt es eine bewusst zeitgenössische Präsenz.

Bien que la maison ait été construite à partir de murs existants, le recours au béton pour remplacer la partie supérieure en bois lui assure une forte présence contemporaine.

The house sits beneath the sheer cliff faces that rise above Chamoson, connecting its stone base to the site in an almost literal way.

Das Haus liegt unterhalb der Fels-wände über Chamoson, die einen geradezu buchstäblichen Bezug zwischen dem steinernen Sockel des Hauses und der Umgebung herstellen.

La maison se dresse sous une paroi de pierre qui s'élève au-dessus de la commune de Chamoson ; la connexion au site semble presque littérale.

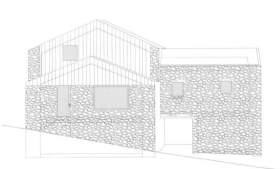

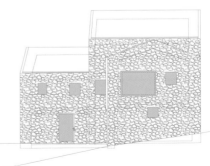

The interior of the house is largely made of concrete, with an austerity frequently seen in contemporary "Swiss box" architecture.

Beton dominiert das Interieur des Hauses, eine Strenge, die bei zeitgenössischer „Swiss Box"-Architektur oft zu beobachten ist.

L'intérieur de la maison est en grande partie en béton. Ce type d'austérité est fréquent dans l'architecture contemporaine de la « boîte suisse ».

The orange color in the kitchen was selected by the client. Other tones in the house are decidedly muted. Below, right, the master bedroom with an overhead window that looks out to the cliffs above.

Das Orange in der Küche wurde vom Bauherrn ausgewählt. Die übrigen Farben im Haus sind entschieden gedämpfter. Rechts unten das Hauptschlafzimmer mit einem Dachfenster mit Blick auf die aufragenden Felsen.

La couleur orange de la cuisine a été choisie par le client. Les autres couleurs présentes dans la maison sont nettement plus assourdies. Ci-dessous, à droite, la chambre principale à fenêtre de toit qui donne sur les falaises.

SELGASCANO

SELGASCANO
Guecho 27
28023 Madrid
Spain

Tel: +34 91 30 76 481
E-mail: selgascano1@gmail.com
Web: www.selgascano.net

JOSÉ SELGAS was born in Madrid in 1965. He got his architecture degree at the ETSAM in 1992 and then worked with Francesco Venecia in Naples, Italy (1994–95). **LUCÍA CANO** was also born in Madrid in 1965, and received her degree from the ETSAM in 1992. She worked with Julio Cano Lasso from 1997 to 2003. Selgas and Cano created their present firm in 2003. They have won a number of First Prize awards in competitions, including: Ideas Competition for Social Housing (Madrid, 1993); the competition for the Badajoz Center (1999–2006); for the Cartagena Conference and Auditorium (2001–08); and for a similar facility in Plasencia (2005–09), all in Spain. They also participated in the "On-Site: New Architecture in Spain" exhibition at the Museum of Modern Art (New York, 2006). After the Silicon House (La Florida, Madrid, 2006, published here), the architects are presently completing the construction of 20 garden villas in Vallecas, Madrid, Spain.

JOSÉ SELGAS wurde 1965 in Madrid geboren. Sein Architekturstudium schloss er 1992 an der ETSAM ab; anschließend arbeitete er für Francesco Venecia in Neapel (1994–95). **LUCÍA CANO** wurde ebenfalls 1965 in Madrid geboren und machte ihren Abschluss 1992 an der ETSAM. Von 1997 bis 2003 arbeitete sie für Julio Cano Lasso. Ihr gegenwärtiges Büro gründeten Selgas und Cano 2003. Sie haben bereits mehrfach erste Preise bei Wettbewerben gewonnen, darunter bei einem Ideenwettbewerb für ein Sozialbauprojekt (Madrid, 1993), einem Wettbewerb für das Badajoz Center (1999–2006) sowie für das Konferenzzentrum und Auditorium in Cartagena (2001–08) und eine ähnliche Einrichtung in Plasencia (2005–09), alle in Spanien. Darüber hinaus waren sie auch in der Ausstellung „On-Site: New Architecture in Spain" am Museum of Modern Art vertreten (New York, 2006). Seit der Fertigstellung der Casa de Silicona (La Florida, Madrid, 2006, hier vorgestellt) arbeiten die Architekten zurzeit an 20 Gartenvillen in Vallecas, Madrid, Spanien.

JOSÉ SELGAS, né à Madrid en 1965, est diplômé en architecture de l'ETSAM (1992). Il a ensuite travaillé pour Francesco Venecia à Naples, Italie (1994–95). **LUCÍA CANO**, également née à Madrid en 1965, est diplômée de l'ETSAM (1992). Elle a travaillé avec Julio Cano Lasso de 1997 à 2003. Selgas et Cano ont créé leur agence en 2003. Ils ont remporté un certain nombre de premiers prix lors de concours en Espagne dont : un concours d'idée pour des logements sociaux (Madrid, 1993) ; celui du centre de Badajoz (1999–2006) ; celui pour le centre de conférences et auditorium de Cartagène (2001–08) et un autre projet similaire à Plasencia (2005–09). Ils ont également participé à « On-Site : New Architecture in Spain », exposition organisée au Museum of Modern Art (New York, 2006). Après la maison Silicone (La Florida, Madrid, 2006, publiée ici), ils achèvent actuellement la construction de 20 villas-jardin à Vallecas, Madrid, Espagne.

SILICON HOUSE

La Florida, Madrid, Spain, 2006

Floor area: 160 m². Client: SELGASCANO.
Cost: not disclosed

The architects started by plotting the location of trees on their site, and built this house around them, basing the design on two main platforms. Since the owners have planted even more trees, José Selgas says that, with time, he imagines that the house will become almost invisible. "The only thing we can say about the interior space is that it goes unnoticed," say the architects; "this is a project that is only related to the exterior." Colored orange and dark blue with paints designed for oil rigs, the rather freely formed platforms circle partially around a large exterior terrace that also allows for trees to emerge. The platforms are essentially divided between night and day. The partially buried living room, with its large collection of books, looks out on the natural setting through a continuous band of Plexiglas windows, while light also comes from above through Plexiglas bubbles in the roof. Plastic or rubber is present almost everywhere—with recycled tires being used as roofing material, and Verner Panton objects within. There is a curious opposition between a house made largely of synthetic materials and the extreme respect for nature displayed in the location and openness of the house.

Die Architekten kartierten zunächst den Standort der Bäume auf ihrem Grundstück und bauten das Haus, das im Wesentlichen auf zwei Plattformen ruht, schließlich um sie herum. Da die Bauherren inzwischen noch weitere Bäume gepflanzt haben, geht José Selgas davon aus, dass das Haus mit der Zeit geradezu verschwinden wird. „Das Einzige was wir über den Innenraum sagen können, ist, dass man ihn übersieht", sagen die Architekten. „Dieses Projekt sucht seine Bezüge ausschließlich im Außenraum." Die frei geformten Plattformen sind orange und dunkelblau gestrichen worden, Farben, die sonst bei Bohrinseln verwendet werden. Sie schmiegen sich zum Teil um eine große Außenterrasse, aus der ebenfalls Bäume herauszuwachsen scheinen. Die Plattformen teilen sich mehr oder weniger in Tag und Nacht. Vom teilweise in den Boden versenkten Wohnraum mit seiner umfangreichen Büchersammlung erlaubt ein durchgängiges Band von Plexiglasfenstern Ausblicke in die Umgebung, Licht fällt zudem durch Plexiglasbullaugen in der Decke ein. Kunststoff und Gummi sind nahezu allgegenwärtig – recycelte Autoreifen dienen als Dachmaterial, im Innern des Hauses finden sich Verner-Panton-Möbel. Es ist ein eigentümlicher Gegensatz zwischen dem überwiegend aus synthetischen Materialien gebauten Haus und dem außerordentlichen Respekt vor der Natur, der sich in der Anlage und Offenheit des Hauses spiegelt.

Les architectes ont commencé par noter l'implantation des arbres sur le terrain et construit la maison tout autour sur deux plates-formes principales. Comme les propriétaires ont continué à planter de nouveaux arbres, José Selgas pense qu'avec le temps leur maison sera presque invisible. « La seule chose que nous pouvons dire de l'espace intérieur est qu'il se déploie sans se faire remarquer, précise l'architecte, c'est un projet en relation unique avec l'extérieur. » Colorées en orange et bleu sombre à l'aide de peintures utilisées pour les exploitations pétrolières, les plates-formes, de contours assez libres, entourent partiellement une vaste terrasse extérieure transpercée de quelques arbres. Elles sont divisées en zone de jour et zone de nuit. Le séjour, en partie enterré, qui se caractérise par une importante collection de livres, donne sur la nature par des fenêtres en bandeau, en Plexiglas. La lumière provient également de petites bulles en Plexiglas qui traversent le toit. Le plastique ou le caoutchouc sont des matériaux omniprésents. Des pneus recyclés ont servi à recouvrir la toiture, et l'on trouve des créations de Verner Panton à l'intérieur. L'opposition est curieuse entre cette maison réalisée en grande partie en matériaux synthétiques et l'extrême respect de la nature manifesté dans son implantation et son ouverture.

The bright color or plastics used in the house are in intentional contrast to the natural setting, but the house is willfully integrated into its site.

Die kräftigen Farben und Kunststoffe am Haus sind ein gewollter Kontrast zur umgebenden Natur. Dennoch ist das Haus bewusst in das Grundstück integriert.

La couleur vive et les plastiques utilisés sont en contraste volontaire avec le cadre naturel, mais la maison s'intègre heureusement à son site.

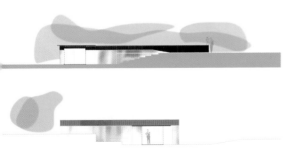

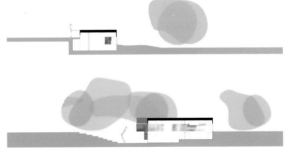

The house is an unexpected combination of clean modern lines and a brightly colored roof slab with spherical windows that looks like it might have come directly out of the 1960s.

Das Haus ist eine überraschende Kombination aus moderner Linienführung und einer knallbunten Dachplatte mit sphärischen Oberlichtern, die wirken, als seien sie direkt den 1960er-Jahren entsprungen.

La maison est une combinaison inattendue de lignes nettes et modernes et d'une toiture plate à verrières sphériques d'un style inspiré des années 1960.

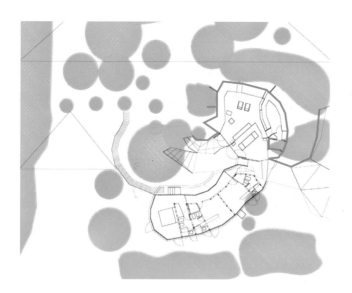

A site plan shows how the house was integrated into existing groups of vegetation. The kitchen (below) has a broad strip window looking out to the garden.

Ein Lageplan illustriert, wie das Haus in die bestehende Begrünung integriert wurde. Die Küche (unten) hat ein breites Fensterband mit Ausblick in den Garten.

Le plan du terrain montre l'intégration de la maison dans la végétation existante. La cuisine, ci-dessous, possède une importante fenêtre en bandeau qui donne sur le jardin.

Furniture, often in plastic, animates
the interior and continues the theme
of intentional playfulness.

*Das Mobiliar, oft aus Kunststoff,
belebt das Interieur und setzt das
spielerische Gesamtthema fort.*

*Souvent en plastique, le mobilier
anime l'intérieur et reprend le thème
ludique du projet.*

SHIM-SUTCLIFFE

Shim-Sutcliffe Architects Inc.
441 Queen Street East
Toronto
Ontario M5A 1T5
Canada

Tel: +1 416 368 3892
Fax: +1 416 368 9468
E-mail: info@shimsut.com
Web: www.shim-sutcliffe.com

Brigitte Shim was born in Kingston, Jamaica, in 1958. She received her B.Arch and her Bachelor of Environmental Studies degrees from the University of Waterloo in Ontario. She worked in the office of Arthur Erickson (1981), and Baird/Sampson in Toronto, before creating her own firm, Brigitte Shim Architect (1988–94). She is a principal and co-founder of **SHIM-SUTCLIFFE**, created in Toronto in 1994. She is presently an Associate Professor at the University of Toronto's Faculty of Architecture and Design. Howard Sutcliffe was born in Yorkshire, England, in 1958. He also received his B.Arch and his Bachelor of Environmental Studies degrees from the University of Waterloo in Ontario. He worked in the offices of Barton Myers (1984–86) and Merrick Architecture until 1993, creating Shim-Sutcliffe with Brigitte Shim the following year. Their projects include the Ravine Guest House (Don Mills, Ontario, 2003–04, published here); the house on Hurricane Lake (Haliburton, Ontario, 2004–05); the Craven Road Studio (Toronto, 2006); and the Massey College in the University of Toronto (2002–06), all in Canada. Their current work includes the Bet Ha'am Synagogue (Portland, Maine, USA); and the Integral House (Toronto, Canada).

Brigitte Shim wurde 1958 in Kingston, Jamaica, geboren. Sie absolvierte ihren B.Arch. sowie ihren Bachelor of Environmental Studies an der University of Waterloo in Ontario. Shim arbeitete für Arthur Erickson (1981) und Baird/Sampson in Toronto, bevor sie ihr Büro Brigitte Shim Architect (1988–94) gründete. Sie ist Seniorpartnerin und Mitbegründerin von **SHIM-SUTCLIFFE**, gegründet 1994 in Toronto. Derzeit ist sie außerordentliche Professorin an der Fakultät für Architektur und Design an der Universität Toronto. Howard Sutcliffe wurde 1958 in Yorkshire, England, geboren. Auch er absolvierte seinen B.Arch. und seinen Bachelor of Environmental Studies an der University of Waterloo in Ontario. Bis 1993 arbeitete er für Barton Myers (1984–86) sowie Merrick Architecture und gründete mit Brigitte Shim im darauffolgenden Jahr Shim-Sutcliffe. Zu ihren realisierten Projekten gehören das Ravine Guest House (Don Mills, Ontario, 2003–04, hier vorgestellt), das Haus am Hurricane Lake (Haliburton, Ontario, 2004–05), das Craven Road Studio (Toronto, 2006) sowie das Massey College an der Universität Toronto (2002–06), alle in Kanada. Aktuelle Projekte sind u. a. die Synagoge Bet Ha'am (Portland, Maine, USA) sowie das Integral House (Toronto, Kanada).

Brigitte Shim, née à Kingston, Jamaïque, en 1958, a reçu un B.Arch et un Bachelor of Environmental Studies de l'University of Waterloo en Ontario. Elle a travaillé dans l'agence d'Arthur Erickson (1981) et chez Baird/Sampson à Toronto, avant de créer sa propre structure, Brigitte Shim Architect (1988–94). Elle est directrice et cofondatrice de **SHIM-SUTCLIFFE**, agence fondée à Toronto en 1994. Actuellement, elle est professeure associée à la faculté d'architecture et de design de l'université de Toronto. Howard Sutcliffe, né dans le Yorkshire, Grande-Bretagne, en 1958, a fait les mêmes études que Brigitte Shim en Ontario. Il a travaillé dans les agences de Barton Myers (1984–86) et de Merrick Architecture jusqu'en 1993, fondant Shim-Sutcliffe avec Brigitte Shim l'année suivante. Ils ont réalisé la Ravine Guest House (Don Mills, Ontario, 2003–04, publiée ici) ; une maison sur le lac Hurricane (Haliburton, Ontario, 2004–05) ; le Craven Road Studio (Toronto, 2006) et le Massey College à l'université de Toronto (2002–06). Actuellement, ils travaillent sur la synagogue Bet Ha'am (Portland, Maine, États-Unis) et l'Integral House (Toronto, Canada).

RAVINE GUEST HOUSE

Don Mills, Ontario, Canada, 2003–04

Floor area: 42 m². Client: not disclosed. Cost: not disclosed.
Team: Brigitte Shim, Howard Sutcliffe, Tony Azevedo, Min Wang

This guesthouse is located in the 1.2-hectare grounds of a Toronto property near a ravine. According to the architects, "It is conceived of as a glowing lantern in the forest, typologically related to greenhouses and traditional garden outbuildings." There is a bedroom, sitting room, bathroom, and kitchen in the Ravine Guest House, but the architects insist on ambiguity between indoor and outdoor spaces, despite the rigorous winter climate of Toronto. A large central "indoor-outdoor" fireplace confirms this effort. Folding wood and glass doors allow the living space and bedroom to open to the exterior in warm weather. A wooden footbridge, reflecting pool, and wooden terrace complete the 111 square meters of exterior space that are part of the project.

Das Gästehaus liegt auf einem 1,2 ha großen Grundstück in Toronto unweit einer Schlucht. Den Architekten zufolge wurde es „als leuchtende Laterne im Wald entworfen, typologisch angelehnt an Gewächshäuser und traditionelle Gartenhäuser". Das Ravine Guest House umfasst Schlafzimmer, Wohnzimmer, Bad und Küche. Die Architekten beharren auf der Mehrdeutigkeit von Innen- und Außenraum, ungeachtet der strengen Winter in Toronto. Ein großer zentraler „Innen-/Außen"-Kamin unterstreicht dieses Anliegen. Falttüren aus Glas und Holz erlauben, Wohnraum und Schlafzimmer bei warmem Wetter vollständig nach außen zu öffnen. Eine Holzbrücke, ein Teich und eine Terrasse aus Holz vervollständigen die 111 m² großen Außenanlagen des Projekts.

Cette maison d'hôtes est implantée sur un terrain de 1,2 hectare près de Toronto, à proximité d'un ravin. « Elle est pensée comme une lanterne éclairée en forêt, et peut se relier typologiquement aux serres et aux cabanes de jardin traditionnelles », expliquent les architectes. Elle comprend une chambre, un salon, une salle de bains et une cuisine. Ses auteurs insistent sur l'ambiguïté de la relation entre les espaces intérieurs et extérieurs, malgré la rigueur des hivers de Toronto. La grande cheminée « intérieure/extérieure » renforce cet aspect. Des portes pliantes en bois et verre permettent d'ouvrir l'espace de séjour et la chambre sur la nature par beau temps. Une passerelle en bois, un bassin et une terrasse également en bois complètent les 111 m² d'espaces extérieurs qui font partie intégrante du projet.

Certainly not a typical holiday cabin,
the small guest house orchestrates
opaque, translucent and transparent
surfaces to create a shelter that is
in communion with the natural surroundings.

Das kleine Gästehaus, sicherlich kein
typisches Ferienhaus, orchestriert
opake, transluzente und transparente
Flächen zu einem schützenden Ort,
der sich harmonisch in sein natürliches Umfeld fügt.

Résidence de vacances atypique,
la petite maison des invités orchestre
savamment les plans opaques, trans-
lucides ou transparents pour créer un
abri en communion avec l'environnement naturel.

ÁLVARO SIZA VIEIRA

Álvaro Siza Arquitecto, Lda
Rua do Aleixo 53 2
4150–043 Porto
Portugal

Tel: +351 22 616 72 70
Fax: +351 22 616 72 79
E-mail: siza@mail.telepac.pt

Born in Matosinhos, Portugal, in 1933, **ÁLVARO SIZA** studied at the University of Porto School of Architecture (1949–55). He created his own practice in 1954, and worked with Fernando Tavora from 1955 to 1958. He has been a Professor of Construction at the University of Porto since 1976. He received the European Community's Mies van der Rohe Prize in 1988 and the Pritzker Prize in 1992. He has built a large number of small-scale projects in Portugal, and has worked on the restructuring of the Chiado (Lisbon, Portugal, 1989–); the Meteorology Center (Barcelona, Spain, 1989–92); the Vitra Furniture Factory (Weil am Rhein, Germany, 1991–94); the Porto School of Architecture, (Porto University, Portugal, 1986–95); and the University of Aveiro Library (Aveiro, Portugal, 1988–95). Other projects include the Portuguese Pavilion for the Expo '98 in Lisbon; the Serralves Foundation (Porto, 1998); and the Adega Mayor Winery (Argamassas Estate, Campo Maior, 2005–06), all in Portugal. He designed the 2005 Serpentine Pavilion (Kensington Gardens, London) with Eduardo Souto de Moura; the house in Pego (Sintra, Portugal, 2005–07, published here); and the Museum for the Iberê Camargo Foundation in Porto Alegre (Brazil, 2008).

ÁLVARO SIZA, 1933 im portugiesischen Matosinhos geboren, studierte von 1949 bis 1955 Architektur an der Universität Porto. Sein eigenes Büro gründete er 1954, von 1955 bis 1958 arbeitete er mit Fernando Tavora zusammen. Seit 1976 ist er Professor für Bauwesen an der Universität Porto. 1988 erhielt er den Mies-van-der-Rohe-Preis der Europäischen Gemeinschaft, 1992 den Pritzker-Preis. Neben zahlreichen kleineren Bauprojekten, die Siza in Portugal realisierte, wirkte er zudem seit 1989 am Wiederaufbau des Lissabonner Chiado-Viertels, baute ein meteorologisches Zentrum (Barcelona, 1989–92), eine Produktionshalle für Vitra (Weil am Rhein, 1991–94), die Architekturfakultät der Universität Porto (Portugal, 1986–95) sowie die Universitätsbibliothek von Aveiro (Portugal, 1988–95). Weitere Projekte sind u. a. der portugiesische Pavillon für die Expo '98 in Lissabon, die Stiftung Serralves (Porto, 1998), das Weingut Adega Mayor (Herdade das Argamassas, Campo Maior, 2005–06), alle in Portugal. Gemeinsam mit Eduardo Souto de Moura entwarf er den Serpentine Pavilion des Jahres 2005 (Kensington Gardens, London), das hier vorgestellte Haus in Pego (Sintra, Portugal, 2005–07) sowie das Museum für die Stiftung Iberê Camargo in Porto Alegre (Brasilien, 2008).

Né à Matosinhos, Portugal, en 1933, **ÁLVARO SIZA** a étudié à l'école d'architecture de l'université de Porto (1949–55). Il a créé son agence en 1954 et travaillé avec Fernando Tavora de 1955 à 1958. Il est professeur de construction à l'université de Porto depuis 1976. Il a reçu le prix Mies van der Rohe de la Communauté européenne en 1988, et le Pritzker Prize en 1992. Il a réalisé un grand nombre de projets de petites dimensions au Portugal, et a travaillé sur la restructuration du quartier du Chiado (Lisbonne, Portugal, 1989–) ; le centre de météorologie (Barcelone, Espagne, 1989–92) ; l'usine de meubles Vitra (Weil am Rhein, Allemagne, 1991–94) ; l'école d'architecture de Porto (université de Porto, Portugal, 1986–95) et la bibliothèque de l'université d'Aveiro (Aveiro, Portugal, 1988–95). Autres projets : le Pavillon portugais pour l'Expo '98 à Lisbonne ; la fondation Serralves (Porto, 1998) ; et le chais Adega Mayor (domaine d'Argamassas, Campo Maior, 2005–06). Il a conçu le pavillon 2005 de la Serpentine Gallery (Kensington Gardens, Londres) en collaboration avec Eduardo Souto de Moura ; une maison à Pego (Sintra, Portugal, 2005–07, publiée ici) et le musée pour la fondation Iberê Camargo à Porto Alegre (Brésil, 2008).

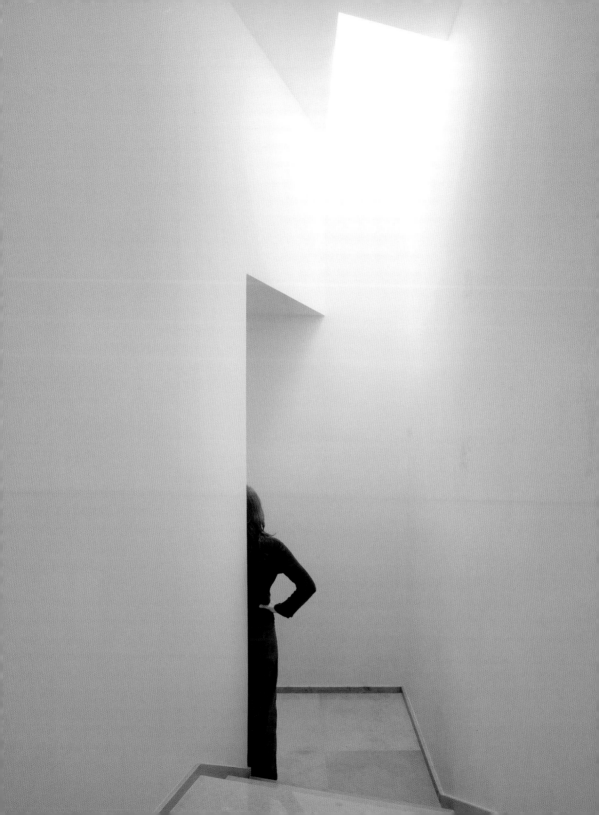

HOUSE IN PEGO

Sintra, Portugal, 2005–07

Floor area: 340 m². Client: Carlos Alemáo. Cost: not disclosed.
Project Architect: António Madureira

Although the articulated volumes of the house are typical of the architecture of Álvaro Siza, the use of vertical wooden slats for the cladding is more surprising.

Während die Gliederung der Baukörper durchaus typisch für die Architektur Álvaro Sizas ist, wirkt die vertikale Holzverblendung eher überraschend.

Sur ces volumes articulés qui rappellent bien l'architecture d'Álvaro Siza, le recours au lattis de bois vertical est plutôt surprenant.

This residence is set on a sloping 21 680-square-meter site facing the Atlantic Ocean. There is a 35-meter difference in height between the upper part of the site and the bottom. The house contains five bedrooms, a study, living room, and kitchen. These spaces are "arranged as semi-independent elements along an internal route, which connects the whole house, from the external arrival space, to the most private accommodation." A number of "semi-private" patios are arrayed along this irregular internal path. Given the slope in the terrain, the house is arranged on four different levels "organized as a single story." The load-bearing masonry walls are covered in timber, while the roof is made of a concrete slab covered in metal sheeting. A covered car park and an open-air swimming pool complete the installation.

Das Anwesen liegt auf einem 21 680 m² großen abfallenden Grundstück mit Blick auf den Atlantik. Zwischen dem oberen und unteren Teil des Grundstücks liegen 35 m Höhenunterschied. Das Haus umfasst fünf Schlafzimmer, ein Arbeitszimmer, ein Wohnzimmer und eine Küche. Die Räume sind „als halbautonome Bereiche angeordnet, entlang eines Pfads durch das Innere des Hauses, der das Ganze verbindet, vom außen gelegenen Eingangsbereich bis hin zu den privatesten Schlafräumen". Entlang dieses unregelmäßigen Gangs im Inneren sind mehrere „halb private" Höfe angelegt. Angesichts des Grundstücksgefälles erstreckt sich das Haus über vier Ebenen, die „wie eine einzige Etage organisiert sind". Die tragenden Wände aus Mauerwerk wurden mit Holz verkleidet, das Dach hingegen besteht aus einer mit Metall verblendeten Betonplatte. Ein überdachter Parkplatz und ein Außenpool vervollständigen das bauliche Ensemble.

Cette maison, qui contient cinq chambres, un bureau, un séjour et une cuisine, est implantée sur un terrain 21 680 m² qui descend vers l'océan Atlantique. Un dénivelé de 35 mètres sépare le haut du bas du terrain. Les espaces de vie sont « disposés en éléments semi-autonomes le long d'un cheminement interne qui parcourt toute la maison de l'arrivée de l'extérieur jusqu'aux parties les plus privées ». Un certain nombre de patios « semi-privés » sont aménagés le long de cette circulation intérieure de forme irrégulière. Compte tenu de la pente, la maison s'étage sur quatre niveaux différents « organisés comme un seul ensemble ». Les murs porteurs en maçonnerie sont habillés de bois. Le toit est une dalle de béton recouverte de tôle métallique. Un garage couvert et une piscine découverte complètent les installations.

A site plan for the house (below) shows its willful complexity, integrated into a sloping site. Left, the side of the residence near the swimming pool is lifted up on a simple concrete plinth.

Ein Lageplan des Hauses (unten) veranschaulicht die gewollte Komplexität des Baus, der in einen Hang eingebettet ist. Die zum Pool weisende Seite des Hauses (links) ruht auf einem schlichten Betonsockel.

Le plan au sol de la maison (ci-dessous) montre une composition volontairement complexe intégrée à la pente. À gauche, le côté de la maison face à la piscine repose sur une simple plinthe en béton.

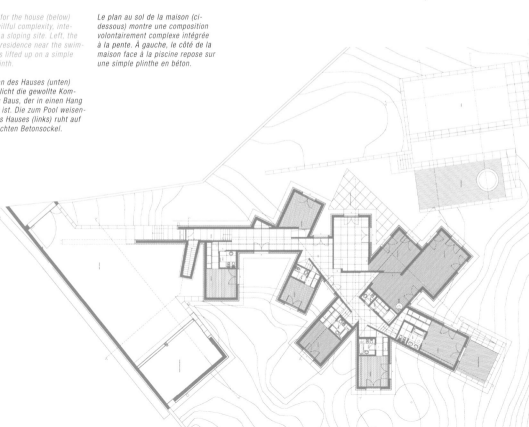

The interior reveals the kind of play on geometric forms and expansion of the Modernist vocabulary for which Álvaro Siza is justifiably famous. Windows frame the views of the garden.

Das Interieur zeugt vom spielerischen Umgang mit geometrischen Formen und einer Erweiterung des modernistischen Vokabulars, für die Álvaro Siza zu Recht berühmt wurde. Fenster rahmen den Blick in den Garten.

L'intérieur exprime le type de jeu sur les formes géométriques et le vocabulaire moderniste qui ont rendu Álvaro Siza si célèbre. Les fenêtres cadrent des perspectives sur le jardin.

PHILIPPE STUEBI

Philippe Stuebi Architekten GmbH
Hardstr. 219
8005 Zurich
Switzerland

Tel: +41 44 440 7777
Fax: +41 44 440 7779
E-mail: ps@philippestuebi.ch
Web: www.philippestuebi.ch

PHILIPPE STUEBI was born in Lausanne, Switzerland, in 1963, and received his degree in Architecture from the Swiss Federal Institute of Technology (ETH) in Zurich in 1993, where he studied under Hans Kollhoff. He set up his own office, Philippe Stuebi Architekten, in Zurich in 1996, with the goal of creating "networked architecture," linking issues like art, ecology, and economics, designing every project down to the smallest interior details. Philippe Stuebi was a co-founder and associate of the Kunstclub HeiQell in Zurich (1988–93), a gallery for contemporary art. His built work includes the Restaurant/Bar Josef und Maria (Zurich, 1998); the Maison Draeger (Korsika, 2000); the Villa Polana (Uitikon, 2000); Beaufort 12, Expo '02 Pavilion (Neuchâtel, 2002); the Würzgraben Housing Estate for the building authority of Zurich (2003); the Levy-Fröhlich House (Zollikon, 2005); and the O House on Lake Lucerne (2005–07, published here). He is currently working on a chapel in Unterbäch; a beachhouse at Zurich Obersee; and a beachhouse on the island Silba in Croatia.

PHILIPPE STUEBI wurde 1963 in Lausanne, Schweiz, geboren und schloss sein Architekturstudium 1993 an der Eidgenössischen Technischen Hochschule (ETH) in Zürich ab, wo er bei Hans Kollhoff studiert hatte. Sein Zürcher Büro Philippe Stuebi Architekten gründete er 1996 mit dem Ziel, eine „vernetzte Architektur" zu schaffen, bei der Fragen wie Kunst, Ökologie und Ökonomie miteinander verbunden werden sollten und jedes Projekt bis ins kleinste Detail der Innenausstattung vom Architekten selbst betreut würde. Philippe Stuebi war Mitbegründer und Teilhaber des Kunstclubs HeiQell in Zürich (1988–93), einer Galerie für zeitgenössische Kunst. Zu seinen gebauten Projekten zählen u. a. Restaurant/Bar Josef und Maria (Zürich, 1998), Maison Draeger (Korsika, 2000), Villa Polana (Uitikon, 2000), Beaufort 12, Pavillon für die Expo '02 (Neuchâtel, 2002), Wohnsiedlung Würzgraben für das Amt für Hochbauten Zürich (2003), die Villa Levy-Fröhlich (Zollikon, 2005) sowie das Haus O am Vierwaldstättersee (2005–07, hier vorgestellt). Aktuelle Projekte sind u. a. eine Kapelle in Unterbäch, ein Haus am Ufer des Zürichsees und ein Strandhaus auf der kroatischen Insel Silba.

PHILIPPE STUEBI, né à Lausanne, Suisse, en 1963, est diplômé d'architecture de l'Institut fédéral suisse de technologie (ETH) à Zurich à 1993, où il a étudié sous la direction de Hans Kollhoff. Il a créé sa propre agence, Philippe Stuebi Architekten, à Zurich en 1996, afin de créer une « architecture en réseau » traitant d'enjeux comme l'art, l'écologie et l'économie, et concevant chaque projet jusqu'aux plus petits détails d'aménagement intérieur. Il a été cofondateur du Kunstclub HeiQell à Zurich (1988–93), une galerie d'art contemporain. Parmi ses réalisations : le Restaurant/Bar Josef und Maria (Zurich, 1998) ; la maison Draeger (Corse, 2000) ; la villa Polana (Uitikon, 2000) ; Beaufort 12, Pavillon pour Expo '02 (Neuchâtel, 2002) ; les immeubles de logement de Würzgraben pour l'organisme de construction de Zurich (2003) ; la maison Levy-Fröhlich (Zollikon, 2005) et la maison O sur le lac des Quatre-Cantons (2005–07, publiée ici). Il travaille actuellement sur les projets d'une chapelle à Unterbäch; d'une maison sur le lac de Zurich et d'une autre sur l'île de Silba en Croatie.

O HOUSE

Lake Lucerne, Switzerland, 2005–07

*Floor area: 700 m². Client: not disclosed. Cost: not disclosed.
Team: Philippe Stuebi with Eberhard Tröger*

An unexpected and powerful pattern of large regular circular openings marks a façade of the house (below)

Ein überraschendes und ausdrucks- starkes Muster aus regelmäßigen Kreisöffnungen dominiert die Fassade des Hauses (unten).

Un puissant et surprenant motif d'ouvertures circulaires marquent la façade de la maison (ci-dessous).

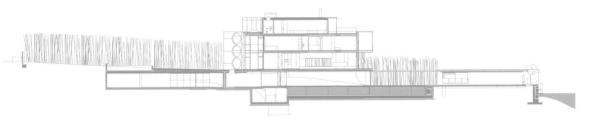

A broad window and simple interior finishes place the emphasis on the remarkable view of the lake seen in the image above of the living room.

Das breite Fenster und die schlichte Inneneinrichtung lenken die Aufmerksamkeit auf den eindrucksvollen Ausblick, den man im Wohnzimmer auf den See hat.

Une énorme baie et la simplicité de l'aménagement intérieur magnifient la vue remarquable sur le lac que l'on perçoit du séjour.

The front and lake sides of this large house are characterized by "sculptural elements" imagined by the architect—large round openings facing Mount Pilatus and "protruding, glistening loggia made of round glass bricks" on the side facing the lake, the Rigi and the Bürgenstock. A regular pattern three large circles high gives a decidedly sculptural appearance to the entry side of the house, echoed in smaller circles shielding the balconies, but opening out onto the spectacular lake view. The side façades are rendered in a rougher way. Despite its ample size, the house is furnished in a spare, modern way, with such touches as a glass balustrade on the main stairway confirming the modernity expressed in the façades and overall layout of the house. The basement includes a 25-meter, partially covered swimming pool and a generous fitness area. A walkway leads past the pool to a concrete boat jetty that extends into the water, allowing direct access from the lake. The somewhat angular plan of the house fits well into its site and maximizes the lake views.

Vorder- und Seeseite der großen Villa werden von „skulpturalen Elementen" dominiert – auf der zum Pilatus gewandten Vorderseite von großen runden, vom Architekten entworfenen Maueraussparungen sowie zur Seeseite mit Rigi und Bürgenstock von einer „auskragenden, funkelnden Loggia aus runden Glasbausteinen". Ein regelmäßiges Muster, drei große Kreise übereinander, lässt die Eingangsseite des Hauses besonders plastisch wirken, was von kleineren Kreismotiven aufgegriffen wird, die die Balkone abschirmen. Zum See jedoch öffnet sich das Haus der spektakulären Aussicht. Die seitlichen Fassaden sind rauer gestaltet. Trotz seiner großzügigen Dimensionen ist das Haus sparsam und modern möbliert. Elemente wie ein Glasgeländer an der Haupttreppe knüpfen an die moderne Anmutung der Fassaden und der gesamten Anlage des Hauses an und unterstreichen sie. Auf der unteren Gebäudeebene liegen ein teilüberdachter Pool mit 25-Meter-Bahnen sowie ein großzügiger Fitnessbereich. Ein Pfad führt am Pool entlang zu einem Bootssteg aus Beton, der über das Wasser ragt und vom See direkten Zugang zum Haus erlaubt. Der eher geradlinige Grundriss des Hauses fügt sich optimal in das Grundstück ein und maximiert den Ausblick auf den See.

La façade d'accès de cette vaste demeure et celle donnant sur le lac sont caractérisées par des « éléments sculpturaux » imaginés par l'architecte : de grandes ouvertures circulaires face au Mont Pilate et « une loggia, projection scintillante faite de briques de verre rondes » face au lac, au Rigi et au Bürgenstock. L'alignement régulier des grandes formes circulaires confère une apparence très sculpturale à la façade d'entrée, et ce motif se retrouve dans les petits cercles de verre qui protègent les balcons ouvrant sur de spectaculaires perspectives du lac. Les façades latérales sont moins sophistiquées. D'importantes dimensions, la maison est meublée avec parcimonie dans un style moderne avec quelques touches originales comme une balustrade de verre le long de l'escalier principal qui confirme la modernité des façades, comme le plan d'ensemble de la maison. Le sous-sol comprend une piscine de 25 mètres en partie couverte et de généreuses installations de remise en forme. Un passage le long de la piscine conduit à une jetée qui permet un accès direct au lac. Le plan, assez anguleux, est bien adapté au terrain et optimise les vues sur le plan d'eau.

Left page, a view toward the boat jetty. Above, the pattern of large circular openings is here echoed by screens and ceiling finishes that also employ circles.

Blick zum Bootsanleger (linke Seite). Das große Lochmuster (oben) wird hier in Wandschirmen und Deckenplatten aufgegriffen, die ebenfalls kreisrunde Muster aufweisen.

Page de gauche, vue vers la jetée. Ci-dessus, le motif des ouvertures circulaires de la façade repris par les écrans et le décor des plafonds.

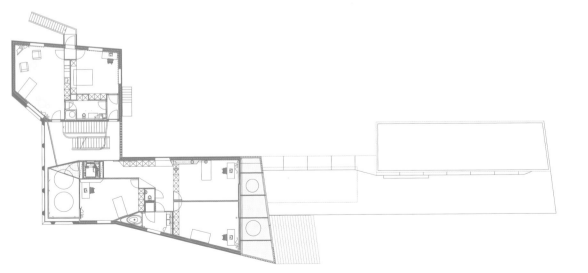

Below, a bedroom with a partial
perforated screen looks out on the
lake. Right, the glass balustrade and
successive chandeliers of the main
stairway.

Ein Schlafzimmer (unten) mit teilweise perforiertem Wandschirm
und Aussicht auf den See. Rechts
die Glasgeländer und Lüster an der
Haupttreppe.

Ci-dessous, une chambre. L'écran de
protection du balcon, en partie perforé,
cadre une vue sur le lac. À droite, un
garde-corps en verre et des lustres
dans la cage de l'escalier principal.

PETER STUTCHBURY

Peter Stutchbury Architecture
5/364 Barrenjoey Road / Newport Beach, NSW 2106
Australia

Tel: +61 2 9979 5030 / Fax: +61 2 9979 5367
E-mail: info@stutchburyandpape.com.au / Web: www.stutchburyandpape.com.au
info@peterstutchbury.com.au / www.peterstutchbury.com.au

A graduate of the University of Newcastle, Australia, in 1978, as a child **PETER STUTCHBURY** lived "on the land" and with aborigines on the banks of the Darling River, and with tribes in the highlands of New Guinea. He works on houses "that nurture their occupants and celebrate a palpable spirit of place." The firm has been given 26 awards by the Royal Australian Institute of Architects (RAIA) since 1999. In 2003, Peter Stutchbury was the first architect ever to win both the top National Architecture Awards from the RAIA for residential and non-residential projects with the Robin Boyd Award for houses for the Bay House at Watson's Bay, Sydney, and the Sir Zelman Cowan Award for Public Buildings for Birabahn, the Aboriginal Cultural Center at the University of Newcastle. Architect of the Sydney 2000 Olympics Archery Pavilion, he has also built several structures on the University of Newcastle campus, including the Design Building and the Nursing Building (with EJE Architecture); the Aboriginal Center (with Richard Leplastrier and Sue Harper); and the Life Sciences Building (with Suters Architects). His built work includes: the Israel House (Paradise Beach, NSW, 1982–92); the Treetop House (Clareville, NSW, 1991); the McMaster Residence (Hawk's Nest, NSW, 1995–98); the Kangaroo Valleys Pavilion (Kangaroo Valley, NSW, 1996–98); the Reeves House (Clareville Beach, NSW, 1997–99); and the Wedge House (Whale Beach, NSW, 2001). More recent works are the Beach House (Newport Beach, NSW, 2002–06); the Outcrop House (Northern Beaches, Sydney, NSW, 2006–07, published here); the Avalon House (Avalon, NSW, 2007); and the Flying Museum (Cessnock, NSW, 2004–08), all in Australia.

PETER STUTCHBURY schloss sein Studium an der University of Newcastle, Australien, 1978 ab. Als Kind lebte er „auf dem Land", mit den Aborigines am Ufer des Darling River und mit verschiedenen Stämmen im Hochland von Neuguinea. Er realisiert Häuser, die „ihre Bewohner hegen und nähren und den spürbaren Geist des Ortes würdigen". Seit 1999 hat das Büro 26 Preise des Royal Australian Institute of Architects (RAIA) erhalten. 2003 war Peter Stutchbury der erste Architekt, der jemals die beiden höchsten nationalen Architekturpreise des RAIA für Wohn- bzw. öffentliche Bauten erhielt: Ausgezeichnet wurden das Bay House in der Watson's Bay, Sydney, mit dem Robin Boyd Award für Wohnbauten sowie das Birabahn Aboriginal Cultural Center an der Universität Newcastle mit dem Sir Zelman Cowan Award für öffentliche Bauten. Stutchbury war der Architekt des Bogenschützenpavillons für die Olympischen Spiele in Sydney (2000) und entwarf außerdem verschiedene Bauten auf dem Campus der Universität Newcastle, darunter die Schulen für Design und für Krankenpflege (mit EJE Architecture), das Aboriginal Center (mit Richard Leplastrier und Sue Harper) sowie das Institut für Biowissenschaften (mit Suters Architects). Zu seinen realisierten Bauten zählen das Israel House (Paradise Beach, NSW, 1982–92), das Treetop House (Clareville, NSW, 1991), die McMaster Residence (Hawk's Nest, NSW, 1995–98), der Kangaroo Valleys Pavilion (Kangaroo Valley, NSW, 1996–98), das Reeves House (Clareville Beach, NSW, 1997–99) sowie das Wedge House (Whale Beach, NSW, 2001). Jüngere Projekte sind u. a. das Beach House (Newport Beach, NSW, 2002–06), das Outcrop House (Northern Beaches, Sydney, NSW, 2006–07, hier vorgestellt), das Avalon House (Avalon, NSW, 2007) sowie das Flying Museum (Cessnock, NSW, 2004–08), alle in Australien.

Diplômé de l'université de Newcastle, Australie, en 1978, **PETER STUTCHBURY** avait vécu enfant « à l'intérieur des terres » avec des Aborigènes sur les rives de la Darling River et dans les tribus des plateaux de Nouvelle-Guinée. Il travaille sur des projets de maisons « qui enrichissent leurs occupants et célèbrent un esprit palpable du lieu ». L'agence a reçu pas moins de 26 prix du Royal Australian Institute of Architects (RAIA) depuis 1999. En 2003, Peter Stutchbury a été le premier architecte à remporter à la fois les National Architecture Awards du RAIA pour des projets résidentiels et non résidentiels ; le Robin Boyd Award pour les maisons (Bay House à Watson's Bay, Sydney) ; et le Sir Zelman Cowan Award pour les bâtiments publics pour le Birabahn, le centre culturel aborigène de l'université de Newcastle. Architecte du pavillon de tir à l'arc pour les jeux Olympiques de Sydney en 2000, il a également construit plusieurs bâtiments sur le campus de l'université de Newcastle, dont celui des études de design et d'infirmerie (avec EJE Architecture) ; l'Aboriginal Center (avec Richard Leplastrier et Sue Harper) et le bâtiment des sciences de la vie (avec Suters Architects). Il a également réalisé : la maison Israel (Paradise Beach, NSW, 1982–92) ; la maison Treetop (Clareville, NSW, 1991) ; la résidence McMaster (Hawk's Nest, NSW, 1995–98) ; le Pavillon Kangaroo Valleys (Kangaroo Valley, NSW, 1996–98) ; la maison Reeves (Clareville Beach, NSW, 1997–99) et la maison Wedge (Whale Beach, NSW, 2001). Plus récemment, il a construit la Beach House (Newport Beach, NSW, 2002–06) ; la maison Outcrop (Northern Beaches, Sydney, NSW, 2006–07, publiée ici) ; la maison Avalon (Avalon, NSW, 2007) et le Flying Museum (Cessnock, NSW, 2004–08), tous en Australie.

OUTCROP HOUSE

Northern Beaches, Sydney, NSW, Australia, 2006–07

Floor area: 285 m². Client: not disclosed. Cost: not disclosed.
Team: Richard Smith, Sacha Zehnder

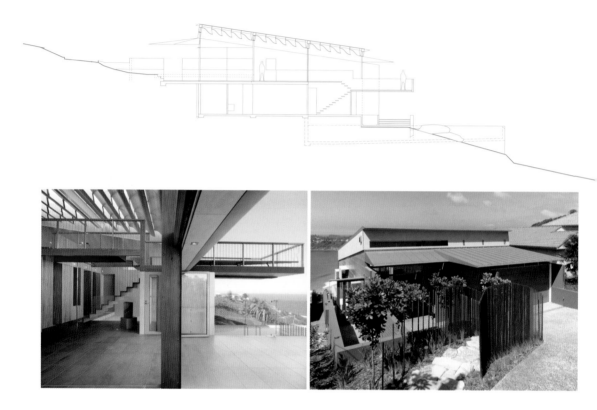

The Outcrop House is located on a typical exposed sandstone escarpment edge above Whale Beach, and yet it is in a suburban environment on the landside. Indeed, seen from its entrance façade, the house seems to resemble typical suburban residences. Facing south and subject to the ocean winds, the house has a northern courtyard "designed for winter comfort," and has "a single powerful aperture to the view" on the southern side. A balcony and pool extend toward the beach. Despite its exposure to the ocean, the house is considered "one of restraint—an enclave that offers the users comfort, ease, place, and dreaming." The roof is designed to allow "controlled vertical light" into the house, and especially into its primary space.

Das Outcrop House liegt auf einer typischen Sandsteinsteilwand über Whale Beach, zur Landseite hin ist es jedoch in ein vorstädtisches Umfeld eingebunden. Tatsächlich wirkt das Haus auf der Eingangsseite wie ein typisches Vororthaus. Das nach Süden orientierte, den Winden des Meeres ausgesetzte Haus hat einen Nordhof „für angenehmen Aufenthalt im Winter" sowie auf der Südseite eine „beeindruckende Öffnung zum Panorama". Ein Balkon und ein Pool erstrecken sich in Richtung Strand. Trotz seiner Öffnung zum Meer wird das Haus als „zurückhaltend" empfunden – „eine Enklave, die ihren Bewohnern Komfort, Ungezwungenheit, Raum und Platz zum Träumen lässt". Das Dach ist so gestaltet, dass es „regulierten vertikalen Lichteinfall" in das Haus ermöglicht, insbesondere in den Hauptwohnbereich.

La maison Outcrop (maison saillie) se dresse sur un escarpement de grès caractéristique au-dessus de la plage de la Baleine, tout en appartenant à un environnement de banlieue côté terre. Vue de la façade de l'entrée, la maison ressemble d'ailleurs aux résidences habituelles de cette banlieue. Mais face au sud et aux vents de l'océan, elle possède une cour « conçue pour assurer le confort en hiver » et « une ouverture unique, mais de forte présence vers le paysage » côté sud. Un balcon et la piscine se projettent vers la plage. Malgré son exposition à l'influence de l'océan, la maison est considérée comme « retenue – une enclave qui offre à ses occupants le confort, l'aisance, un lieu et des rêves ». Le toit a été dessiné pour faciliter « l'éclairage vertical contrôlé » de l'intérieur de la maison, et en particulier de ses volumes principaux.

A cantilevered balcony juts out toward the beach, connecting the interior and exterior of the house to its site.

Ein auskragender Balkon in Richtung Strand schafft eine Verbindung von Innen- und Außenräumen des Hauses mit der Umgebung.

Un balcon en porte-à-faux se projette vers la plage et connecte au site l'intérieur et l'extérieur de la maison.

Interior forms show a carefully orchestrated play on degrees
of transparency or opacity that allow
natural light to penetrate the house
in a controlled way.

Die Gestaltung des Interieurs zeugt
von einem orchestrierten Spiel mit
Transparenz und Opazität, was
zugleich kontrollierten Lichteinfall
in das Haus ermöglicht.

L'intérieur est un jeu soigneusement orchestré sur divers degrés de
transparence et d'opacité qui laissent
pénétrer la lumière naturelle de façon
contrôlée.

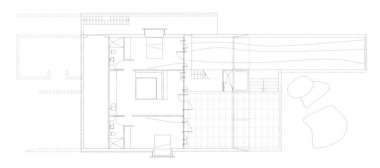

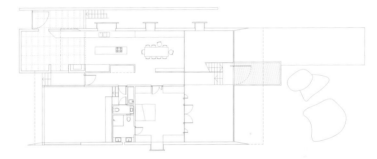

Subtle overhead natural light comes into the living spaces, where a contrast of materials giving emphasis to wood creates a warm atmosphere.

Von oben fällt auf subtile Weise natürliches Licht in die Wohnräume. Dort sorgen Materialkontraste und das dominierende Holz für eine warme Atmosphäre.

La lumière naturelle pénètre dans le séjour de manière subtile. Le contraste des matériaux met l'accent sur le bois pour créer une atmosphère chaleureuse.

TNA

TNA Co., Ltd.
9–7–3F Sumiyoshityou
Sinjuku-ku,
Tokyo 162–0065
Japan

Tel: +81 3 3225 1901
Fax: +81 3 3225 1902
E-mail: mail@tna-arch.com
Web: www.tna-arch.com

Makoto Takei was born in Tokyo in 1974. He graduated from the Department of Architecture of Tokai University in 1997. Between 1997 and 1999 he was at the Tsukamoto Laboratory, Graduate School of Science and Engineering, Tokyo Institute of Technology, and worked with Atelier Bow-Wow. Between 1999 and 2000 he worked in the office of Tezuka Architects, before establishing **TNA (TAKEI-NABESHIMA-ARCHITECTS)** with Chie Nabeshima. Chie Nabeshima was born in Kanagawa in 1975 and graduated from the course in Habitation and Space Design, Department of Architecture and Architectural Engineering, College of Industrial Technology, Nihon University (1998), before working at Tezuka Architects (1998–2005) and co-founding TNA. Their projects include the Wood Wear House (Hayama, Kanagawa, 2005); the Color Concrete House (Yokohama, Kanagawa, 2005); the Ring House (Karuizawa, Nagano, 2006, published here); the Wood Ship Café (Hayama, Kanagawa, 2007); and the Mosaic House (Meguro-ku, Tokyo, 2007), all in Japan.

Makoto Takei, 1974 in Tokio geboren, schloss sein Architekturstudium 1997 an der Universität Tokai ab. Zwischen 1997 und 1999 war er am Tsukamoto-Labor der Graduate School of Science and Engineering am Tokyo Institute of Technology tätig und arbeitete mit dem Atelier Bow-Wow. Von 1999 bis 2000 war er für Tezuka Architects tätig, bevor er mit Chie Nabeshima das Büro **TNA (TAKEI-NABESHIMA-ARCHITECTS)** gründete. Chie Nabeshima wurde 1975 in Kanagawa geboren und schloss den Studiengang Wohnbau und Raumgestaltung am Institut für Architektur und Bauwissenschaften am College of Industrial Technology der Universität Nihon ab (1998), bevor sie für Tezuka Architects tätig war (1998–2005) und TNA mitbegründete. Zu ihren Projekten zählen das Wood Wear House (Hayama, Kanagawa, 2005), das Color Concrete House (Yokohama, Kanagawa, 2005), das Ring House (Karuizawa, Nagano, 2006, hier vorgestellt), das Wood Ship Café (Hayama, Kanagawa, 2007) sowie das Mosaic House (Meguro-ku, Tokio, 2007), alle in Japan.

Makoto Takei, né à Tokyo en 1974, est diplômé du département d'architecture de l'Université Tokai (1997). De 1997 à 1999, il a travaillé dans le Laboratoire Tsukamoto de l'école supérieure de sciences et d'ingénierie de l'institut de technologie de Tokyo et a collaboré avec l'Atelier Bow-Wow. De 1999 à 2000, il est architecte chez Tezuka Architects avant de créer **TNA (TAKEI-NABESHIMA-ARCHITECTS)** avec Chie Nabeshima. Chie Nabeshima, né en Kanagawa en 1975, a été diplômée de conception d'espace et de l'habitat du département d'architecture et d'ingénierie architecturale du collège de technologie industrielle de l'université Nihon (1998), avant d'entrer chez Tezuka Architects (1998–2005) et de fonder TNA. Parmi leurs projets : la maison Wood Wear (Hayama, Kanagawa, 2005) ; la maison Color Concrete (Yokohama, Kanagawa, 2005) ; la maison Ring (Karuizawa, Nagano, 2006, publiée ici) ; le Wood Ship Café (Hayama, Kanagawa, 2007) et la maison Mosaic (Meguro-ku, Tokyo, 2007), tous au Japon.

RING HOUSE

Karuizawa, Nagano, Japan, 2006

Floor area: 102 m². Client: Hill Karuizawa.
Cost: not disclosed

This unusual house was built in a forest setting. It is a laminated lumber structure with a basement and two levels above ground, for a total height of 9.37 meters. Its site covers a total of 1387 square meters. The forest clearly inspired the architects to design in a different way than they would have in the city. "Rather than having a single-directional view, a space where one is able to see the forest milieu from every direction and height is achieved." The "ring" referred to in the name of the house does not refer so much to its shape as to the 360° views its interiors offer. Made of wood and glass, with burnt cedar siding positioned in bands whose width and number are unrelated to floor levels, the Ring House has an enigmatic presence. Its largely empty interiors, with their birch floors, almost dissolve into the forest background creating an impression of suspended volumes or weightlessness.

Das ungewöhnliche Haus wurde in einer Waldgegend errichtet. Die Konstruktion aus laminiertem Holz mit Keller und zwei oberirdischen Geschossen hat eine Höhe von insgesamt 9,37 m. Das Grundstück ist 1387 m² groß. Der Wald inspirierte die Architekten ganz offensichtlich zu einem gänzlich anderen Designansatz, als sie ihn in der Stadt gewählt hätten. „Statt eine auf einen Punkt konzentrierte Aussicht zu haben, wurde hier ein Raum geschaffen, von dem aus das Waldumfeld aus jeder Richtung und von jeder Höhe aus zu sehen ist." Der Begriff „Ring" bezieht sich weniger auf die Form des Hauses, als auf den 360-Grad-Ausblick, den es erlaubt. Das aus Holz und Glas gebaute Ring House besitzt eine rätselhafte Präsenz. Die Verkleidung aus rußgeschwärztem Zedernholz wurde zu Bändern angeordnet, deren Breite und Anzahl jedoch nicht mit den Etagen des Hauses korrespondieren. Die überwiegend leeren Innenräume mit ihren Birkenholzböden verschmelzen geradezu mit dem Waldhintergrund und erzeugen den Eindruck von schwebenden Volumen oder Schwerelosigkeit.

Cette étonnante maison s'élève dans un cadre forestier. De trois niveaux, dont un en sous-sol, pour une hauteur totale de 9,37 mètres, sa structure est en bois lamellé-collé. Le terrain couvre une surface de 1387 m². La forêt a évidemment inspiré aux architectes une solution différente de ce qu'ils auraient pu construire en ville. « Plutôt que de privilégier une vue dans une seule direction, nous avons abouti à un espace d'où l'on peut voir la forêt dans toutes les directions et sur différentes hauteurs. » Le « ring » ou anneau, qui a donné son nom à la maison, ne se réfère pas à la forme, mais à la vue panoramique à 360°. Les façades, en bois et en verre, sont habillées de cèdre brûlé posé en bandeaux, dont le nombre et la largeur sont indépendants des niveaux, ce qui confère à cette maison une présence énigmatique. L'intérieur aux sols de bouleau est presque vide et se dissout dans le fond de la forêt, donnant ainsi une impression de volumes suspendus ou d'absence de poids.

The house sits on a hilly site in the forest, its irregular black banded exterior giving little hint as to the real location of the floors.

Das Haus liegt auf einem hügeligen Waldgrundstück. Der mit unregelmäßigen schwarzen Bändern überzogene Außenbau verrät wenig über die tatsächliche Lage der Stockwerke.

La maison est implantée en forêt sur un terrain mouvementé. Ses façades à bandeaux noirs de largeur variée ne donnent que peu d'indications sur la répartition des niveaux.

The inside of the house is characterized by an extreme lightness, with views of the forest all around. Wooden floors, steps and furniture contrast with the clean white ceiling or wall band surfaces.

Das Innere des Hauses zeichnet sich durch große Helligkeit aus und bietet zu allen Seiten hin Ausblick in den Wald. Böden, Treppen und Mobiliar aus Holz bilden einen Kontrast zur weißen Decke oder den bandförmigen Wandflächen.

L'intérieur de la maison se caractérise par une luminosité extraordinaire et une vue panoramique sur la forêt environnante. Les sols, les escaliers et le mobilier en bois contrastent avec le plafond blanc ou les murs en bandeaux.

Although the plan of the house is
a perfect square, the disposition of
interior elements, including the bedroom or bathroom seen on this page
defy any rigorous pattern.

Obwohl der Grundriss des Hauses
ein perfektes Quadrat ist, folgt
die Anordnung des Innenausbaus,
einschließlich Schlafzimmer und Bad
auf dieser Seite, keineswegs einem
strengen Muster.

Bien que le plan de la maison soit
un carré parfait, la disposition des
éléments intérieurs, y compris la
chambre ou la salle de bains repré-
sentées ici, défient toute implantation
rigoureusement logique.

ZHANG LEI

AZL Atelier Zhanglei
Architecture Design Institute, NJU
Hankou Road 22
210093 Nanjing, Jiangsu
China

Tel: +86 25 5186 1369
Fax: +86 25 5186 1367
E-mail: atelierzhanglei@163.com

ZHANG LEI was born in 1964 in the Jiangsu province of China. He was the founder of AZL Atelier Zhanglei, and is a Professor and Vice Dean of the School of Architecture at Nanjing University. He studied architecture at Southeast University in China (1981–88) and then at the ETH Zurich (1991–93). His major projects include the Brick Houses and the Concrete Slit House published here (Nanjing, 2006–07); the Jiangsu Software Park (Nanjing, 2006–08); the Shantang Villas (Suzhou, 2006–08); and the Fang LIjun Art Gallery (Chengdu, 2007–08), all in China.

ZHANG LEI wurde 1964 in der chinesischen Provinz Jiangsu geboren. Er war Gründer von AZL Atelier Zhanglei und ist Professor und Vizedekan der Architekturfakultät der Universität Nanjing. Sein Architekturstudium absolvierte er an der Southeast University in China (1981–88) sowie an der ETH Zürich (1991–93). Zu seinen wichtigsten Projekten zählen die hier vorgestellten Brick Houses und das Concrete Slit House (Nanjing, 2006–07), der Jiangsu Software Park (Nanjing, 2006–08), die Shantang Villas (Suzhou, 2006–08) sowie die Fang LIjun Art Gallery (Chengdu, 2007–08), alle in China.

ZHANG LEI, né en 1964 dans la province du Jiangsu en Chine, est le fondateur d'AZL Atelier Zhanglei, et professeur et vice-doyen de l'école d'architecture de l'université de Nankin. Il a étudié l'architecture à l'université du Sud-Est en Chine (1981–88), puis à l'ETH à Zurich (1991–93). Parmi ses principales réalisations, toutes en Chine : les maisons de brique et la maison de béton fendu, publiées ici (Nankin, 2006–07) ; le parc de logiciels du Jiangsu (Nankin, 2006–08) ; les villas Shantang (Suzhou, 2006–08) et la galerie d'art Fang Lijun (Chengdu, 2007–08).

BRICK HOUSE 01

Gaochun, Nanjing, Jiangsu, China, 2006–07

Site area: 1650 m². Floor area: 850 m². Client: Wang Yongjun. Cost: €68 000

Zhang Lei explains, "Brick House 01 and Brick House 02 are separate projects with two different clients who are close friends. Together with two other families they bought a property along the lake and built four houses, two other houses in between these two brick houses were designed by another local architect." Both of these large houses were built for a remarkably low cost per square meter of 80 euros. The architect acknowledges the difficulties posed by this budget, but praises the clients, who were closely involved in the entire process. Zhang Lei regards these two residences as an "evolution from the prototype of the Chinese courtyard house." He paid particular attention to the relationship of the houses to the lake that lies to the northwest of the sites. Locally produced red bricks were used for the main structures because they are the most readily available and typical construction materials in the region. The "pattern of the brick façades reflects a logic of opening, or openness," concludes Zhang Lei.

Zhang Lei erklärt: „Brick House 01 und Brick House 02 sind separate Projekte für zwei verschiedene, eng befreundete Auftraggeber. Gemeinsam mit zwei weiteren Familien hatten sie ein Grundstück am See gekauft und vier Häuser gebaut, wobei die zwei Häuser dazwischen von einem anderen ortsansässigen Architekten entworfen wurden." Die beiden großen Häuser wurden für bemerkenswert niedrige Baukosten von 80 Euro pro Quadratmeter realisiert. Der Architekt räumt ein, dass dieses Budget schwierig war, lobt jedoch die Bauherren, die in den gesamten Prozess eng eingebunden waren. Zhang Lei versteht die beiden Häuser als eine „Weiterentwicklung des Prototyps des chinesischen Hofhauses". Besondere Aufmerksamkeit galt der Beziehung der Bauten zum See nordöstlich des Grundstücks. Für die Hauptbauten wurden regional gefertigte rote Ziegelsteine verwendet, da sie am einfachsten erhältlich waren und ein für die Region typisches Baumaterial sind. Abschließend bemerkt Zhang Lei: „Das Muster der Backsteinfassaden spiegelt eine Logik der Öffnung, der Offenheit."

Zhang Lei explique que les « Brick House 01 et Brick House 02 sont des projets indépendants pour deux clients différents qui sont ses proches amis. Avec deux autres familles, ils ont acheté une propriété en bordure d'un lac et construit quatre maisons, deux étant conçues par un autre architecte local ». Ces deux grandes résidences ont été édifiées pour le prix étonamment bas de 80 euros le mètre carré. L'architecte reconnaît les difficultés posées par un tel budget, mais félicite ses clients de s'être étroitement impliqués en permanence dans le processus du projet. Zhang Lei considère ces deux résidences comme « une évolution du prototype de la maison à cour chinoise ». Il a porté une attention particulière à la relation avec le lac qui s'étend au nord-ouest des terrains. Les constructions principales sont en briques rouges produites localement, parce qu'elles étaient plus facilement disponibles, et matériaux typiques de construction de la région. La « disposition des briques en façade reflète une logique d'ouverture, ou d'ajouré », conclut Zhang Lei.

A site plan shows the location of the two Brick Houses within an existing neighborhood. Brick House 01 is to the right on the plan (light blue) and Brick House 02 roughly in the middle of the plan.

Der Lageplan veranschaulicht die Position der beiden Brick Houses in der bestehenden Nachbarschaft. Brick House 01 ist rechterhand zu sehen (hellblau), Brick House 02 etwa in der Mitte des Plans.

Ce plan d'ensemble montre la situation des deux « maisons de brique » dans leur environnement existant. La Brick House 01 est à droite sur le plan (en bleu clair) et la Brick House 02 au centre.

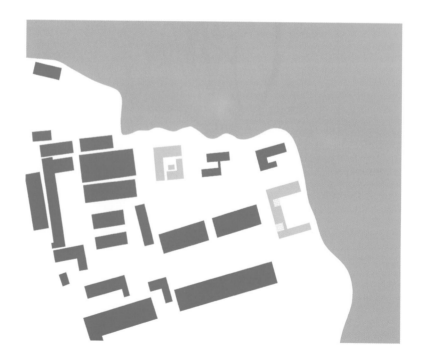

Elevations of the house show its rectilinear form and irregular pattern of openings. Above, a broad square opening, framed by the brick surface of the house, has a simple elegance. The brick pattern gives a relief and roughness to the exterior surfaces.

Aufrisse des Hauses veranschaulichen die geradlinige Form und die unregelmäßigen Wandöffnungen. Eine breite, quadratische Maueröffnung (oben), gerahmt von der Backsteinfassade, ist von schlichter Eleganz. Das Backsteinmuster verleiht den Außenfassaden reliefartige Rauheit.

Des élévations de la maison montrent sa forme orthogonale et l'implantation irrégulière des ouvertures. Ci-dessus, simple et élégante, une grande ouverture carrée cadrée de briques. Les motifs des briques confèrent un relief et une irrégularité aux surfaces extérieures.

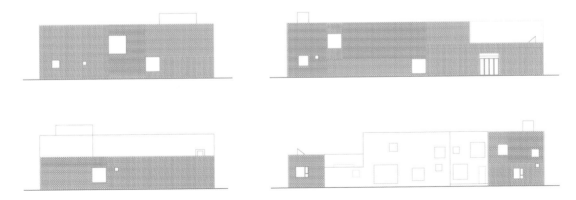

The basic plan of the house is an irregular "U" shape. The smoother white interiors contrast with the roughness of the exterior brick surface. Irregular openings, some allowing for natural overhead lighting, animate the interior space in the daylight.

Der Grundriss des Hauses ist ein unregelmäßiges „U". Die glatten weißen Interieurs kontrastieren mit der Rauheit der Backsteinflächen am Außenbau. Unregelmäßig angeordnete Fensteröffnungen, durch die natürliches Licht zum Teil auch von oben einfällt, beleben den Innenraum bei Tag.

Le plan de la maison est en forme de « U » irrégulier. Les intérieurs blancs et lisses contrastent avec la rudesse des façades. Les ouvertures de formes variées, dont certaines en position zénithale, laissent l'éclairage naturel animer le volume intérieur pendant le jour.

BRICK HOUSE 02

Gaochun, Nanjing, Jiangsu, China, 2006–07

Site area: 1200 m². Floor area: 680 m². Client: Ye Hui. Cost: €52 800

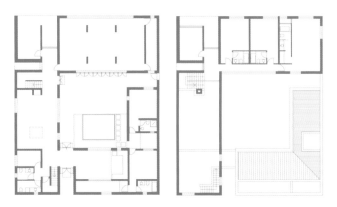

This second house shares with the architect's other nearby residence a contrast between the austere brick façade and smooth, bright interior spaces.

Das zweite Haus zeichnet sich ebenso wie der Nachbarbau des Architekten durch den Kontrast von strenger Backsteinfassade und hellen Innenräumen aus.

Cette seconde maison reprend le contraste voulu par l'architecte entre les austères façades en brique brute et les intérieurs lisses et lumineux.

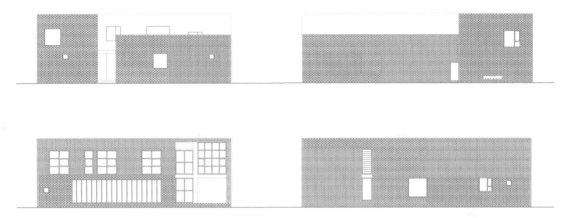

The house has a very simple design, as the elevations and the images demonstrate. Window placement is again irregular. The gray sky in these images reinforces an overall impression of strict austerity.

Der Entwurf des Hauses ist äußerst schlicht, wie die Aufrisse und die Abbildungen zeigen. Auch hier ist die Anordnung der Fenster unregelmäßig. Der graue Himmel auf den Bildern unterstreicht den Gesamteindruck von strenger Nüchternheit.

Le plan de la maison est d'une grande simplicité, comme les élévations et les photographies le montrent. Le positionnement des fenêtres est, là aussi, irrégulier. Le ciel gris renforce une impression générale de rigoureuse austérité.

CONCRETE SLIT HOUSE

Nanjing, Jiangsu, China, 2006–07

*Site area: 320 m². Floor area: 270 m². Client: Xie Mingrui.
Cost: € 108 000*

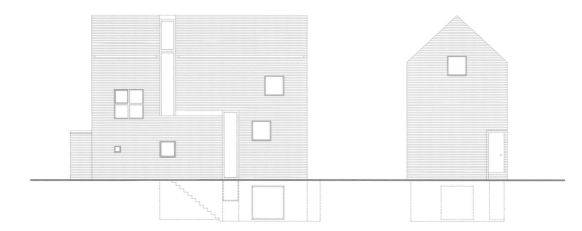

Although somewhat deformed by a wide-angle lens (right) the house is rigorously rectilinear, pierced in an unusual way by the entrance and the slit that gives the residence its name.

Trotz der leichten Verzerrung durch ein Weitwinkelobjektiv (rechts) ist das Haus streng geradlinig. Ungewöhnlich durchbrochen wird das Haus vom Eingang sowie dem Einschnitt („slit"), dem es seinen Namen verdankt.

Bien que légèrement déformée par une prise vue au grand angle, la maison est parfaitement orthogonale. Elle est percée de façon surprenante par son entrée dans l'angle et la fente (« slit ») qui lui donne son nom.

This residence, with a substantially higher construction cost per square meter than the Brick Houses (400 euros), "fits into the historical context formulated in the beginning of the 1920s in the center of Nanjing with a new form," according to Zhang Lei. Indeed, the house adapts the scale and typology of neighboring houses, while remaining decidedly different. The public areas of the house are intended to be "transparent" or open, while preserving the privacy of the spaces through "limited openings to the surroundings" in the densely built site area. This apparently contradictory result is achieved through the use of a zig-zagging slit that almost appears to cut the house in two, admitting light and views out without sacrificing privacy. Concrete was used for the entire structure, including the roof, although the exterior areas around the house offer a wooden terrace. The architect's insistence on the material can be seen as a commentary on the building boom in China. He says, "Even though we use half the world's cement, this is the first real concrete building in Nanjing, a city that has built 1300 high-rise concrete towers in the last 25 years."

Der Bau dieses Hauses war mit erheblich höheren Kosten von 400 Euro pro Quadratmeter verbunden als die Brick Houses. Zhang Lei zufolge „fügt es sich mit seiner neuen Form in den historischen Kontext ein, der im Stadtzentrum von Nanjing in den 1920er-Jahren entstand". Und tatsächlich orientiert sich das Haus in Größe und Typologie an den angrenzenden Bauten, bleibt jedoch zweifellos etwas völlig anderes. Obwohl die Gemeinschaftsbereiche des Hauses „transparent" bzw. offen gestaltet wurden, wurde die Privatsphäre gewahrt, indem nur „begrenzte Öffnungen zum Umfeld" der dicht besiedelten Wohngegend eingesetzt wurden. Dieser scheinbar widersprüchliche Effekt wurde durch einen Zickzackschnitt erzielt, der das Haus geradezu in zwei Hälften zu teilen scheint. Er lässt Licht ins Haus und ermöglicht den Blick nach draußen, ohne dabei Privatsphäre zu opfern. Die gesamte Konstruktion, einschließlich des Dachs, wurde aus Beton gefertigt, wobei zum Außenbereich auch eine hölzerne Terrasse gehört. Das Beharren des Architekten auf diesem Baumaterial lässt sich als Kommentar zum chinesischen Bauboom verstehen. Er merkt an: „Obwohl wir die Hälfte des gesamten Zementverbrauchs der Welt beanspruchen, ist dies der erste wirkliche Betonbau in Nanjing, einer Stadt, die in den letzten 25 Jahren 1300 Hochhausbauten realisiert hat."

Cette résidence, qui a coûté nettement plus cher au mètre carré que les maisons de brique (400 euros), « s'intègre au contexte historique du centre de Nankin datant du début des années 1920, avec une forme pourtant nouvelle », précise Zhang Lei. La maison est en effet en harmonie avec l'échelle et la typologie des maisons voisines, tout en se montrant résolument différente. Les parties de réception sont « transparentes » ou ouvertes, en préservant l'intimité des espaces par « des ouvertures limitées sur l'environnement » de ce quartier très densément construit. Ce résultat apparemment contradictoire est atteint grâce à une fente en zigzag qui semble pratiquement couper la maison en deux, laisse passer la lumière naturelle et ouvre des perspectives, sans compromettre l'intimité de l'intérieur. La construction tout entière est en béton, y compris le toit. Une terrasse en bois a été aménagée à l'extérieur. L'insistance de l'architecte sur le choix du matériau peut être interprétée comme un commentaire sur l'explosion du secteur de la construction en Chine : « Même si nous utilisons la moitié du ciment du monde, c'est le premier bâtiment réellement en béton édifié à Nankin, une ville qui a construit 1300 tours de grande hauteur en béton au cours des 25 dernières années. »

The house adapts itself to the essential form of neighboring residences, but stands out in its austere grayness. Interiors are animated by the unexpected placement of openings and the use of wood.

Obwohl sich das Haus formal grundsätzlich in die Nachbarschaft integriert, hebt es sich durch sein strenges Grau von den übrigen Bauten ab. Die ungewöhnliche Anordnung der Wandöffnungen und die Nutzung von Holz beleben das Interieur.

La maison est adaptée à la typologie des résidences voisines, mais se détache d'elles par son austère couleur grise. Les intérieurs sont animés par la disposition inattendue des ouvertures et la présence du bois.

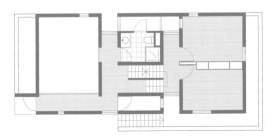

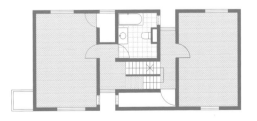

RENÉ VAN ZUUK

René van Zuuk Architekten b.v.
De Fantasie 9
1324 HZ Almere
The Netherlands

Tel: +31 36 537 9139
Fax: +31 36 537 9259
E-mail: info@renevanzuuk.nl
Web: www.renevanzuuk.nl

RENÉ VAN ZUUK received an M.Sc. degree from the Technical University of Eindhoven (1988), and created his own firm in 1993. He has a design staff of five persons. Prior to 1993, he worked for Skidmore, Owings & Merrill in London and Chicago (1988–89), and at Facilitair Bureau voor Bouwkunde Rotterdam, Hoogstad, van Tilburg Architecten (1989–92). His notable completed projects include: Eight Bridges (Nieuwsloten, 1993); the Lock House "Oostersluis" (Groningen, 1995); the Villa van Diepen (Almere, 1995); Four Canal Houses (Java Island, Amsterdam, 1997); the Educational Farm "Griftsteede" (Utrecht, 1999); the Center for Plastic Arts "CBK" (Alphen aan de Rijn, 2000); the Art Pavilion "De Verbeelding" (Zeewolde, 2001); and the ARCAM Architectural Center (Amsterdam, 2003). Other work includes: Blok 16 housing and fitness complex (Almere, 2003); the Bridge for bicycles and pedestrians (Almere, 2003); the Bridge Keeper's House (Middelburg, unbuilt); and the Office Building "Zilverparkkade" (Lelystad, 2004). Furthermore, he has worked on a group of 20 houses (Bosrijk, Eindhoven, 2005); a 10-story apartment building (Dudok, Hilversum, 2006); a multi-functional first-aid post (Dordrecht, 2007); Project X (Almere, 2004–08, published here); and a villa in Wageningen (2008), all in the Netherlands.

RENÉ VAN ZUUK erwarb seinen Master of Science an der Technischen Universität Eindhoven (1988) und gründete sein eigenes Büro 1993. Er hat fünf Mitarbeiter. Vor 1993 arbeitete er für Skidmore, Owings & Merrill in London und Chicago (1988–89) und am Facilitair Bureau voor Bouwkunde Rotterdam, Hoogstad, van Tilburg Architecten (1989–92). Zu seinen wichtigsten Projekten zählen acht Brücken (Nieuwsloten, 1993), das Schleusenhaus „Oostersluis" (Groningen, 1995), die Villa van Diepen (Almere, 1995), vier Kanalhäuser (auf Java, Amsterdam, 1997), der Kinderbauernhof „Griftsteede" (Utrecht, 1999), das Zentrum für bildende Künste „CBK" (Alphen aan de Rijn, 2000), der Kunstpavillon „De Verbeelding" (Zeewolde, 2001) sowie das Architekturzentrum ARCAM (Amsterdam, 2003). Weitere Projekte sind u. a. Blok 16, ein Wohnkomplex mit Fitnesseinrichtungen (Almere, 2003), eine Fahrrad- und Fußgängerbrücke (Almere, 2003), ein Brückenwächterhaus (Middelburg, nicht gebaut) sowie das Bürohaus „Zilverparkkade" (Lelystad, 2004). Zudem arbeitete er an 20 Hausbauten (Bosrijk, Eindhoven, 2005), einem zehnstöckigen Apartmenthaus (Dudok, Hilversum, 2006), einer multifunktionalen Erste-Hilfe-Ambulanz (Dordrecht, 2007), am Projekt X (Almere, 2004–08, hier vorgestellt) sowie einer Villa in Wageningen (2008), alle in den Niederlanden.

RENÉ VAN ZUUK, M.Sc. de l'Université technique d'Eindhoven (1988), a créé son agence en 1993. Il emploie cinq collaborateurs. Avant cette date, il avait travaillé pour Skidmore, Owings & Merrill à Londres et Chicago (1988–89), et pour Facilitair Bureau voor Bouwkunde Rotterdam, Hoogstad, van Tilburg Architecten (1989–92). Parmi ses réalisations les plus importantes, toutes aux Pays-Bas : huit ponts (Nieuwsloten, 1993) ; la maison-écluse « Oostersluis » (Groningen, 1995) ; la villa van Diepen (Almere, 1995) ; quatre maisons de Canal (Ile de Java, Amsterdam, 1997) ; la ferme éducative « Griftsteede » (Utrecht, 1999) ; le centre d'arts plastiques « CBK » (Alphen aan de Rijn, 2000) ; le pavillon d'art « De Verbeelding » (Zeewolde, 2001) et le centre architectural ARCAM (Amsterdam, 2003). Il a réalisé également : le Blok 16, complexe de logements et centre de remise en forme (Almere, 2003) ; un pont pour piétons et bicyclettes (Almere, 2003) ; la maison du gardien de pont (Middelburg, non construite); l'immeuble de bureaux « Zilverparkkade » (Lelystad, 2004); un ensemble de 20 maisons (Bosrijk, Eindhoven, 2005) ; un immeuble d'appartements de 10 niveaux (Dudok, Hilversum, 2006) ; un poste de premiers secours polyvalent (Dordrecht, 2007) ; le Project X (Almere, 2004–08, publié ici) et une villa à Wageningen (2008), tous au Pays-Bas.

PROJECT X

Almere, The Netherlands, 2004–08

Floor area: 185 m². Clients: René van Zuuk and Marjo Körner.
Cost: not disclosed

Despite its enigmatic name, this project is nothing other than the architect's design for his own home. René van Zuuk's former home, called Psyche, is on an adjacent lot and now serves as his office. Both are located in an experimental housing area called De Fantasie (The Fantasy), and they now share a common garden along a canal. The new house fits into the local building pattern, which includes a "box-like" appearance. The architect has also made an effort to interpret the Dutch Building Decree that restricts floor area but makes exceptions in certain circumstances, which René van Zuuk has taken advantage of. Clad in thin cement panels with a branch-like pattern that somewhat alleviates the rectilinear repetition of the design, the house has roof windows that bring natural light into the upper story bedrooms. The ground floor includes living areas, while the rectangular upper floor has three bedrooms.

Trotz des rätselhaften Namens verbirgt sich hinter diesem Projekt nichts anderes als der Entwurf des Architekten für sein eigenes Haus. René van Zuuks früheres Domizil „Psyche" liegt auf einem angrenzenden Grundstück und dient ihm inzwischen als Büro. Beide liegen in einem experimentellen Wohngebiet, De Fantasie, und teilen sich ein Gartengrundstück am Kanal. Das neue Haus fügt sich in das örtliche Baumuster ein, das u. a. ein „kastenförmiges" Erscheinungsbild vorgibt. Der Architekt bemühte sich zudem, die niederländische Bauordnung zu interpretieren, die die Geschossfläche beschränkt, jedoch Ausnahmen für bestimmte Fälle vorsieht, von denen van Zuuk Gebrauch macht. Das Haus ist mit dünnen Zementplatten mit einem zweigähnlichen Muster verblendet, was die geradlinige Wiederholung des Entwurfs etwas auflockert. Dachfenster lassen natürliches Licht in die Schlafzimmer im Obergeschoss. Im Erdgeschoss liegen die Wohnbereiche, darüber, im rechteckigen oberen Stock, drei Schlafzimmer.

Malgré sa dénomination énigmatique, ce projet est tout simplement la privée maison de l'architecte. Son ancienne résidence, appelée Psyché, qui se trouve sur une parcelle adjacente, lui sert maintenant de bureaux. Toutes deux sont situées dans une zone de construction de logements expérimentaux appelée « De Fantasie » et partagent un même jardin le long d'un canal. La nouvelle maison s'intègre dans la typologie locale qui intègre les constructions de style « boîte ». L'architecte s'est également livré à une réinterprétation d'un règlement néerlandais de la construction, qui réduit les surfaces au sol, mais prévoit des exceptions dans certaines circonstances, ce dont René van Zuuk a tiré parti. Habillée de panneaux de ciment coulé à motifs de branches qui allège un peu la répétitivité de l'ensemble, la maison possède des verrières zénithales qui éclairent naturellement les chambres du niveau supérieur. Le rez-de-chaussée comprend les zones de séjour et l'étage compte trois chambres.

The house is characterized by a powerful upper block clad in cement sitting over a lower zone that is almost completely glazed.

Das Haus zeichnet sich durch einen imposanten oberen Block aus, der mit Zement verblendet wurde und auf einem fast vollständig verglasten unteren Bereich sitzt.

La maison se caractérise par une pesante partie supérieure habillée de béton qui repose sur une base presque entièrement vitrée.

An earlier house by the architect neighbors the new residence near a canal and beneath high-tension wires, signs of the high population density of the Netherlands.

Ein früheres Gebäude des Architekten liegt neben dem neuen Wohnhaus am Kanal und unter Hochspannungslei-tungen, einem Hinweis auf die hohe Bevölkerungsdichte der Niederlande.

Également en bordure du canal, la maison voisine a elle aussi été réalisée par l'architecte. La ligne de haute-tension est un signe de la forte densité de population aux Pays-Bas.

Interior spaces are as austere as the outside of the house might suggest, but the architect plays on light and darkness in a masterly way.

Die Innenräume sind so streng wie der Außenbau vermuten lässt. Dennoch spielt der Architekt meisterlich mit Licht und Dunkel.

Les volumes intérieurs sont aussi austères que l'extérieur de la maison le laisse imaginer, mais l'architecte joue magistralement du clair-obscur.

The plan of the house is made of rectangular volumes, but sloping angles (above) and broad openings to the garden bring it to life.

Der Grundriss setzt sich aus rechteckigen Volumen zusammen, doch Schrägen (oben) und große Öffnungen zum Garten hin beleben das Haus.

Le plan de la maison se compose de volumes rectangulaires que des éléments inclinés (ci-dessus) et de larges ouvertures sur le jardin réussissent à animer.

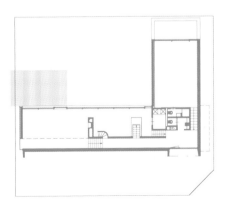

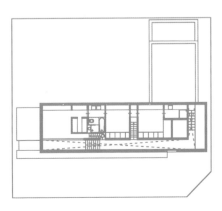

INDEX OF ARCHITECTS, BUILDINGS, AND PLACES

CREDITS